AF576662

© 2002
Royal Caribbean Cruises Ltd.

All rights reserved.
No part of this publication may be reproduced, stored in a retrieval system or transmitted, in any form or by any means electronical, mechanical, photocopying, recording or otherwise, without the prior written permission of the copyright holder.

All requests for copyright should be adressed to:
Royal Caribbean Cruises Ltd., 1050 Caribbean Way, Miami, Florida 33132, U.S.A.;
or to Anders Wilhelmsen & Co AS, P.O. Box 1583 Vika, NO-0118 Oslo;
or to the publisher Andresen & Butenschøn AS, P.O. Box 1153 Sentrum, NO-0107 Oslo.

Photos by Fin Serck-Hanssen unless credited in the captions.

The publisher has, with assistance from LCA (London Contemporary Art), BONO (Norwegian Visual Artists Copyright Society) and the individual photographers, made best efforts in clearing all rights to the use of copyright works as included in this book. If you are an author or a holder of copyright and have any questions regarding rights clearance of a work included in this book, please feel free to contact the publisher Andresen & Butenschøn AS, P.O. Box 1153 Sentrum, N-0107 Oslo, Norway.

The use of the abbreviations RCI, RCL and RCCL

RCI Royal Caribbean International owns and operates the fleet of Royal Caribbean Cruise ships. RCI is the term used in this book for this brand.

RCL Royal Caribbean Cruises Ltd. is the holding company listed on the New York Stock Exchange and the Oslo Stock Exchange for the two brands Royal Caribbean International and Celebrity Cruises.

RCCL was previously used for RCI.

Design: Bruno Oldani Kommunikasjonsdesign, Oslo
Editor: Hans B. Butenschøn
Translation: Catherine Stein and Linda Sivesind
Printed in Finland 2002 by Gummerus Printing, Jyväskylä
Paper: Galerie Art Silk 150 gr.

ISBN 82-7694-060-9

Distribution:
Copies are for sale onboard Royal Caribbean Cruise ships
Norsk Sjøfartsmuseum and in all Norwegian bookstores.

Trade orders from: Sentraldistribusjon ANS, Østre Aker vei 61, NO-0286 Oslo.

Vision of Art

How art enhances Royal Caribbean Cruise ships

by Jon Lie and
Fin Serck-Hanssen (photo)

Published by Andresen & Butenschøn
for Royal Caribbean Cruise Lines

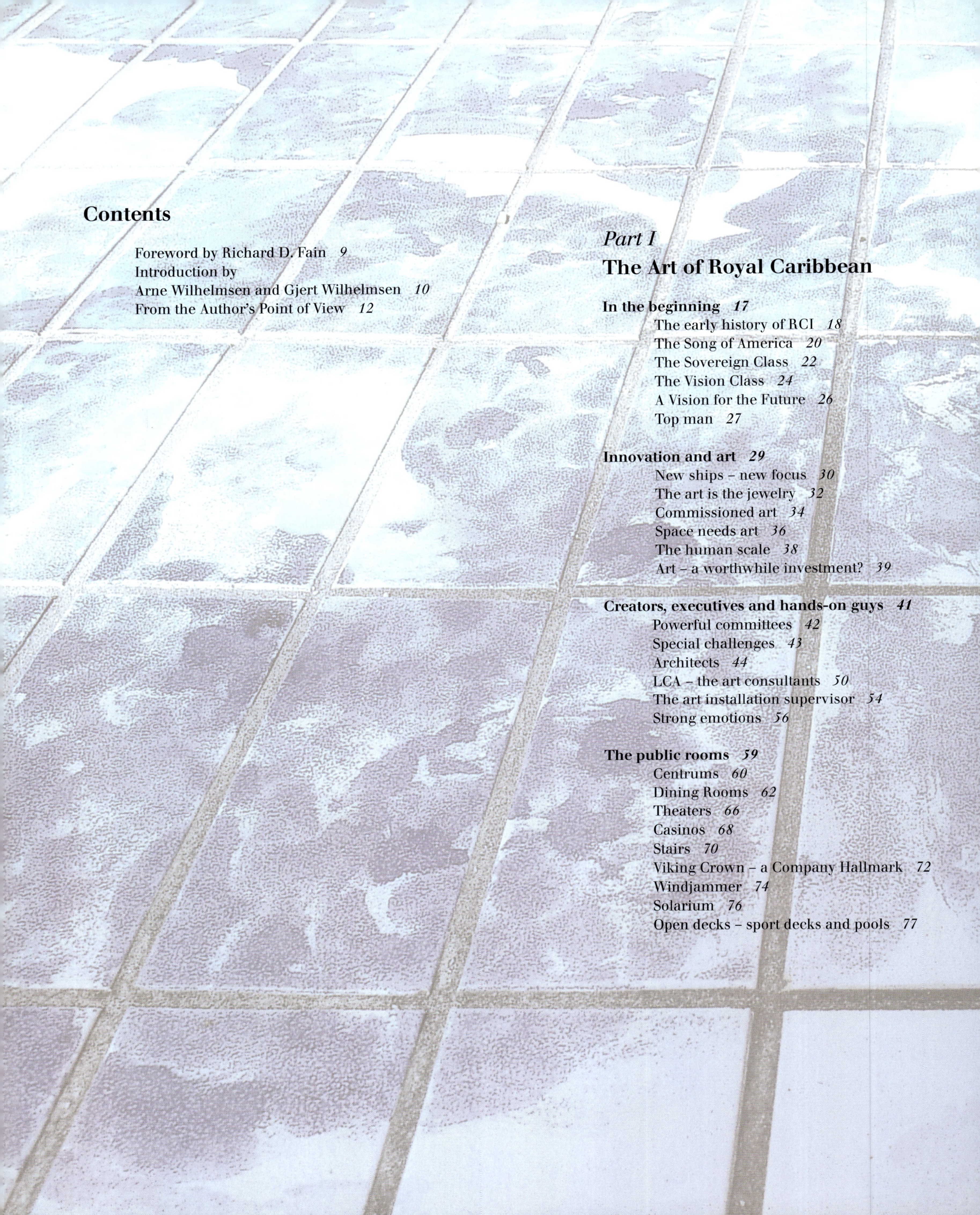

Contents

Part II
Onboard

Part III
Artists and Artisans

Knut Steen (cv p 331): "Moon".

"RCI's emphasis on artwork aboard their ships is a great idea. It's like a floating gallery of easy access for everybody, not just a chosen few. More and more the acquisition of serious art has become very exclusive, reserved for a few elite collectors, many of whom buy for the sole purpose of speculation. Even in a museum, one has only limited access, being pushed along so that others can also see, forbidden to touch the art or even get close.

RCI could have engaged in speculation; instead they made a conscious choice to obtain a great quantity of very good serious art and exhibit it throughout the ship. Art that invites people's understanding instead of alienating and intimidating them.

I think it's wonderful that people have the opportunity not only to see so much original art, but to be able to live with it, and to go back again and again to look at something that interests them for the duration of their trip on board."

Knut Steen
Norwegian sculptor

Knut Steen in Pietrasanta.
(Photo: Morten Krogvold)

Royal Caribbean's Chairman and Chief Executive Officer, Richard D. Fain.

Foreword

**Vision of Art -
indicating new examples
of artworks to be mentioned**

I've learned from experts and experience that building a ship is a highly collaborative process, and that everyone, from architects and engineers to outfitters and designers, has a part to play in the choreography of crafting a ship.

Watching these master craftsmen breathe life into our ships has broadened my concept of art. Growing up, I held the fairly traditional view that art was something you framed and hung on the wall. Later, I conceded that a piece of sculpture could qualify as art, but I absolutely held the line at that – until the cruise industry got a hold of me.

I now know that ships can be works of art, and we at Royal Caribbean International and Celebrity Cruises ships have an entire fleet of masterpieces. I now see art in the graceful curve of a staircase and the detailed etching on a nineteenth-century panel. I now look at the centrums and Royal Promenades on Royal Caribbean and the AquaSpas and conservatories on Celebrity and see art in its much larger context – in the architecture, in the design, even in the lighting .

Just as our ships are floating works of art, they are also showcases for some of the finest works of art on land or at sea. We are very proud of the gallery of artists and artisans we have assembled on our ships. I am convinced that a mural admired in the dining room or a statue drawing you to a stairwell can contribute just as much to one's cruise experience as other amenities.

It is hard to imagine a more dramatic backdrop for a collection of art than the vast oceans and the open skies. The monumental Pool sculpture by George Cutts on Enchantment of the Seas looks even more imposing in that setting.

We select our art to set a mood and to create an environment. Many of our art pieces are highly integrated into the area. Obviously that's most significant with Centrum pieces, such as the breathtaking artworks by Larry Kirkland on Splendour of the Seas and Voyager of the Seas, Knut Steen's wonderful floating sculpture in the Centrum of Grandeur of the Seas or Jonathan Clowe's impressive work on the Rhapsody. The list of important artworks is indeed very long.

This book pays tribute to the hundreds of artists and craftsmen who contribute their inspired skills to enhance the beauty of our ships and to increase the satisfaction of our guests. I am grateful to them for raising my own horizon in art, and for sharing their passion and creativity with all of us. ■

Richard D. Fain
Chairman and CEO
Royal Caribbean Cruises Ltd.

Introduction

Nautical art and design

Since time immemorial, there has been a vital link between ships and artistic expression in Norway. Indeed, the first visual artistic expressions were rendered in the prehistoric stone carvings found in many places along the extensive Norwegian coastline; many of them depicted ships.

As time went on, the ship, and the way it was constructed, developed as a work of art. We see this in the sleek lines of the Viking ships.

Most seagoing Viking ships were utilitarian objects, necessary for a livelihood that depended on the sea. In a mountainous country with little arable land, the ocean offered the main basis for survival. Ships and boats were used for fishing, transport, trade and war.

But there were also ships created for leisure. In addition to being artistically shaped, they were decorated with some of the most exceptional ornaments created at that time. Perhaps the first known cruise ship in Norwegian waters was the Oseberg ship, a vessel built for and used by a Norwegian Viking queen for excursions in the coastal waters of Viken, now known as the Oslo Fjord.

In Viking times it was customary to bury prominent people in their ships. Thus the Oseberg queen was laid to rest in her pleasure boat along with her most precious belongings, including her jewelry, preserving a treasure trove of artistic expression to be discovered a millennium later.

Today's sleek Norwegian cruise liners are a link to the past, to another age when state-of-the art vessels, rich in ornamentation and artistic expression, were created for people of leisure.

A modern cruise ship has been described as a naval architect's dream, contrasting sharply with the utilitarian cargo ships and tankers of our time. Although the exteriors of the most modern cruise ships tend to be less sleek and more boxy than the romantic passenger ships of the past, the essence of the dream remains.

In fact, the interiors of modern cruise ships have evolved into extravagant, luxurious seaborne resorts, catering to every whim of today's passengers. And all this lavishness is beautifully accentuated by unique, top-quality art.

At Royal Caribbean, quality and innovation have been the keystones of corporate development since the company was founded more than 30 years ago.

Art has consistently occupied a central position on Royal Caribbean vessels. Every ship has been carefully crafted so that each has her own soul, expressed both in the exterior lines of the ship and in the interior layout and ornamentation.

It has always been important that Royal Caribbean ships set themselves apart from other passenger vessels. Upon viewing or experiencing one of Royal Caribbean's vessels, passengers and observers alike should be

Prehistoric rock carvings were used as motifs for captets onboard the Song of Norway.

able to say: “This must be a ship from the Royal Caribbean fleet!”

At the same time, care has been taken to make each Royal Caribbean ship different from the other ships in the fleet. Each must have her own identity. It is here that art has played an especially crucial role. In the development of every Royal Caribbean vessel, artistic outfitting has been central to creating the ship’s identity and soul.

This extensive art program has been made possible by the wholehearted engagement of a great number of experts, including artists, architects and art consultants.

We wish to render hommage to the creative effort by all involved, and can think of no better way than to publish a lavishly illustrated book giving examples of the art onboard the ships and to present a selection of the people behind the art and their ideas by interviews.

Arne Wilhelmsen Gjert Wilhelmsen

The Oseberg ship in all her glory. Thanks to the blue clay and tightly-packed turf, in which she was buried, the wood of the ship was hermetically preserved for over 1100 years.

From the author's point of view

This book is not about art history. It is instead an account of some aspects of the world's largest floating art collection as experienced onboard the six Vision ships and the first of the giant Voyager series by an author and a photographer. *Vision of Art* was written on the basis of meetings with the most important artists, architects, art consultants, those who install the works of art, those who make the decisions, and those who sail the seas on these floating repositories of art.

Our aim is to give an impression of what happens from the time the idea of a ship is conceived until the finished vessel sails out of the shipyard on her "maiden" voyage. This is a complex process. A ship is not created on a conveyor belt in a factory. It is built by human beings, people with differing priorities and values.

This is why we have allotted space on these pages for many different voices to be heard, expressing a variety of viewpoints and opinions. These are the voices that contribute to the shipbuilding process. This is not to say that all the various participants in the creative process have been given space, but many are represented in one way or another.

The art presented in this book is a selection of the most important works onboard each featured ship. Some of the works illustrate the overall themes of each ship. There is a broad selection of international artists, although some emphasis has been placed on British, American, and Norwegian artists. This reflects the representation of their works onboard the ships.

Splendour of the Seas *in Oslo harbor. (Photo: Knut Vadseth)*

The photographs are of superb quality thanks to the artistic eye of photographer Fin Serck-Hansen. We hope the pictures and text tempt the readers of this book to travel and experience this very special atmosphere and art at first hand.

One natural question may be: "Where is the ship's soul?" Our experience is that it pervades the entire ship, and can often be found wherever an individual feels most comfortable. We found it in many places, including:

- a deck chair in the sunshine off the coast of Alaska with a view of the glaciers from deck 10 onboard the *Rhapsody of the Seas*;
- the Champagne Bar in the Centrum on the *Vision of the Seas* with a view through large windows of the sea and of Peter Layton's shining 5-deck-high Centrum sculpture, or Inger Sitter's impressive "floating" marble reliefs in the Main Staircase;
- the beautiful, light Windjammer Café on the *Grandeur of the Seas* on her way out of the harbor in San Juan, Puerto Rico;
- a deep armchair in the Viking Crown on the *Splendour of the Seas* as it cascades onto the Oslo Fjord at 24 knots on a sunny summer day, with the Akershus Fortress astern and Copenhagen dead ahead;
- at the Captain's dinner in the "Romeo and Juliet" Dining Room under Nini Anker Dessen's wonderful tapestry series, with a five-course meal heading into the sunset in the straits between Sardinia and Corsica onboard the *Legend of the Seas*;
- the dance floor in the Aft Lounge on *Enchantment of the Seas* sailing through deep blue Caribbean waters towards Charlotte Amalie in the US Virgin Islands;
- Or with a wide-open wallet while shopping on the Royal Promenade onboard the world's largest cruise ship, the *Voyager of the Seas*, departing from Miami and bound for an adventure in the Caribbean.

This book was created in Finland, UK, France, Italy, Alaska, the Caribbean, Connecticut, Miami, Washington DC and Oslo. There are many who deserve thanks. Some 100 people have contributed to the contents of this book through conversations and interviews. Special thanks to: Norwegian sculptor Nini Anker Dessen, who conceived the idea for this book; Gro Nesjar and Joan Blackman for inspiration, knowledge, and all they contributed from their memory; Bruno Oldani for artistic design; Njål Eide for an introduction to the mysteries of ship design; Hans B. Butenschøn for perseverance and an unwavering determination to find the "red thread" through an overwhelming amount of material. Last, but absolutely not least, we thank shipowners Gjert and Arne Wilhelmsen for showing the patience and generous resolve which have made this project a reality.

Jon Lie

SPLENDOUR
SEAS

Part I

The art of Royal Caribbean

"The art is like no other art
and the ships
are like no other ships."

Nicola Elstone
London Contemporary Art

In the beginning

"The Song of Norway led to a creative process so important that it has influenced this company for more than 30 years."

Arne Wilhelmsen
Shipowner

Left: Viking Crown, Sovereign of the Seas.
Mayan Sculpture (copy), Vision of the Seas.

Mogens Hammer and Martin Hallen at the railing on the Song of America.

The early history of RCI

Royal Caribbean Cruise Line AS was conceived in a burst of creative activity.

The concept was simple: to create a new line based on ships tailor-made for cruising the warm waters of the Caribbean.

The idea came from Edwin Stephan who had hotel and cruise line operating experience from Miami, Florida. He came to Norway in 1968 to find shipowners who would back his ideas financially and operationally. And he wanted to have Norwegian seagoing officers, deck and engine crew.

His idea quickly caught on with two family owned shipping companies in Oslo, I.M. Skaugen and Anders Wilhelmsen & Co., later to be joined by the US based Gotaas Larsen Shipping Corporation Inc.

A contract was signed with the Finnish shipyard OY Wärtsilä AB to build a 700 passenger cruise liner for delivery in 1970 with an option for a second vessel to be delivered in 1971. And Royal Caribbean Cruise Line AS was established as a company.

A key person at the outset was Sigurd Skaugen, the senior owner in the firm I.M. Skaugen. He was a remarkable man, full of creative energy and enthusiasm. He was childless and came, in a way, to look upon the new buildings, as his children.

The naval architects from the owner's side were Gjert Wilhelmsen of Anders Wilhelmsen & Co., and Martin Hallen, the technical director of I.M. Skaugen, assisted by Olav Eftedal.

Arne Wilhelmsen came to work closely with Kristian Pahle, the commercial director of I.M. Skaugen, on the development of the new company.

RCI started more or less from scratch. Skaugen and Gotaas Larsen had some experience with passenger vessels, however, having been involved with the postwar emigrant trade to Australia. Entering the cruise business was still an altogether new and different business for all involved.

"However, starting from scratch was an advantage because we felt free to develop a new concept. Almost all ships cruising in the Caribbean were former transatlantic liners which had been converted for cruising. Those that had been built more recently were hybrids with a lot of the conventional liner features. This was true of the *QE 2*, commissioned in 1966 and deployed in the Caribbean during the winter. A book about this vessel and the way it was developed became compulsory reading for us all, to illustrate how not to develop our vessels," muses Arne Wilhelmsen.

The main architects at the outset were Norwegian Geir Grung, who designed the exterior, and Danish Mogens Hammer, who was responsible for interior design.

In the beginning there were many "brainstorming sessions" in Oslo, Miami and Helsinki. People were brought in from the outside – consultants, architects and experts on all aspects of the business, and many creative ideas in the field of shipbuilding and design were produced.

The first RCI vessel, *Song of Norway*, came out with sleek lines and a clipper bow. To make

With three ships in service, the world of Royal Caribbean seemed complete for a while.

it different from all existing passenger ships, an observation lounge was placed around the funnel. This lounge was called the "Viking Crown" and was to become the hallmark of the new cruise line.

The interior featured a dining room and lounges with decor based on musical themes from famous musicals such as "The King and I", "My Fair Lady" and "South Pacific".

Notable among the first artists were the well-known Norwegian sculptor Ørnulf Bast, who adorned the reception area with bas-reliefs of Norwegian Viking ships, and Cato Strøm, who made large zinc etchings of Norwegian landscapes for the main stairways.

The *Song of Norway* was soon followed by two sister ships, the *Nordic Prince* in 1971 and the *Sun Viking* in 1972.

RCI were successful in creating a unique atmosphere on these vessels. The *Song of Norway* soon became the most popular cruise-ship in the US market in spite of the fact that the company was new and did not have an established brand name.

Its name gave the vessel a flying start. It so happened that the musical "Song of Norway" was being launched in the US market as a movie. RCI made an agreement with ABC, which produced the movie, to have joint publicity and thus RCI went on a roadshow introducing the ship and the company in 52 movie theater markets all over the United States. The very first showing of the movie took place in Miami on the day the vessel went on its maiden voyage. This contributed to making the ship *Song of Norway* an instant success. ■

Shipowner Sigurd Skaugen (1907–1975) played an active role in creating the "soul" of the new ships, and he set a standard of innovation fantasy that has since become an important RCI feature.

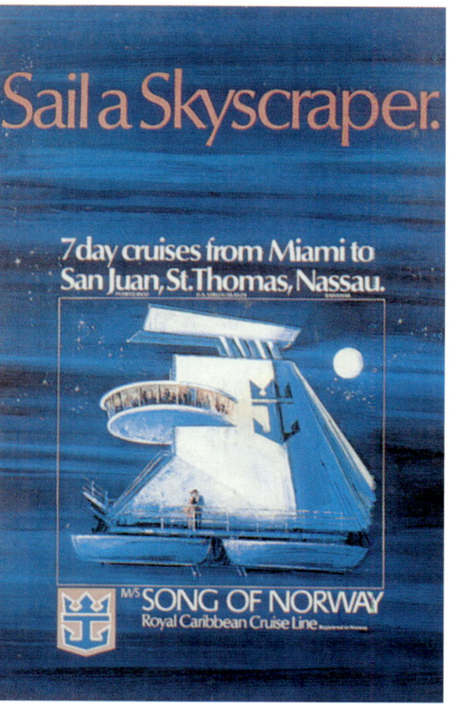

"Sail a Skyscraper" was one of the hard-selling ads for Song of Norway *in the early 1970's, focusing on the Viking Crown Lounge around the funnel.*

Ørnulf Bast: Bronze Viking ships in relief on a golden mosaic background. Song of Norway, *Main entrance hall. The Norwegian sculptor Ørnulf Bast, who was a close friend of Sigurd Skaugen, was commissioned to make major pieces for the main entrance of the* Song of Norway. *Bast's huge Viking ship in bronze relief on golden mosaic dominates the main entrance halls on all the first three vessels. This was also where the three shipping companies' flags waved proudly under the Norwegian pennant. Bast also made monumental works for the Camelot Dining Room on the* Nordic Prince. *Bast was quite a character. He once went to Hallen with his assistant to collect some money. Hallen was certain he had already paid that particular bill. "The money is probably in your top hat," suggested the sculptor's assistant. "No, I keep nothing but bills there!" responded the artist.*

Original Japaneese woodblock prints from the 1890's, aquired for the Madame Butterfly Dining Room onboard the Song of America. *These prints showed the impulses that foreigners brought to the Far East: Western clothing, trains, steamships – all being new to the Japanese after 250 years of isolation.*

The Song of America

Shipowners and founders of RCI, Arne and Gjert Wilhelmsen initiated this book as a hommage to the many artists and architects who have contributed significantly to create a distinct identity for the Royal Caribbean fleet.

The development of the *Song of America*, although based on experience from the initial vessels, was a new breakthrough in design and architecture. The advantage of several years of operative experience gave new options in planning and development. Accomodating over 1,400 passengers she had twice the capacity of previous ships. This made it necessary to have much larger and a greater variety of public rooms which again created new opportunities for architects, designers and artists. Mogens Hammer was still going strong and designed the impressive theater lounge in addition to an intimate piano bar with a distinct nautical flavor called America's Cup. Geir Grung who was responsible for exterior designs, created a new Viking Crown which was much larger and more elegant than its predecessors. The Norwegian artist Jørleif Uthaug, with his intimate knowledge of Norse mythology, did an outstanding job in decorating this room. Two new architects were brought in with the building of the *Song of America*. Finn Nilsson from the well-known firm Arnstein Arneberg, did the Madame Butterfly Dining Room while another Norwegian architect, Njål Eide, was responsible for a lounge called Oklahoma. This latter was to become central in the development of the public spaces on the later RCI vessels.

From the very the beginning, the shipowners themselves were actively involved in the creative process while the vessels were developed. When Sigurd Skaugen, who had been the creative genious in developing the "soul" of the first three vessels, passed away in 1975, his partners became even more active as to the art program.

For example, when the *Song of America* was developed in the early 1980's, Arne Wilhelmsen and his wife Lise, who was educated as an interior decorator, made a special effort to assist the architects and artists. When Finn Nilsson wanted some authentic art for the Madame Butterfly Dining Room, Arne Wilhelmsen, who was a frequent traveller to the Far East, was commissioned to visit Kyoto. Here he engaged Baido Minami, the only surviving Ka-No artist, to make paintings on silk paper with the traditional bird and flower motifs. He also searched print shops to find woodblock prints depicting the arrival of Americans and Europeans to Japan in the early Meiji period in the 1870's.

Arne Wilhelmsen also introduced Mogens Hammer to the New York Yacht Club in order to find pictures and half models of the racing yachts participating in the America Cup races for the piano bar and visited the Metropolitan Museum of Art to find various memorabilia for the vessel's decor.

When Njål Eide had a problem in establishing appropriate decor for the Oklahoma Lounge, Jørleif Uthaug was brought in. But he knew little of musicals and had to be "educated" on the relevant themes. "The result became the most beautiful lounge afloat," states Arne Wilhelmsen. ■

The Sovereign Class

Sovereign of the Seas *was the first "megaship" to be introduced into the cruise market.*

The *Song of America* provided a platform for the next series of vessels developed by RCI. In spite of the fact that the "megaship" concept was developed jointly by RCI and Wärtsilä, the first actual "megaship" was built by Chantiers d'Atlantique in St. Nazaire, France. With a capacity of over 2,200 passengers at the time of delivery in 1987, the *Sovereign of the Seas* was the largest cruiseship ever built, three times larger than the original *Song of Norway.*

The new vessel was not only larger, it was also different from its predecessors in the sense that it offered the traveling public a more varied onboard environment. This was reflected in the vessel layout, the choice of decor and coloring, and in the art. The ship became more sophisticated throughout in order to have a stronger appeal to a more discerning traveler.

Sovereign of the Seas was to be followed by two sister ships, *Monarch of the Seas* in 1991, and the *Majesty of the Seas* in 1992.

A new era had begun. ■

Sovereign of the Seas *in the Panama Canal. This series of ships was built nearly as wide as a Panamax – the maximum size for sailing through the Canal to the Pacific coast.*

Centrum, the multi-deck atrium, was first designed by Njål Eide for Sovereign of the Seas, *and was to become the epitome of the "megaships". (Photo: Knut Vadseth)*

The Vision Class

The next project to evolve was the development of the *Vision Class* vessels which was to be an entirely new concept. In contrast to the existing vessels which had been tailor-made for the Caribbean, these new vessels were to be designed to cruise anywhere in the world.

As before when new vessels were developed, a lot of innovation and new thinking went into the development of the *Vision Class* ships. In order to include itineraries which heretofore had not been feasible, greater speed became a feature of some of these vessels. In order to allow for longer voyages and more time at sea, the cabins were made larger and more comfortable. Balconies, which had already been introduced on some ships, were built into a greater number of cabins. The public rooms were presented in a greater variety and style to please the more experienced cruiser. New features, such as a spacious solarium with a sliding roof and the first ever golf course onboard a ship, represented interesting innovations.

More than ever the importance of art onboard was reflected in the new ships of the *Vision Class* and how that was done will be the main subject of this book. ■

The Solarium on Rhapsody of the Seas. *The Solariums were a new feature for the* Vision Class *ships.*

"Glass ship". Made by Norsk Kunstglass for Viking Crown, Rhapsody of the Seas.

David Gordon Smith (British, b. 1945): "Harlequin". Welded sheet bronze. Entrance, Masquerade Theater, Vision of the Seas.

Galia Amsel: "Niche sculpture", Main Stairs, Vision of the Seas.

The Voyager of the Seas *being built in Turku, Finland.*

A vision for the future

RCI has always encouraged innovation. This has run like a 'red thread' through the operations since the company began to plan the *Song of Norway* in the late 1960's. The *Song of Norway* was a new concept at the time: the first ship tailor-made for cruises in tropical waters, with open sundecks and air-conditioning, and a great deal of emphasis on the décor and art onboard.

Every ship was to have her own identity, and each series was to be different from the preceding series. At the same time, RCI wanted to maintain continuity. It had to be clear that all the ships belonged to the same company. This is why there are some common denominators like the Viking Crown, the vast lounges around the funnel found in a wide variety of styles on all Royal Caribbean vessels.

When RCI went from the *Sovereign* series to the *Vision Class*, even more emphasis was placed on art and architecture. New ships have always been planned well in advance in this company. The RCI team now created a series of six ships in which each vessel was unique. Each ship was built as a new creation that bore certain similarities to those built before.

The *Vision Class* ships were built in pairs at two different shipyards. Although in many ways they were sister ships they convey different impressions to the passengers. This is because their themes vary in their many public rooms, especially the dining rooms, show lounges and casinos.

The *Vision Class* ships became the optimal type of cruise ship. With a 2,000 passenger capacity, the ships could sail fully booked all year round. Royal Caribbean moved outside the Caribbean for the first time. Today, the *Vision* ships are in service in the Caribbean, South America, Europe, Alaska, the Far East and worldwide.

With *Voyager* the company has – in a sense – returned to its origins. The *Voyager Class* vessels are tailor-made for the Caribbean, which continues to be an extremely important market for the company's operations. These ships are designed to attract new types of passengers. They have vast capacity, make good profits and generate about 2.5 times as much revenue per year as the *Vision* ships.

Top man

Royal Caribbean's CEO, Richard D. Fain.

RCI's powerful CEO, Richard D. Fain has been involved in all levels of planning and building these ships. He is a very skilled negotiator who doesn't give up easily. His first major task at RCI was to chair the Steering Committee for building the *Sovereign of the Seas*. In 1988, he was named Chief Executive Officer and Chairman of the Board. His responsibilities and influence have been considerable. The *Vision* ships became his "babies". He monitored their development and was closely involved in everything related to these ships. "He inherited a legacy consisting not only of everything we had put into the ships, but also our corporate business philosophy and way of doing things," remarks Arne Wilhelmsen.

Richard D. Fain doesn't think he deserves to be called the 'Father' of the *Vision Class* series: "When you tell the history of a creative effort, it often sounds like a series of inspirations or critical moments. In fact, what has been so exciting about every step of this journey is how many people are involved and how exciting the process has been. And I think everybody involved, including myself, felt that this was an opportunity to create something really great. We had an opportunity to do things differently. With sufficient focus, we were able to do some wonderful things.

"We had terrific success with the *Sovereign Class* of ships. We learned a lot in the creation of those ships, both in terms of what the passengers wanted, and in terms of technology. The technical team was headed by Martin Hallen, a genius when it comes to building cruise ships. Part of his genius is not just his ability to calculate stresses and allocate spaces, but to hear what people want, that is, to listen to them and translate their suggestions into something that works from the engineering point of view.

"In every class of ships there are certain things you try to accomplish. With the *Vision Class* one of the goals was to make it easy for passengers to find their way around. That had to do with the layout of the ship, and with the big increase in the number of choices of where to go and find activities. The upshot is that the *Vision* ships have a far more flexible layout than previous vessels.

"And flexibility is becoming increasingly important in the industry", says Fain. "The cruise industry will be different in five years. I think we have seen something between a revolution and an evolution when it comes to offering passengers more choices. I think it is likely that Cuba will open up within the next five years. That will have a dramatic impact. We will see growth in destinations in South America and new destinations in the Caribbean. And we'll see more new ships going to the Far East, and to European/Mediterranean and Scandinavian waters." ■

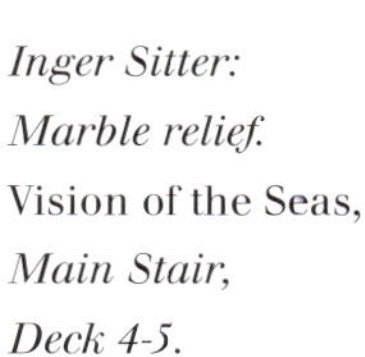

Inger Sitter: Marble relief. Vision of the Seas, *Main Stair, Deck 4-5.*

Innovation and Art

"Making demands on artists is neither impossible nor illogical. We insist that art has to work in a certain context ..."

Gro Nesjar
London Contemporary Art

Giovanni Arico:
"Two Glass Blowers".
Detail. Enchantment of the Seas.

Pearl Levy:
"L'Afriquaine II".
Patinated bronze
Sculpture.
Voyager of the Seas.

New ships – new focus

One of the most radical innovations on the *Vision* vessels was architect Njål Eide's further development of a unifying Centrum of mind-boggling dimensions. It was onboard the *Splendour of the Seas* that American artist Larry Kirkland made his splendid sun-disc "Celestium" for the Centrum, an installation five decks high. "This idea of large sculpture installations continued throughout the six-vessel series. The works of art on the various decks seem to flow from this spectacular Centrum, and it was the Centrum itself that acted as the catalyst for the process," says Richard D. Fain.

As far as the owners' personal involvement is concerned, today's process is a far cry from the time the first ship, the *Song of Norway*, was built. Now a number of ships are under construction or on order at the same time. "It doesn't make sense for us to go about choosing art for the ships as a kind of hobby," remarks Arne Wilhelmsen. "Now things must be done professionally. Of course, we provide some inspiration, and follow the process, but these days it is the architects, in close collaboration with our capable partners at London Contemporary Art, who choose the art. They provide complete project management, including budget responsibility".

LCA enters the scene

Quality is a major prerequisite onboard all RCI vessels. Great effort is invested in ensuring this. According to Nicola Elstone of LCA: "We were fortunate to be able to work on five of the six *Vision Class* ships, and we learned a lot from ship to ship. For us, it was very satisfying that the last of the sister ships turned out to be just as widely acclaimed by the passengers as the first in the series had been three years earlier – especially satisfying when one realizes that each ship featured new interior decors and artwork programs."

London Contemporary Art's relationship with RCI started with an art program for the Legend of the Seas. "We went in with very modern ideas. Some liked our approach and some didn't. We had to make adjustments, and take a more traditional approach including figurative art. By the last ship, we gained acceptance for a more contemporary abstract approach. The experience of working with the ships and the different architects was quite an education," continues Nicola Elstone.

"One of our selling points was that we could help to unite the visual aspects of the ships. We were working with all seven architects spread around the world who propounded very different schemes. The art was able to unite all those architects and all those schemes to create a sense of unity in the ships. In addition, we were able to make a visual statement to accentuate the differences between the ships. We created a new overall concept for each vessel.

"The names of the areas onboard are generally chosen by the marketing department while the themes are often suggested by the architects. These themes often proved helpful since they gave us a framework for our work.

"I think it would be a mistake to do things radically different on every ship. A repeat passenger should know that they are walking onto a Royal Caribbean ship. We don't want the same artwork, but we do want the same feel, supplemented by new artists and techniques."

Architect Howard Snoweiss, seasoned Casino and Theater architect after more than 20 years' cooperation with Royal Caribbean, says: "There is continuity in RCI's choice of artists from ship to ship. Helaine Blumenfeld, Knut Steen, Inger Sitter, Larry Kirkland and Jonathan Clowes are household names. Choices are not haphazard; they are by design. Architect Njål Eide works close with these artists. Because Njål is responsible for the Centrums, he is at the core of the way our ships feel. He also does the stairways, which are also key public spaces. We achieve this visual continuity because he works so well with the artists." ■

Larry Kirkland (cv p 299): "Celestium", Centrum, Splendour of the Seas.

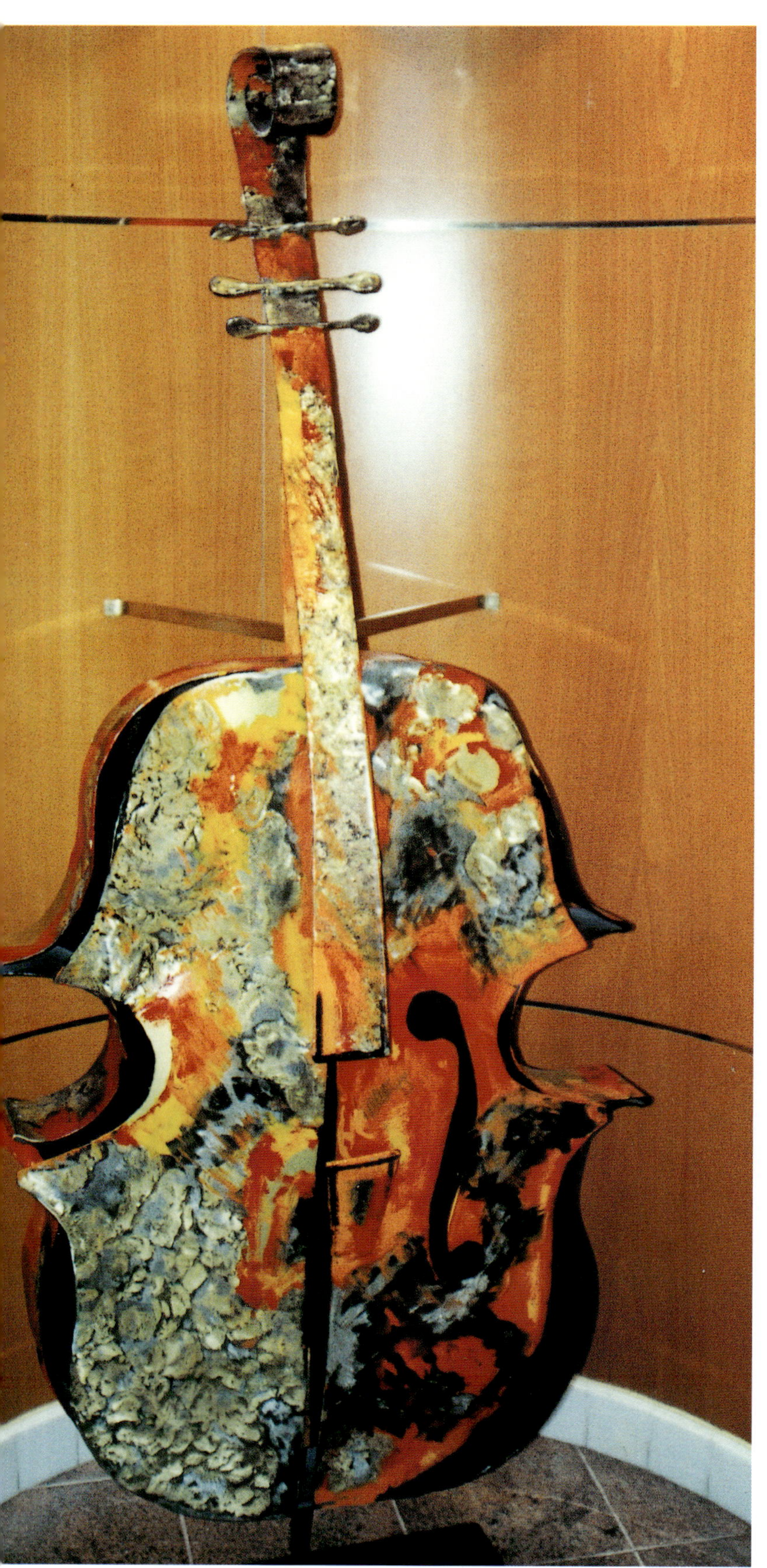

The art is the jewelry

"We look at the art onboard as the jewelry," says architect Howard Snoweiss. "It's what people actually see and remember. It glamorizes a space. But we have to distinguish between the kind of art that's being used on these ships and other art. I think most of this is quite different from what you will find in a Madison Avenue art gallery. We do pieces that are themed and geared to work in the spaces."

The artists must be integrated into the building process. "We can no longer build a ship and buy the art afterwards," says the architect Njål Eide. "The art must be planned together with the architecture. There must be a close relationship because in the end, it is the architect who is responsible – also for the success of the space.

"But we have art consultants to assist us. We discuss things until we come up with a list of artists we feel suit the project. Overall, this method works very well. Building – as we did – nine ships at the same time, all in different stages of construction, demands tight management at every level.

"We're working in a borderline area between art and decoration. The purpose of the artwork is to enchance the space, and this can sometimes create a conflict with the artists and their egos. In the end, it will be RCI who has the final word – and considering the number of ships built and amount of artwork commissioned, the process goes very smoothly," explains Eide.

"Each architect receives a number of operational briefings about what his or her area will be used for", says Petter Yran, another architect involved in the RCI ships. "Then we make proposals for themes or décor, for example classic interiors, an Art Deco interior, a traditional English interior. We have the overall responsibility for all construction and finishes for the space.

"We make suggestions about where to put art and we either agree or disagree with the art consultant's proposals. As far as the artwork is concerned, we are obviously concerned that the color range the artists work with also compliments the space." ■

Marc Berlet (cv p 259): "Espanola Drive". Painted metal and wood. Rhapsody of the Seas, *Deck 6 Starboard by entrance Broadway Melodies Theatre.*

Mike Newby (cv p 310): "Festivals", one of three panels of stained glass in main stairs, Enchantment of the Seas.

Commissioned art

"Our work must be consistent and stand up to high standards across my disciplines: quality, safety, technical, and not the least aesthetics," states LCA's Gro Nesjar. "This applies to all art onboard, even decor elements. Obviously, it's fundamental to be able to differentiate between good and bad quality. We have to select the good; we must never underestimate our audience. The passengers have paid for an experience based on quality, so quality must be reflected in the food, service, decor, furniture and absolutely in the level of art onboard. We must never believe that 'average' people don't experience art. Experiencing art is not reserved for 'the in-crowd'. Cruise passengers are observant and have plenty of free time. Most spend at least a week on the ship."

Janet Stayton (cv p 327): "Moonlight Bay". Oil paintings on canvas. Midship Lounge, Deck 6, Rhapsody of the Seas. *Moonlight Bay is the all time classic song written by Edward Madden and Percy Wenrich for the 1939 film "Babes in Arms", which caused a sensation in 1939 as the biggest box office hit that year. Janet Stayton's paintings celebrate the classical theme of moonlight over water. She feels that in this series she has captured something pure; there isn't the nostalgia she painted previously but rather a dimension of space, of night, bringing forth the eternal questions of man and nature.*

An artist's view

The American painter Janet Stayton, who lives and works in Pietrasanta, Italy, has executed several large commissions for RCI. "I am my own boss," says Stayton. But she adds: "If you are working for a client you have to swallow your pride and listen to them when they make comments, and you must do it with great respect. You do things the way you want to, but you must respect their wishes. The first commission I made was 'The Moonlight Bay' onboard the *Rhapsody of the Seas.* I was a little nervous when I arrived at the ship. You never really know what to expect until the actual walls are in place since they are curved. They mounted the paintings before I arrived. There's a step there that you were unable to see. They made changes that you didn't know about, even in the colors.

"When I arrived at the hotel, they said: 'Everything is already up. But there is one thing you won't like.' A deep silence followed. 'We had to cut one of your paintings.' That ruined my evening. I didn't know which painting they were talking about.

"The next day I went to the ship. There was a wall where they had to fit a door, so they had cut a painting into three panels. Thank God it looked absolutely fabulous. And it was the only painting that could possibly be treated that way.

"All the lighting and the wood finishes on the walls sucked some of the colors out of the paintings. I had to reinforce some of the lines in the glowing moonlight. Instead of black or gray, I had muted them to keep the moonlight idea and they just vanished. They said: 'Don't be angry, don't be hurt. But we have to talk to you.' I was not afraid of them, but I could sense my pride welling up. I was used to having large New York shows, and there I was sitting on a ship in a French yard and nasty things were happening. I had to push this down, all this ego and pride. I was going through an incredible growing process. Right on the spot this whole thing began and ended. I took a deep breath, swallowed and said I would be happy to do the changes required.

"Of course they were right. It's a site piece. It's part of an organic space, not a studio with white cool walls. There was very little to do, but it had to be done. I guess one could have been a prima donna, but you don't gain anything by it. It may make you feel better, but you are not completely autonomous. If you are a prima donna, you pretend to have control over things that are not controllable. It's a public place – it's not yours. You have to let go and do your job. And that becomes a level of professionalism.

"But after they cut my painting in three on *Rhapsody*, and after they put three paintings in the wrong order on *Vision*, I have found it best to make my paintings interchangeable, so that they work no matter which way you cut them or arrange them.

"A big commission means a lot of work. You have to do away with the artist's luxury of being able to work at your own pace, when you want to lock yourself up in the studio, spending hours sitting in a chair looking at your work, thinking, being autonomous, being your own boss and working the hours you want to work.

"You can find lots of good artists for a ship but many of them can't deliver. This entails a responsibility: If you get a job, you have to do it. The ship will sail on schedule. It doesn't matter if you make a beautiful painting or sculpture if the work is not finished on time. You have to bury your ego because you're working for someone. That is, you don't exactly bury it, but you hide it. When you do commissions, you have to work many, many, many hours a day. You have to be disciplined with your time, and you have to keep going even when you don't want to." ■

Space needs art

"Any space needs art to be complete," says Richard D. Fain, Royal Caribbean's CEO. Shipowner Gjert Wilhelmsen agrees with Fain: "These ships aren't floating art galleries. The purpose of the art is to be a part of the overall atmosphere. A good example is the Centrum – a huge and dominating space which extends upward through as many as seven decks, with an eye-catching piece of art that blends well into this tall space, sculpturally speaking. These sculptures must be big enough, dominant and striking. Larry Kirkland set the tone with his Sun Disc on the *Splendour of the Seas.* The art is part of what gives the ship her identity. This is also clear in the Dining Rooms, with their central sculptures, and the theaters, with their beautiful stage curtains that take many months to create at Paramount Parks. We learned early on from Sigurd Skaugen. It started out as decor, but eventually became a great deal of stunning art."

"We wouldn't mind going more in the direction of integrating art into the ship's structure, forging it into the steel, so to speak," says Lars Iwdal, head of Arkitektbyrån AB in Gothenburg, Sweden. Arkitektbyrån has created all the solariums for the *Vision Class* ships and the sports deck/solariums for the *Voyager Class* ships. Iwdal prefers to look at a ship as a large piece of art in its own right. He would like to see even closer cooperation between the architects and the artists in the development of the ship.

However, he concedes that it is difficult to find the right artists. "We have to bear in mind that we are creating artificial environments which are supposed to remind us of something real in another place. But we're on a ship. There's a limit as to how much freedom you can take without it becoming excessive, and that has been known to happen. But we learn and we improve. And we learn to become stronger as architects in dealing with the owners."

Architect Howard Snoweiss has designed casinos for seven ships and theaters for six: "We are happy about having an art consultant involved in this. I think it's important that there be someone who acts as a liaison between the designer and the artist; someone who knows how to handle artists. They comprise a special group of egos, and they need a lot of handholding. Sometimes they are dependable and sometimes they are not. One little crisis in their personal life can affect everything they do." ■

Helaine Blumenfeld (cv p 265): "Wrapped figure 1". Red travertine sculpture. Vision of the Seas. *Niche, Main Stairs, Deck 5-6. Starboard side.*

Bruce McLean: Powder Coated Faint on Steel Panels. Voyager of the Seas.

Maria Veronica L. Solem (cv p 323): Oil paintings. Purser's Desk on Vision of the Seas.

The human scale

Richard D. Fain: "Njål Eide and the other architects have managed to make architecture on a human scale so that people feel comfortable. They have done more than just make beautiful rooms and structures. One of the dangers of size is that you feel awe. I remember the old Intercontinental Hotel in the Port of Miami. It was a fancy hotel. The owner said: 'I must spare no expense'. He ended up making an enormous lobby, which was awe-inspiring and grand, but cold and unwelcoming. I think that's one of the reasons it went bankrupt. Afterwards they went back in and covered it with carpets and put up little partitions to break up the space. It was still impressive, but on a more human scale.

"As we were building the *Sovereign Class* ships, we went over to look at that hotel. We realized this was very impressive, but we needed a place where our passengers would enjoy spending time. One of the comments I love to hear is: 'Gee. It was not until I got ashore that I realized how big the ship was.' Too often architects want people to walk in and say 'WOW!'. Our architects want people to walk in and say 'WOW', and still be saying that seven days later." ■

Carl Nesjar (cv p 308): Sculpture for Centrum, Enchantment of the Seas.

Art – a worthwhile investment?

David Stanley is Vice President Casino and Onboard revenue and sponsor for the Artwork Program.

In 1970, Royal Caribbean paid USD 13,5 million for the *Song of Norway*. Thirty years later RCI spent some USD 12 million on art alone for the *Voyager of the Seas*. Some people say they could have spent half that amount and still had a decent ship. David Stanley, Vice President Onboard Revenue and sponsor for the Artwork Program, doesn't agree: "I think it's money well spent. Our ships are spectacular because of our public spaces. There's no other company that makes its public spaces look as beautiful as Royal Caribbean. The product we offer and the value that we give is very good. We just need to communicate that value to the people. The art alone is obviously not the reason passengers purchase a cruise, but people are amazed at the beauty of these ships. That's part of exceeding their expectations."

Stanley also explains that the art budget covers far more than just paintings and wall decorations: "We basically do three types of art. One is architectural art, which is art decor that is an integral part of the architecture. For example, if an architect wants to feature a frieze around a door, that would count as art and go into the art budget. The second is the thematic art, where the architects use the art budget to reinforce the theme of a room. This can be wall murals, floor mosaics, even ceiling domes. The third is what we call 'art-art' which includes the traditional pictorial art, paintings, sculptures – artwork that can be moved easily to another location.

"The art budgets are generally split evenly between the three types of art as defined; however, the trend with the newer ships is more toward 'art-art'.

David Stanley admits that he doesn't know how much difference the art makes to the average guest.

"I know it makes a lot of difference to some guests, and I'm sure it makes no difference to others. What do the people in between feel about the art? I certainly think they notice a feeling about a room, they notice a theme – and they would definitely notice if it weren't there. But some people love the ships for the art. They look at all the pieces and they are hugely impressed. People are relaxed on a cruise. They have time to look at the details of the decor of our ships. The idea behind our art program is to stimulate the passengers, make them think and feel and react."

Richard D. Fain agrees: "Very few people come back and say 'I took this cruise because of the beautiful art onboard.' Most people wouldn't list the art as being a significant feature of Royal Caribbean. But I think when people are onboard, and when people walk around enjoying themselves, they appreciate the ambiance – a feeling not only of elegance but also of interest.

"The great architects that we have used to design our ships, Njål Eide, Robert Tillberg, Lars Iwdal, Howard Snoweiss, create spectacular spaces. But any space needs art to be complete. And I think the art compliments it. The architecture is great, but the architecture is even greater when it is filled with beautiful works of art. And the architecture also makes the art better. The setting is an important element of a good piece of art. And many of our art pieces are highly integrated into their arenas. Obviously, that's most significant with some of our Centrum pieces.

"People get an image of quality from many features on the ship. If you look at moldings and the fine detail of the woodwork, the wall materials and the ceilings, they are some of the most complex, but also the most elegant ceilings at sea. The artwork is an integral part of the image, conveying a sense of quality even if the passengers are not consciously aware of it. The art makes a Royal experience even more enjoyable." ■

Creators, executives and hands-on guys

"To be part of creating something as rich and complicated as a modern cruise ship gives me an incredible feeling of pride."

Gro Nesjar
London Contemporary Art

Maria Veronica L. Solem painting the last strokes in the Golf Bar onboard the Voyager of the Seas.

Christiane Pettersen (b. 1943, French): Sculpture. Brass. Vision of the Seas.

Powerful committees

Two separate bodies, each representing the owners in different ways, oversee and direct the work on new buildings. These are the Steering Committee and the Inspection Team. The latter is comprised of ships' officers who inspect the construction of the ships on site at the various yards.

A Steering Committee includes owners, technical teams and key Miami management; designers and architects attend by invitation. The committees meet regularly throughout the entire planning and building process. This means that they meet continuously since Royal Caribbean is building or designing a number of ships at any given time. Headed by Richard Fain, the Steering Committee has emerged as one-third think-tank, one-third watchdog and one-third coordinator. The committee looks after the entire ship, from engines to the standard of cabins, from dining room layout to passenger flow in the public areas.

Kelly Gonzales is Manager New Building Department and member of the RCI Steering and Art Committees.

Says architect Howard Snoweiss: "It's always a give-and-take process. We sometimes go to the Steering Committee with two alternative concepts. I think that Royal Caribbean in particular uses the design of the ships as part of their marketing approach. Each time you go there, they are looking for something new – a new slant, a new twist, another way of doing something."

Architect Petter Yran says: "The Steering Committee uses a lot of money on architecture, models, drawings, perspectives, etc. to give all involved the best possible impression of what the passengers will experience when they come onboard. We work on our proposals until we come up with something the committee is satisfied with."

Architect Bjørn Storbraaten says: "The Technical Director Harry Kullivara and Richard Fain are especially good at noticing problems. They can read drawings and see right away if things are in balance or not, and if the margins are too small for anything – from washing to corridor traffic. I was impressed by how much they understood from just sitting and observing. After all, it isn't easy to understand an architect's drawings."

Kelly Gonzales, Manager, New Building Design and member of the Steering and Art Committees, says: "Until some years ago, the artwork was presented to the entire Steering Committee. That has now been narrowed down to the Art Committee, consisting of 6–7 persons headed by our Chairman and President. All artwork presentations are presented by the art consultants to the architects before being presented to us. Knowing that what is presented to us already has the architects' and the designers' blessings, we try to narrow the art presentations down to a select group of people to keep it more streamlined and productive."

Says Gro Nesjar of London Contemporary Art: "We present our concept to the Art Committee, which is independent in its decisions. Once we went through the art for *Vision of the Seas*, with 70 boards, in 2 1/2 hours! Generally, money is not the focus of our discussions. They'd rather pay a little more and be impressed with what they get."

Vice President David Stanley elaborates: "The major objects of art are usually approved around 18 months before the delivery of the ship so that the artists have time to construct the piece, test it, ship it over to the yard and install it. We're pretty well organized. There are minimal last-minute changes," he says.

"Last-minute stuff is for men like Chris Gottelier. He is the hands-on miracle maker who solves those problems. He's terrific. He knows what he's doing and he knows how to do it. He is a huge asset to Royal Caribbean and LCA. The artists love him and he loves their art," says Stanley. ■

Special challenges

Gro Nesjar adds: "You can't plan for every contingency. Often things turn out differently than we had first imagined and we have to take that in stride. It's challenging and it demands flexibility on the part of everyone. Everything that goes on the ship must be approved by DNV, the ship classification society. The standards set for the Vision and Voyager vessels were tougher than ever before. When it comes to safety, little or no latitude is allowed. The artists have to conform to a multitude of restrictions: safety, weight, fire regulations and what the engineers tell them about how their art must be able to move or not move. Passenger safety is always paramount. But sometimes we make mistakes. It's impossible to think of everything. A sharp little metal bit in a relief on a stairway may be in exactly the right place for a guest to catch his arm. Commissioned art for cruise ships requires many more considerations than normal decorative artwork."

Art Installation Supervisor Chris Gottelier refers to the Aurora Borealis in the Viking Crown on the *Vision of the Seas*: "It's 350 pieces of glass sticking up 2.5 meters above the deck. You couldn't reach them by hand – but they were sharp. Somebody came to inspect and said: 'Those pieces are sharp, somebody is going to injure themselves.' I said: 'Show me someone who can jump 2.5 meters and hit it.'" Kelly Gonzales adds: "By nature, artists require a certain amount of freedom to be able to express themselves. And on the ships there are so many rules and regulations that have to be taken into consideration. They have to strike a fine balance, and it takes an artist with particular attention to detail to help us work out an installation suitable for a ship." ■

The security standards also apply to the artwork onboard the ships. Their installation must be approved by the ship classification society and US Coastguard. Huge installations like Larry Kirklands "The Dancer and Tutu" on Voyager of the Seas *are no exception.*

Architects

Njål Eide, sculptor Warren Seelig, his wife and co-worker Sherry Gibson with Espen Viksjø during their first meeting about the Centrum sculpture for Radiance of the Seas. *The meeting took place two years before the ship made her Maiden Voyage. (Photo: Jon Lie)*

The modern cruise ship is often described as a first-class floating resort. In addition, it must embody the technology and resource processes necessary to be self-sustaining for varying periods at sea. Creative and often unique solutions are required to respond to the complex logistic, technical, functional and safety demands this entails. It is within these challenging constraints that cruise ship designs and concepts are being developed. Current commitments at the forefront of this development include a great number of ships currently ordered and being built by RCI.

Multiple architects

One may wonder why Royal Carribean employs so many architects for its ships. Other companies give the job to one or two firms. Richard D. Fain explains: "Very early on, we made a conscious, unanimous decision to divide the responsibilities for the design of the ship, interior and exterior alike, among different architects. First of all, we wanted to create differentiation. It is not that one is better than the other, but with only one firm of architects, there is a danger that the ship will have too much of the same feeling all over. You want different atmospheres in different places; at one moment you might want a quiet, elegant space, and the next you might want something with rockers and a bit whimsical. There's no doubt that any one of our architects could create a series of different spaces, but I think we get more differentiation and variety by having the different inputs.

"In addition, different architects have different strengths. Some architects and firms of architects have particular expertise on the technical requirements for the theater, while others seem to have a better sense of working with space, and still others seem more comfortable dealing with colors and textures.

"Another reason for hiring multiple firms is that there is a limit to the creativity any man or woman can apply to any given project. RCI thinks that at some point enthusiasm and excitement wane. But people still have to work together. What we found is that they all accept the challenge and come up with solutions that are better than anyone could have come up with on his own. It has its pluses and minuses, but if they can't work together, we can end up with compromises, and they usually feel like – compromises."

Competition and cooperation

Shipbuilding is a complicated process that entails conflicts of interest. But there should be conflicts in a creative process if the result is to be good. There should be a certain competitive element and an overall desire to deliver the best possible results. This is one of the reasons why architects have to compete to get a job. At the same time, architects must be able to cooperate so that the end result, the ship, can be perceived as a whole. Architects not chosen in the first round are allowed to criticize those who win the bid in their subsequent work. This leads to a lot of good input in the various areas.

"After we have submitted our drawings, the yard comes with its proposal and sub-contractor drawings," explains architect Petter Yran. "These must be proofed. The yard is interested in driving down standards and costs, while we are preoccupied with keeping them as high as possible.

"The process goes quickly. Ship plans and work for USD 350–400 million are carried out in 30 months. A project like this would take twice as long on land. Both the planning period and the construction period have become much shorter since we entered the scene in this industry. The yards always want more time to negotiate procurement, etc., so they pressure us and the owners, who approve the time schedule, to cut 'our' time. As a result, the planning period is about half what it was just a few years ago. But the total number of man-hours hasn't declined. You just need more people working on the project. This means that an architect must have a larger firm today in order to complete such contracts," explains Yran.

The Head Architect

The Norwegian Njål Eide is rated among the world's most experienced and creative cruise ship designers. The *Vision Class*, the *Voyager Class* and the *Radiance Class* all bear Eide's hallmark. These cruise liners constitute a fleet of 15 ships ranging from 70,000 to 142,000 gross tons.

Njål Eide's role at Royal Caribbean Cruise Lines began with the *Song of America* over 20 years ago. "From very early on, there was strong cooperation between the shipowners and architects regarding the artwork onboard," says Eide. "In the beginning, the artwork onboard was predominantly Norwegian – Norwegian artists were closest. As time went on, the ships' interiors became more and more influenced by international contemporary art, although Norway is still strongly represented.

Njål Eide describes the long and involved road to building a cruise ship – long before art becomes a factor: "When RCI decides to build a new ship, they go to the shipyard first. They define the specifications for the kind of ship they want and what functions it must fulfill. Once the program is laid out, they might contact me. But in the first phase, the project is worked out internally, with RCI and a shipyard that is experienced at managing cruise ship projects.

"Ship engineering has clear parallels with being a land-based architect. You have to know how to construct a large building; none the less, you use consultants in specialized areas. In this case, it is the ship's engineer who dominates and defines the technical criteria.

"The shipowner goes out to different shipyards and asks for bids on the concept they have developed.

"I never give up. There's no use coming to me with something that isn't good enough. Everyone knows that."

Njål Eide

The Head Architect
Although many architects have made significant contributions to the Royal Caribbean ships, one architect holds a special, very important place in the history of RCI: Njål Eide.

The owners get a number of responses, and at this point I have also had the pleasure of being brought into the picture to evaluate and discuss the proposed ideas. In the end, a shortlist is drawn up of about three or four yards that are asked to bid for the job. Each yard has its own special way of building. As a result, the end result will be different from yard to yard. I am often involved in several phases of evaluation and adapting the solutions to satisfy the owners' interests. A certain number of the architect's intentions are incorporated into the project before a contract is signed. This is important because it can have an impact on the price.

After the *Song of America*, Eide participated in the *Sovereign* series, in which the shipowner used three or four architects. Eide had a central role. He was responsible for designing the general areas such as the Main Staircase and Atrium, plus a number of specialty rooms all over the ship. It was also Eide who chose most of the art. The art was selected jointly by the owners and the architects in those days. There were no art consultants then – just a little committee, and proposals usually came from the architects. There was also little artwork compared to the projects today.

The Champagne Bar onboard Grandeur of the Seas *is a typical creation by Eide who also designs the furniture for his spaces.*

"This worked fine," says Eide. "There was still Norwegian dominance, but we had traveled and made contacts with a number of international artists, whom I felt suited the project."

For the *Vision Class* ships, Eide has executed concept design and layout arrangements, detail planning and interior design of major spaces including all Centrums, two double-height Dining Rooms, all Schooner Bars, most Viking Crown Observation Lounge/ Discos, two Windjammer Cafés and most main circulation areas and services.

"With our enormous workload for the shipowner and the demands made on the architecture office, we no longer have time to select art. Having an art consultant, London Contemporary Art, gives us some relief. It's also very useful that a person as efficient and knowledgeable as Gro Nesjar has established a branch office of LCA in Oslo.

"There has to be chemistry with the artist. I know from my own experience that if you work with the art consultants and artists in the early stages of a project, the results will be successful.

"There is usually a theme for parts of the ship. RCI has done this ever since the *Song of Norway*. The themes crystallize after discussions between owners, the architects, and the art consultants. I honestly don't know whether the first proposals come from the art consultants. The best ideas have a tendency to come from the least expected sources at strange times. But the owners maintain a very conscious line of management – in contrast to a normal new-building committee. This also applies to the names on the ships. They have a list of proposed names for the rooms onboard. Sometimes things happen a little bit out of order. First, a ship gets a name, then the common rooms are named, and only then is the ship's theme decided. This can lead to conflicts.

"Njål Eide was like our guru of architecture."

Kelly Gonzales
Manager New Building Design

"The art has to be installed on the ship according to schedule. The shipyard calculates this into its schedule. All of the artwork for all the different areas must be in their crates on the dock at a given time, completely ready for mounting. All the art must be packed and sent in accordance with this schedule. Once the art arrives at the yard, it's the art installation manager along with the yard's project manager who are responsible for the whole process that follows. They are the ones who tell the shipyard that those screws are in the right place and that they've correctly mounted the suspension apparatus – or that they have do it differently so that, for example, it can bear two tons of marble. We used to do this kind of work a lot before, together with the yard. Now the yard has total responsibility for most art installation onboard right up until the ship is delivered and leaves the pier. LCA supervises and makes certain this process works.

"The art must be mounted at the right time, that is, not too early so that it can get damaged. There have been occurrences where artwork has been completely destroyed, or crates exposed to rain on the dock, filling up with water. This happened with a sailing boat model intended for a Schooner Bar, but we managed to dry it out. A lot of strange things happen along the way.

"Then we have to coordinate the electricity and lighting – together with the artist, we agree on how the artwork will be lit, and other electrical requirements. From day one, we specify artwork for the walls. But we don't know what kind. We might decide to install 25 spotlights in the area, but the final placement is just an estimation. All changes from the plan cost money. But that's part of the process. The timetable set in the project plan has to incorporate time for adjustments and fine-tuning.

"There may also be a question of coordinating the lighting with a computer program that allows for variations as the day progresses. For example, at breakfast time, we provide a clear, fine light; at lunch, a little softer light. If cocktails are served at 4.30 p.m., we move on to nice, dramatic lighting – not exactly disco lighting, but a little atmospheric. An orchestra may play lovely, swinging music in this light. Americans love to dance, and they will go straight to the dance floor as soon as they get their drinks. The atmosphere is pleasant, and the passengers wander off to eat. In the stairway to the Dining Room the light will also be adjusted to fit the atmosphere. We create a stage set. The whole ship is basically a theater."

But there are differences among stage sets. Njål Eide didn't want to design a *Titanic* 2: "You won't get me to reconstruct the past. I've only worked with 'reconstructing' once, and that was when I won the competition for the exterior of the *Disney Magic*, a nostalgia ship. Otherwise, my basic principle is 'no reconstruction'. I'm happy this principle has been accepted. Cruise ships are complex creatures. We're building modern floating hotels.

"I'll not reconstruct the past", says architect Njål Eide. He'd rather show his visions for a future cruise ship. Interior from Viking Crown, Splendour of the Seas. *(Photo: Kjartan Prøven Hauglid).*

"There are always people who ask for 'romantic old boats.' I have actually tried to steer clear of splashing around the type of rubbish you see in many cruise ships: the constant repetition of bad cliches and nostalgia. The old ships were made with iron hulls, usually painted, steel girders with a deck on top, usually in the form of a hardwood deck that was thick enough to handle temperature fluctuations. Portholes were the largest windows you could put in. Brass was used because it didn't rust and oiled teak and mahogany were used because they didn't rot. All this was accompanied by rope-work and blocks and lots of white paint.

"Today's technology is completely different. We can build these ships larger and of more durable materials. We still use brass, but on the top decks we use modern materials like saltwater-resistant aluminum. Times have changed, and this is reflected in the architecture. We don't want to sail across the Atlantic in a storm with tiny portholes, a sleek gracious hull at full speed. We build "box-like" ships that contain most hotel facilities, primarily over the water line, with proven bows and sterns. Emphasis is on a well-designed upper deck with funnel and masts. The end result is a whole new world.

"Until the 1950's, ships used a lot of wood paneling. As a result of fire regulations, metal had to replace the use of wood. In the

Vision Series, we were given permission to use a very thin wooden veneer on a specific percentage of the room's total wall space. This was a price calculation. You will see on these ships that I have used a lot of wood, but also metal. We strive for decorative as well as functional effects. That's become the general rule. Everybody associates ocean liners with dark interiors. That's considered 'maritime' and continues to have an influence. I, on the other hand, began designing relatively light boats.

"'We know that Njål designs the most expensive ceilings,' one Steering Committee member said, 'but we just have to have them.' Money isn't an issue when the shipowners earn strong profits. Of course, there are always conflicts between the engineers and the architects. All the arches and the curvatures that are very much a part of my work are important factors in creating an atmosphere onboard. A flat ceiling is the cheapest, but you won't get me to work with one. The flattest things I've done are the Schooner Bars. I even had to put a twist on the Royal Promenade onboard the *Voyager*. I have to be an architect and give people the feeling of streets and buildings. They can't just walk straight ahead all the time.

"I designed all the chairs for the Dining Rooms on the *Legend* and *Splendour*, and I drew all the sketches myself. The rumors about my napkin consumption on airplanes are totally correct.

"The best napkins are the stiff ones on SAS. You could send them home on the fax machine! Every time I get on a plane, if I just have a little space around me and a gin & tonic, I feel fine. These are some of my best moments. You can dream a little. The trip gives inspiration. And the sketch is important.

"Every time somebody tells me that we'll solve this or that problem in the future with a computer, I tell them I don't believe it. The day we can't use a pen, we'll have lost something very important. A computer is exact. Everything comes from a program, but a machine can't replace the connection between the brain and the hand. We fantasize and write and draw. In the end, there's a ship. A ship made by people! And sometimes it has to be changed by the same people.

"For example, while planning the two first *Vision Class* ships, the *Legend* and the *Splendour*, we began considering a built-in bathing area. The area that eventually came to be known as the Solarium was to be very elegant with a retractable moving roof. But it didn't come without a few hitches. RCI's CEO, Richard D. Fain, thought the first glass roof wasn't good enough. We flew to the yard at St. Nazaire, France together with Technical Director Martin Hallen. It's not easy to make this kind of glass roof, with all its arches and angles. And everything has to be built much stronger than on land and has to be able to withstand the ship's movement. In the end, it added up to a lot of tonnage - lots of steel and little glass. Fain didn't like it and I agreed. The end of the story is that we ordered a whole new roof just a few months before the ship was set to sail. It seemed crazy and it was expensive, but it was the right decision.

"We've been able to use enormous resources over many years to develop these giant projects. Now I'm working on a project to put glass along the whole Centrum on both sides. Mistakes are the most expensive thing you can make in this industry, but the projects have become less costly as we have gained experience. You don't make as many mistakes after so many years of experience," says Njål Eide. ■

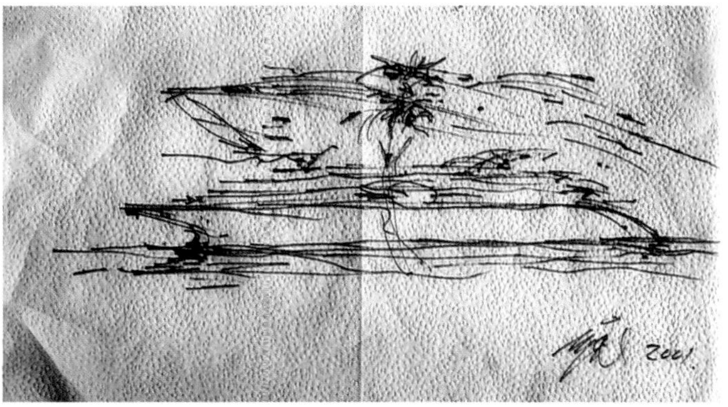

The rumors about Eide's consumption of napkins on airplanes are all correct.

LCA – the art consultants

"Historically, the architect would come up with the artwork for his or her area. But in many cases we felt that the art was an afterstart in their eyes. They focused on 'their space' and the art was an additional bell and whistle, but not really keyed to the space. By bringing in specialists on art – whose sole purpose was the art – we were able to move that to a higher level. The art consultants were more specialized, but we still maintain that the architects are ultimately responsible for their own areas."

Richard D. Fain

Today's head of LCA, Andrew Ingram, joined the company 11 years ago. At that stage there were two operations: a publishing house in London, selling prints to UK, Australia and various other places; and a share in a subsidiary based in Chicago, which sold LCA prints on the US market. They sold about 45,000 prints a year, mostly to the corporate art market. Ingram's appointment coincided with steep economic decline, which was countered by establishing LCA as sellers to galleries in the US. Last year's turnover was about USD 2.8 million. At that time, LCA also bought a small corporate art business. The timing was poor; the market dropped and corporate sales became almost nonexistent.

"Then Nicola Elstone joined us, and two years later, Gro Nesjar joined LCA," recalls Ingram. "At that stage Gro opened up an LCA office in Miami. This was largely because we had seen that there was an incipient auction-print business, which has since become a very big business, and we thought there might be an opportunity here.

"Elstone began chasing Royal Caribbean to establish us as a straightforward supplier of art. Then we heard that they were actually looking for art consultancy for their new ships. They didn't want the architects to bear the sole burden for the art selection.

"What we were able to present was a presence in both London and Miami. We were also fortunate that Gro Nesjar was more experienced than anybody else in dealing with cruise lines and onboard art. The combination of the two factors made RCI quite happy to appoint us. Initially, they chose two art consultant companies for their first two ships; the result was that we did the *Legend* and the other group was to do the *Splendour*. We were later hired for all the *Vision Class* ships. It was one of these curious situations where a combination of coincidences took place at roughly the right time, resulting in the continuation of this business."

"Although we also do work for other cruise companies, we have become the main consultants for RCI's new ships. From our point of view, it became rather clear early on that working with RCI would be a total commitment. We chose this approach because we looked at the RCI business as long-term. The alternative could have resulted in our spreading ourselves too thin – and really not satisfying any client to the fullest. I think we have been right, although we are beginning to pick up other business. Now we have more people and a better spread, so we are better equipped to handle having several balls in the air.

Mostly girls in the corporate art division of London Contemporary Art. Seated at the table from left: Directors and partners Gro Nesjar, Andrew Ingram, Joan Blackman. Standing from left: Claire Burrows, Anne Cecilie Thidemansen, Caroline Rankin, Anne Holtermann, Nicola Elstone, Sissel Hanssen, Leigh Banks, Chris Gottelier. (Photo: Gemma Levine)

We deliver "the icing on the cake"

Gro Nesjar, LCA, Oslo

"We now know how to make it work. We know the bureaucracy of Royal Caribbean. We offer a very wide range of choice and full service. We've got good access to anybody, anywhere, to do anything. We are not the only consultants who have access to quite a number of people, of course. The difficult part is having access to the right people who can do the variety of work required to fill a ship up with good art rather than rubbish."

"When you see a cruise ship, you are amazed by its size and the number of works of art that go into it. Imagine, then, what it is like to work on two or three ships simultaneously. That's what we're doing and each project is at a different stage, whether it is at idea concept stage or installation.

"For an art market, this is an extraordinary phenomenon. It certainly represents the biggest new art market in the world. RCI have been a strong proponent of art and are among the biggest art buyers.

"However, art for ships is an isolated phenomenon. It has no or little influence on other parts of the art market. It's there, and the artists involved make a profit. I would doubt if it has any significant impact, certainly at this stage, on the acceptance of the artists in the national arena. But it certainly would be a pity if RCI said they were not going to showcase art any longer. I don't think they would save a lot of money by not doing it. The build cost for the *Voyager of the Seas* was USD 500 million and USD 12 million for art accounts for only about 2 % of the cost."

Gro Nesjar ran the Miami office and was in charge of art auctions on the ships that LCA handle. She had previously furnished art for cabins on the *Sovereign* ships among other cruise ships. After five years, Nesjar moved to Norway to establish a separate office to assume all contact with the Norwegian architects and RCI's new-building office in Oslo.

Gro Nesjar.

"We deliver the icing on the cake," says Nesjar. "It's an element that seems unnecessary on the surface, but that pleases and surprises the passengers. We have to accept that not everybody sees the value in what we do, but the proof is in the end product - a successful and beautiful ship.

"We have to make demands on the artists, and they have to accept that in these projects, they are important tiles in a larger mosaic," says Nesjar.

"Many artists have questioned how we can come to them with color boards and commission art to satisfy specific demands. From an art history perspective, however, this is nothing new: Most famous art pieces up to the 1800's were ordered specifically for an area with a specific purpose. So, making demands on artists is neither impossible nor illogical. We insist that art has to work in a certain context, both chromatically and thematically. Most professional artists don't find this unreasonable."

Growing up with art

As the daughter of two prominent Norwegian artists, Gro Nesjar had an upbringing that gave her certain advantages: she's not afraid of the artist's status as "holy". She grew up surrounded by art and artists. Picasso taught her to swim one summer in the south of France. She played hide-and-seek with Calder and Hartung, and was dragged around to museums and galleries from the time she could walk. She absorbed Renaissance and Baroque art while her mother viewed modern art.

"A job like this necessarily entails a certain emotional involvement. When a ship is nearing completion, we have to prepare ourselves for criticism. My heart is always heavy when I attend the dinner held onboard the finished vessel, in conjunction with the delivery of a ship. 'Everybody' is there, and everybody has an opinion about the art. It can be difficult not to take it personally. I get a rush every time. To be part of creating something as rich and complicated as a modern cruise ship gives me an incredible feeling of pride. I consider myself extremely fortunate to be a part of it. I am moved and filled with affection for all the ships I've been involved with. These kinds of feelings outweigh many times over all the stress and nervousness experienced during the process."

Joan Blackman and Sissel Hanssen in the London Contemperary Art office in Miami.

This artwork consists of fused glass and steel and shows the shape and size of a boat similar to the small, light boats used in the Viking age. Deck 11 Viking Crown, Rhapsody of the Seas. *Made by Norsk Kunstglass, Norway.*

Joan Blackman who took over the Miami office when Gro Nesjar moved to Oslo, manages the RCI business. "We have a Cruise Auction Division and a Corporate Division. Our responsibility in the latter is communications, liaising with Royal Caribbean and managing all the American architects. 'Our' architects include the Howard Snoweiss Design Group, historically a very active partner for Royal Caribbean.

"With each ship, we got better, and the *Vision of the Sea*s turned out to be the crowning glory. It was a well-managed project and the artwork turned out to be spectacular. We now have a well-tuned formula for developing these projects, but we have to stay on our toes as the harried pace requires professionalism," says Blackman.

"I get so personally involved. Royal Caribbean has a high level of insight, of conceptualizing ideas and visualizing art. You don't have to spoon-feed them. They know what they're doing and they know what we are talking about. It actually makes our job much easier. And there is a lot to be said for a long-term relationship. The most exciting part is working together with the architects, to translate their inspiration into actual art. When we approach these projects our challenge is to coordinate

all of the architects' ideas, looks and areas. Gro works with the Norwegian architects, London works with the Swedes and British, while we work with the Americans. Each architect has his own way of looking at it, but art covers the entire ship. Our challenge is: How do we avoid creating a hodge-podge art collection? How can we tie it all together to ensure continuity?

"When we are first notified about a ship, we spend a month or so to meet with every single architect and find out what their interests are. Then we have our own corporate meetings where we start comparing notes. Before you know it, we have come up with an overall theme or 'red thread' for the vessel. With *Rhapsody* it was music, with *Enchantment* it was theater and entertainment, with *Vision* it was very futuristic and about what art can be – the vision of art. We create a unique selling proposition for tying in all areas, if we are lucky. The themes are also a tool to keep us in line and make sure we are consistent in our approach. Around 95 percent of the art is commissioned. We have to imbue some method into the madness. The themes are cornerstones. They are also great for Royal Caribbean's promotional

efforts. We help create a different personality for each vessel."

Sissel Hanssen, project leader and art consultant for LCA in Miami, says: "As long as you are up front and do your job, including delivery and follow-up, everything goes well. The most important thing is that the owners trust you. You have to pay tremendous attention to detail and be accurate. Let's say that you want to put a heavy antique mirror on a wall. You have to find the right 'look', that is, find it, negotiate a price, order it and be sure it is delivered. If the mirror is old and fragile, you need to take precautions to protect it. How can it be mounted on the wall so that the vibrations of the ship won't ruin it? It also has to be secure so that nobody can steal it. Rule Number One: it has to be secure and safe for the passengers. But it also has to look beautiful. It's an exciting job – lots of work and travel." ■

Last work on Floor Feature, Casino Royale, Voyager of the Seas. *Peter Zsiba with two assistants at the yard in Turku, Finland.*

The art installation supervisor

Chris Gottelier onboard Voyager *at the yard in Turku, Finland. "I went to France to help install a glass sculpture of a woman with a top hat in the* Splendour of the Seas. *It grew from there to be almost a full-time job."*

"The LCA team includes an installation consultant on site, Installment Supervisor Chris Gottelier, who handles and coordinates the art," explains Kelly Gonzales, Manager New Building Design. "In the art meetings that take place at various locations throughout the year, the architects are present because, in the end, they are still responsible for the artwork. But Chris Gottelier has been very influential. He's been involved with all of the *Vision Class, Voyager Class* and *Radiance Class* ships," she reports.

Captain Svein Pettersen of the *Voyager of the Seas* puts it this way: "He (Chris Gottelier) sees solutions that others can't see. Without him, we would not have so much art onboard. He's the one who manages to mount a piece of artwork after the others have given up. He doesn't give in when he meets the first obstacle. He's also a calm and well-balanced guy who understands that it doesn't help to scream and yell. That should be a slogan for the whole building process: It doesn't help to scream and yell."

Chris Gottelier explains how he got involved: "I was working with my brother-in-law, Mike Newby in London. He was commissioned to build a large glass sculpture of Fats Waller, the jazz pianist, for the *Monarch of the Seas.* I was working as a glass artist at that time and the piece was built in my workshop. We assembled it and put it on the ship. Everything that's happened since came out of being involved with the installation of Fats Waller.

It was groundbreaking work. We were effectively pioneering the use of that kind of glue on that scale.

"We worked with LCA on specialist installations and did the trouble-shooting for them on the other ships. On the *Voyager* – and *Radiance – Class* of ships we are acting as on-site eyes and ears for them, and to facilitate art installations, we help the yard with some problems.

"Morten Jensen is the Norwegian part of the trouble-shooting team. He lives with the ship for half a year and sorts out all kinds of practical problems. Most of the workers at Kværner Masa Yards speak only Finnish, but some of them understand and speak a little Swedish, and Morten, like all Norwegians, understands Swedish, which is a big help.

"We don't work primarily as installers anymore. We are facilitators; the ones who make sure that it all happens. If that means we get our hands dirty, that's fine. The primary objective is to make sure

"It's a complex process: Lots of people working together; lots of disappointment, lots of hard work. But you are making a SHIP!

Chris Gottelier

"For the Legend of the Seas *we built a large glass ship. Heavy stuff and hard to get in. Lots of headaches." Ben Jenkins with the stacked glass ship in Mike Newby's workshop in London.*

the artwork is installed. There's always an artist onboard who needs some help. That's why we're here," says Gottelier, adding that they also advise the yard when problems come up with the artwork: "We have to reassure them, deal with them, tell them they can handle it. And they can at the end of the day; these people are craftsmen.

"LCA does an amazing job in commissioning the art, checking it, and cooperating with the architects. But they have no technical expertise, nor have they ever needed to. This means it's difficult, particularly when they are talking to the yard, to have credibility. LCA represents the artists, not the shipbuilders. The yard feels more comfortable dealing with craftsmen – people who get their hands dirty. People who can talk about Sicaflex ...

"We, Morten Jensen, Australian Ben Jenkins and myself, are implants, if you like. On a day-to-day basis we deal mostly with LCA and the New-building office at the various yards. They recognize the need for good solutions because they have to deliver a finished ship. It's their responsibility until hand-over and they want to send the ship out as perfect as they possibly can. Miami expects to receive a finished ship, but they don't care how it happens. And that's fine – that's what they pay for.

"Often we realize that we have a problem only after we open the crate and are ready to install the work. Then you have to react quickly to make the appropriate adjustment, and ensure that it's installed in as ship-shape and secure manner as possible. Anything can be fixed with great big agricultural bolts, but you don't want to do that. The yard people have workshops and materials, so you can often design a solution which can be made on-site very quickly. Most of the very complicated things are easily solved. But all in all, it must be said that after completing art programs for so many vessels, we usually get it right the first time, without too many problems on-site.

"The ships are living things and you become a part of them. When a vessel is handed over and the passengers start embarking, I really resent them. I know that's what the ship is built for. But still, I think 'at least take your shoes off, for goodness sake'! You feel so possessive. These people just don't understand the blood, sweat and tears that have gone into that installation. Our part, the artwork, is just a small part of it compared to all the engineering and everything else. But we know what we've done. And then it sails away.

"You can't explain these emotions to families and friends outside this world of art and shipbuilding. They don't understand. They're impressed by the scale of it. But they haven't seen it half finished. They haven't seen it like it was in wintertime or in the autumn, when you looked at this huge thing and thought: 'This cannot possibly be a floating palace by October. It just can't be. But it will be.'

"This is a complex process: lots of people working together, lots of disappointment, lots of hard work. But you are making a ship, not a dead thing. There's a real sense of achievement. It's very emotional."

Planning and building the ships takes around 2 1/2 years. "Two weeks before the ship's delivery, it's a circus", says Gottelier. "When you're working, you know what to do. But with all these people flying in from all corners of the world, well, they don't know much and they don't help you. It's 24 hours a day. If we have everything onboard we sail with the ship and finish our work during the crossing." ■

Strong emotions

The world's largest cruise ship, Voyager of the Seas, *during Sea Trials in the Baltic Sea.*

Ed Stephan, former president of RCI, says: "I took my marketing people to see the *Sovereign of the Seas* two weeks before delivery. They almost cried, and started to talk about canceling cruises. I told them I'd gone through this before. 'If the yard tells you it will be finished, it's the truth. Believe me, they know what they're doing,' I said.

"A certain amount of re-evaluation takes place even in the last few weeks before the delivery," concurs Kelly Gonzales, Manager New Building Design. "Going onboard the ship is like the moment you walk down the aisle to get married. You have last-minute jitters.

"We walk through and evaluate things as they unfold immediately prior to delivery, just to see if things are up to our expectations, to see if they've understood our vision of what we thought it would be."

And when the ship is delivered and sets out for sea, "It's incredible," says Gonzales. "It is like a delivery; it is like seeing your baby. Even after many years in the industry, it's still sometimes hard to believe that this whole thing can actually happen.

One of the great moments in Richard D. Fain's life was when he arrived by helicopter to the *Voyager of the Seas* during her first sea trials in the Baltic Sea off the coast of Finland in June 1999.

"I was thrilled. I was overjoyed," recalls Richard Fain. "To fly out and see this huge ship at sea – it was magnificent. You must remember that while the ship is being worked on it is covered with scaffolding so you can't see anything. Then all of a sudden, they take away the scaffolding and protective covering, and the ship sails out for sea trials. Seeing this ship in the ocean from the air was mind-boggling. But even more thrilling was when I landed on the ship and walked around it. The crew and all the people onboard kept coming up to me and telling me how excited they were.

"There was never a moment's doubt that she would do all the things that were expected. People told me this was going to be wonderful, and I had absolute confidence that it was going to be. Njål Eide said: 'Richard, I assure you, you will like the proportions of the Royal Promenade.' And Robert Tillberg and Cecilia Kinnisson said to me: 'This Dining Room is going to knock their socks off.' I believed it in my head. But actually seeing it was a wonderful experience for me. Truly gratifying and exciting.

"I make no apologies about being emotional about all this. I believe I'm professional, but there's nothing wrong with loving what you do," concludes Fain. ■

Njål Eide's Royal Promenade is the absolute Centrum on board Voyager of the Seas *with Larry Kirkland's* Main Centrum Sculpture.

The public rooms

*"Wherever you are onboard,
you suddenly see something new –
something that makes you say:
'I never saw that before.' "*

Richard D. Fain
CEO, Royal Caribbean

Maria Veronica L. Solem
(cv p 323):
"A Moment of Eternity".
Oil on canvas.
Rhapsody of the Seas.

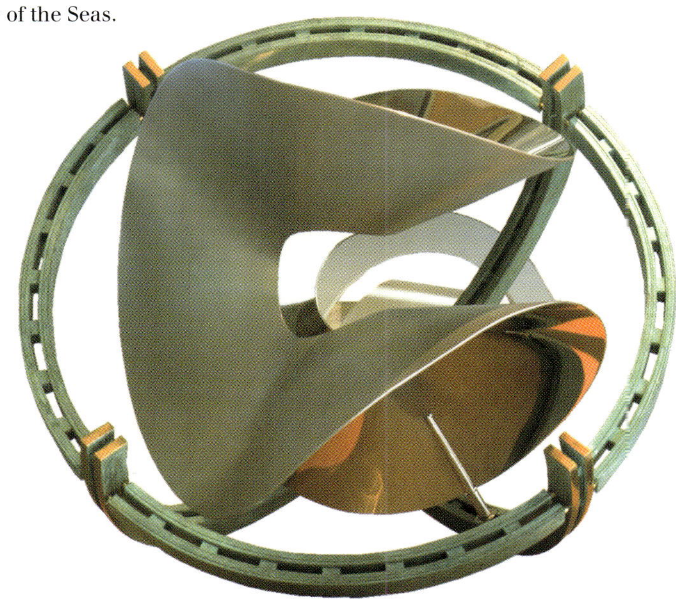

John Ashworth (cv p 257):
"Cross Section III".
Bronze, wood.
Vision of the Seas.

Centrum

"This is a huge, very high space in the middle of the ship. It is similar to the atriums you find in many contemporary hotels like the Hyatt chain of hotels in the US. The Centrum has been deliberately positioned at mid-length of the ship's hull, as it serves as the point where the passengers enter or leave the ship. It is a striking and impressive element of the ship's interior," says Gjert Wilhelmsen.

The tall vertical space of the Centrum soars upwards through seven decks, and the impression of height is underlined by a set of glass elevators moving up and down. At the top of this huge space, the elevators enter the Viking Crown's observation lounge, which is part of the Viking Crown.

The Centrum is a reference point. It is here where guests meet the ship for the first time. One goes to meals via the Centrum as the dining rooms are always adjacent to the Centrum. The Purser's Desk and the Shore Excursions Desk are all a part of the Centrum."

Architect Njål Eide is the man who created the atriums in these ships: "I felt that there was a need for a central place," explains Eide. "The shipowners had to constantly increase the size and capacity of the ships to meet the market need and competition. The increase in size made it necessary to add new features. The same thing happens in every society which grows. Suddenly you need a marketplace, a space which functions as a meeting place and safety feature – in a crisis you don't run for a

corner with a fire roaring behind, you run towards a central spot. The stairs into the Centrum are also escape routes."

In the beginning, however, the Steering Committee was not entirely convinced. They called the atrium the "hole in the doughnut" because it served no purpose. "We built a 1:20 scale model of the Centrum for the *Sovereign of the Seas*," recounts designer and model-builder Halfdan Greve, "with elevators that went up and down, dimmable lights and live plants. It was a marathon. We finished the model at eight in the morning and half an hour later the mighty committee came strolling in, wearing their dark suits. When I came back after a quick shower, all the gentlemen were kneeling on the floor, running the model elevators up and down. The result, as we all know, was positive."

Gjert Wilhelmsen adds: "The best part was that the technical team, headed by Martin Hallen and me, was able to find solutions which meant that the large openings in the upper decks did not weaken the structure of the ship. The hull has to be able to withstand powerful moments of stress. In addition, the ship's superstructure must be a load-bearing construction."

"Now, we had to put something into these huge lovely rooms," says Njål Eide. "Needless to say, it had to be art. ■

Jonathan and Evelyn Clowes (cv p 277): "Diadem". Centrum. Rhapsody of the Seas.

Dining Rooms

The owners have always put strong emphasis on the dining rooms on the ships. "The dining-room experience during a week of cruising is important to the passengers, in particular the women. Here they will be well looked after, thanks to excellent food and service provided by an expert staff. A good dining room is in fact a key element to having happy, satisfied passengers throughout a cruise. The setting and the atmosphere of these rooms are always very important," explains Gjert Wilhelmsen.

Njål Eide designed the "Romeo and Juliet" Dining Room on the *Legend of the Seas*, which is among the best on any of Royal Caribbean's ships. The room is two decks high, with full-height flat glass walls on both sides – giving a panoramic view. "I succeeded in fighting to pull the galleries inward all the way around in such a way that they were freed from the windows," recalls Eide. "Former CEO Ed Stephan said: 'I want the deck to go all the way to the windows.' I said: 'No, just imagine if you can sit a little further in and get a double view.'

"There was a question about what the dining room should be called. Previously we had always used musicals as the theme for each room – one theme per room. But more recently we have had a theme for the whole ship that acts as an umbrella for the other themes. I suggested Romeo and Juliet, knowing full well that it was by no means a musical. And it was accepted. It fits well with the balconies and all.

"On the *Legend*, I got Norwegian textile artist Nini Anker Dessen involved. She actually came in via the Wilhelmsen brothers.

"Nini and I work well together," says Eide. "I like her colors. She is good at combinations. She made many fine pieces which gave a lovely impression. The work were produced in Aubusson in France, home of the world's best weavers, with a centuries-old tradition of artisanship."

Tillberg Design AB of Sweden specializes in ship interiors and has designed dining rooms and Windjammers on the *Sovereign, Majesty* and *Monarch* in the *Sovereign Class*, the *Grandeur, Enchantment, Rhapsody*, and *Vision of the Seas* in the *Vision Class* and on two ships of the *Voyager Class* so far. Architect Cecilia Kinnison who works with architect Robert Tillberg, says: "We have a lot of experience with passenger vessel design. A two deck dining room such as on *Grandeur* has functional and logistical requirements that must be met in order for the room to be successful. The relationship of

Njål Eide designed the elegant Romeo and Juliet Dining Room for Legend of the Seas. *Nini Anker Dessen made the congenial tapestries.*

Thai-inspired decorations in the Dining Room The King and I on Splendour of the Seas. *(Photo: Kjartan P. Hauglid.)*

tables and chairs to each other and waiter service areas are important factors in the overall design. All servers should have the best possible working conditions and the distance to the galley must be as short as possible. 1200 people must be fed hot food fast – and they are! These dining rooms are built according to the total passenger capacity of the ship divided into two seatings.

"So we had two decks to work with – it would be good if they were connected, we thought: although it's two decks, it shouldn't be separated by two different names – we can't have 'The King' downstairs and 'I' upstairs.

"Our basic idea for the *Grandeur's* dining room was to work from the theme of 'The Great Gatsby' – a classic 1920's-1930's inspired interior with warm woods, faux alabaster lightning, warm green carpet and accents of deep plum. For the sister ship, *Enchantment of the Seas* 'My Fair Lady' was chosen, with a traditional, English-inspired style, with black and white colors inspired by Ascot. The basic architecture remained the same, being the sister ship, so it was these new colors and decorative lightning plus new art that gave this dining room its own identity. In both vessels we decided to have a formal, symmetical deck opening and centrally oriented stairway with a sculpture at the base. For the 'Great Gatsby' a bronze sculpture of a beautiful 1920's woman was chosen. For 'My Fair Lady' a sculpture of Eliza dressed in her Sunday best with flowers at her feet was commissioned. The matching element at the other end of the room is composed of a grand piano and a waterfall with an onyx paneling backdrop designed in a straight classical, yet pleasant, style.

"When we came to *Rhapsody* and *Vision* we made things a little more youthful, but 'Hair' or 'Grease' wouldn't do. They were too modern and felt a little out of place for a dining room. We wanted to design a room that was silvery, with matching tones. We went for an interior that was soft, feminine in its forms, romantic but also modern with the theme of 'Edelweiss' from 'The Sound of Music'. The room is not as symmetrical and formal as in the other ships. We also wanted to do something with lighting and crystal, to have a glittering architectural element that also served as art, so we created a wall of glass elements," says Cecilia Kinnison.

"For *Vision* we presented various sketches to the Steering Committee. There were several options for the name of the room but none that were truly in the spirit of the architectual forms we had established for the sister ship. Because it is asymmetrical and somewhat contemporary, I thought it should be called 'Aquarius'. There was some discussion before Mr. Fain challenged me: 'What does the song sound like? If you can sing a little bit of it then we can use it.' I sang as best I could and Mr. Fain accepted the idea. They chose a 'nordic look' with blond beech paneling and a dark blue base for the room. This gave it a somewhat spacey feeling with a hint of astronomy and the universe. We couldn't use a glass wall, as on *Rhapsody*, so we commissioned an art piece based on a wood carving from the 1200s that LCA had found. The pattern was carved out in stone and the grooves filled with gold – very beautiful.

Behind the beautiful antique harp, the painting shows people sitting in an opera house watching the performance. The man with hidden eyes is a self-portrait by the painter, Peter Woodward, Voyager of the Seas.

The *Voyager of the Seas* is among Tillberg Designs' largest commissions for Royal Caribbean, with the Dining Rooms and Windjammer. The ship has dining areas over three decks. With all the tables in use, there is seating for 1,980 guests. This was a new challenge, explains Kinnison. "We had three decks at our disposal. We needed to make one room. A room of that size needs an Ariadne's thread running throughout. We chose Opera – grandeur and magnificence for the overall theme. 'Carmen' on deck three has the darkest color scheme and represents dance within the arts. 'La Boheme' on deck four has medium tones – blue and walnut and expresses painting. And 'The Magic Flute' on the uppermost deck symbolizes music and also has the lightest color scheme.

"A magnificient tromp l'oeil painting on the backdrop wall connects all three decks – it is of people sitting in an opera house leaning forward in their boxes to watch the performance. In addition, we have a beautiful antique harp that LCA found in London. If you stand on the music platform with the piano and look at the people in the painting, you will see a man who has something in front of his eyes. This is artist Peter Woodward's self-portrait." ■

At the base of the elegant stair for the Great Gatsby Dining Room onboard Grandeur of the Seas, *Tillberg chose a bronze sculpture by British sculptor David Norris of a beautiful 1920's flapper.*

Robert Tillberg of Sweden designed the three storey Dining Room onboard Voyager of the Seas.

The Theaters

Theater, Splendour of the Seas. *"We put a piece of artwork at the back as well, so that there is something to focus on as one turns to leave the theater. You can see how the two play off against each other."*

"These rooms have changed a lot as the ships have grown larger, carrying up to 3,500 passengers," says Gjert Wilhelmsen. The fairly straightforward entertainment lounge on the first ships became a theater-style lounge on the *Sovereign Class* of ships, seating more than 900 passengers. On the *Vision Class*, these lounges were further refined to become full-fledged theaters with the latest state-of-the-art light and sound systems capable of handling large Broadway-style shows.

"We were assigned certain spaces on the *Legend of the Seas*, one of which was the theater," says Howard Snoweiss, who has designed all six theaters onboard the *Vision Class* ships. "This was interesting because it was the first time Royal Caribbean did a proper theater. Prior to that, the entertainment lounge was a lounge. We decided to make use of the tradition of theming when planning the artwork for this room.

"At the entryway we established the theme with a piece of artwork, as well as a floor design. Then we placed artwork at critical locations throughout the room. For instance, entering the theater on *Legend*, there is a glass piece by Gianni Arico, the Venetian glass artist.

"I had seen some pieces he'd done in Venice – angels with trumpets. We thought a modification of that was appropriate here because the trumpeting would announce the theater, the showmanship and all the activities.

"The other major feature in the theaters is the stage curtain, which is considered a major piece of artwork in itself, giving the room its character. We didn't want it to be merely a painted backdrop. We wanted a rich curtain. So it was made with appliqués, reflective materials and details that gave life and activity to the piece.

"We also designed the rails and other features to coordinate with the artwork, giving a sense of everything being tied together. We wanted the whole room to work as one unified presentation – artwork, architecture, fabrics, ceiling and detailing.

Entrance to Theater, Splendour of the seas. *"Tribute to New York Skyline" interplays with the stage curtain. Stained, rolled dichroic, bevelled and fused glass by Stanley Hildreth, American, Gaytee Studios, USA.*

Theater, Grandeur of the Seas. *(Photo: Nancy Robinson Watson.)*

Theater, Legend of the Seas. *(Photo: Nancy Robinson Watson.)*

"On *Grandeur* the concept was different. We designed a proper balcony, making it a two-storey theater. Some of the artwork is free-standing and some is built into the architecture. The stage curtain was again a major feature. We surrounded it with artistic glass panels on either side that tie into a chandelier which frames the stage and the proscenium. When you enter the theater it will be down. Then during grand events the chandelier goes up, the curtain goes up and the lights dim.

"For *Rhapsody* we designed a carpet which picks up the musical notes and the art deco motifs that relate to the theme of theater itself. The chandelier was designed in consideration of a special request by the chairman. It can be raised and lowered to create a sense of drama." ■

Casinos

For the *Legend* and *Splendour of the Seas*, Royal Caribbean hired a Las Vegas consultant to design the casinos. The first Snoweiss-designed casino was on the *Grandeur*. "RCI wanted a Las Vegas-style casino. They asked us to go to Las Vegas – to the source – to do research. On the way back we came up with the idea: why not theme the casino as a tribute to Las Vegas? And interestingly, the first art feature we thought of for the casino, has now become an RCI trademark. It's called the Treasure Floor. We took advantage of the raised deck situation to set something into the floor with glass panels on top," explains Howard Snoweiss.

"The Treasure Floor was actually a tribute to Treasure Island, one of the most famous hotels in Las Vegas. You will also see allusions to many other famous Las Vegas spots. Snoweiss will always remember presenting this concept/proposal to the Steering Committee: "Richard D. Fain reluctantly said: 'OK, I'm going to approve this thing, but be prepared to cover it'. Neither we nor anyone else had done anything like this at the time.

"This project was our first exposure to *Zsiba-Smolover*, and as they were designing this fabulous floor, we kept telling them: 'We want jewels, skeletons and everything else, plus all the lighting in there.' The floor became a unique and unexpected art piece. When the ship came in, this floor was literally the biggest hit on the ship.

"There is so much going on in these casinos, but we try to keep it lively. The architectural elements were stylized – we call it 'Sophistiglitz' – throughout the casinos.

"We probably condense as much quality into these smaller casinos as Las Vegas puts into their huge casinos. The number of light-

Floor Feature, Vision of the Seas. *Interior Design and Procurement Services.*

From Grandeur*: Treasure floor feature by Zsiba-Smolover (cv p 319).*

"Pennies from Heaven". Zsiba-Smolover feature from Voyager of the Seas.

Zsiba-Smolover: "Sunken Treasures". Grandeur of the Seas.

ing points, the quantity of lighting effects, the amount of overhead signage, the amount of artwork is comparable to what they do in a large casino in Las Vegas. It's that intense.

"The most spectacular casino is *Voyager*'s, where the design is taken to a new level.

"In this casino we incorporated the art into the overall design; it's the lighting, the music, the tap dance." Snoweiss likes to think of it as environmental art. It creates a total mood and atmosphere. They had quite a time installing artwork as the pieces are technologically very advanced. The lighting for *Voyager* was supplied by the shipyard and it was to be controlled by the *Zsiba-Smolover* dimming boards. The interaction was very difficult, and to bring all the elements together was a demanding task. ■

Ceiling feature, Casino Royale, Enchantment of the Seas. *Architect Howard Snoweiss, artists Zsiba-Smolover.*

Stairs

The main stairways are considered key public spaces. Stairs and corridors are used by the passengers to move between "spaces"; stairwells in traditional ships are therefore often non-spaces. At the same time it is precisely these non-spaces which see the greatest traffic among the ships' guests. RCI has faced up to the challenge of giving stairways and corridors clear identities so that passengers will know immediately where they are in the ship. A stairway should also provide an experience. Simply descending a set of stairs should give a mental "lift". ■

Tertit Prestegaard, Norwegian: "Ocean". Hand woven tapestry. Voyager of the Seas, *Main Stairs, Starboard, Deck 2-3.*

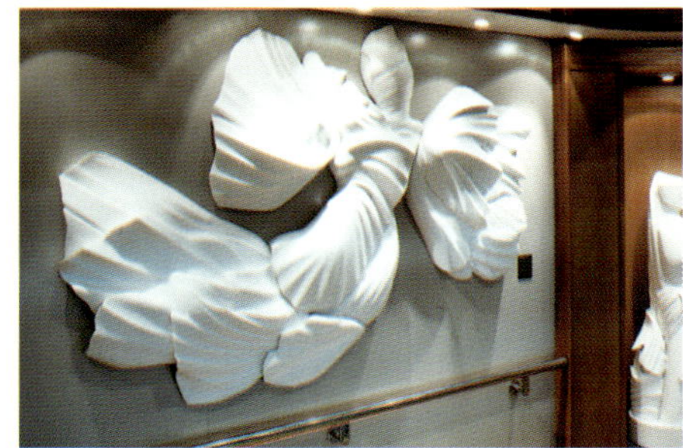

Helaine Blumenfeld (cv p 265): "Angel in Flight". White Carrara marble. Voyager of the Seas, *Main Stairs Starboard, Deck 4-5.*

Inger Sitter (cv p 316): "Floating Cliffs". Marble. Voyager of the Seas, *Main Stairs Starboard, Deck 9-10.*

Rolf Jørgensen, b. 1925, Norwegian: "The Sea". Acrylic on Canvas. Legend of the Seas, *Main Stairs, Deck 7-8.*

Laurence Broderick (cv p 269): "Goddess Athenae". Grandeur of the Seas, *Forward Stairs.*

Tertit Prestegaard: "Painting", Voyager of the Seas.

Viking Crown – a Company Hallmark

Royal Caribbean's earliest groundbreaking design was the profile of their new vessel. John Maxtone-Graham writes: "Two design precedents influenced the decision. The first was the 1962 Seattle World's Fair icon, the 600-foot Space Needle. A large circular room containing a revolving restaurant was impaled near the top of the spire. The second was maritime inspired, from the German Atlantic Line's Hamburg, which boasted a new funnel refinement. It had a large smoke-dispelling platform built atop on tripod legs.

The *Hamburg* funnel established a new super-structure aesthetic. The combined height of the funnel and tripod equaled the height of the bridge/mast assembly forward. Prior to the *Hamburg*, masts had towered over funnels; now funnels and masts became balanced masses at either end of the vessel.

Both the Seattle Space Needle and the *Hamburg* funnel provided inspiration for the new vessel.

The first Viking Crowns like this one on Song of Norway, *had their entrances from an outer deck and were not much loved by ladies after visiting the hairdresser.*

The New York Skyline facing the dance floor onboard Voyager of the Seas *was made by Michael Newby (cv p 310).*

Ed Stephan and his Norwegian partners wanted a public room high in the ship with a panoramic view. The natural location was around an enlarged funnel, a radical departure from conventional architecture.

Architect Geir Grung made several proposals for a Viking Crown. Shipowner Sigurd Skaugen preferred a solution combining two funnels with a panoramic lounge around them. Everyone agreed, but there were so many different sketches, that most were confused. Then quietly, shipowner Gjert Wilhelmsen switched the two sketches and the one-funnel solution became a reality.

The *Vision* ships' Viking Crown is a spacious yet intimate spot which serves as both nightclub and day lounge. The special challenge for the architects was to combine night and day use. It all began with the *Song of Norway* which was given a fairly modest lounge. It was also used in marketing the company. Newspaper advertisements boldly declared: "Sail a skyscraper." Since then, the Viking Crown has developed into a magnificent space between heaven and sea, rising high above the ships' swimming pools and other activity areas.

On the *Voyager*, the Viking Crown is an entire small deck unto itself of 900 square meters, offering a range of different functions. It even has a chapel at the very top. Architect Bjørn Storbraaten of Yran & Storbraaten says that designing the large Viking Crown was a challenge: "We had to stitch together a jazz club, library, card room, and cocktail lounge plus golf bar into one area which was to hang together and at the same time express the special functions of all the parts. That need has played a large part in the rooms' decor."

Storbraaten likes to take part in the artistic process himself:

"I have produced artwork myself as a sideline – and I am fairly good at it. I like to sketch things out the way I think they should be.

"One striking element is Veronica M. Solem's large golf-themed painting for the Golf Bar which is adjacent to the ship's outdoor golf course. Veronica Solem is very professional. While we were designing the golf club, she made a large number of test paintings. I said: 'Not that, perhaps more like that.' She painted several pieces until in the end we said: 'Okay, that's it'. And then she finished it.

"The mosaic wall in the Jazz Club is inspired by the Manhattan skyline. Perhaps it's not especially original, but why must one always be so original? We created depth and lights in the windows and we made the featured dancing couple huge so people would have something to look at. The artist, Mike Newby, made the wall in London.

"And then there was the floor. I had walked across an especially lovely floor at the Miami International Airport which turned out to be made by Michele Oka Doner. My first thought was: 'Who can find me this woman?' At first there was no response, but in the end Gro Nesjar heard about it and found Michele. She is a fantastic person to know, the daughter of the ex-mayor of Miami's South Beach.

"When we discussed that floor in a meeting I said I would like it to be dark blue or black. Fain looked at me and said: 'Are you absolutely sure?' 'Okay,' he said, 'then we must trust the architect.' And so the floor was laid in blue terrazzo with instruments and notes inlaid in bronze medallions." ■

Peter Esdaile (cv p 289). "Aquamarin". Mixed media. Splendour of the Seas.

Inger Sitter (cv p 316) had the idea for the dance floor on Splendour of the Seas, *designed by architect Njål Eide and executed by Hamy Sveis of Norway.*

Windjammer

All the way forward, beautifully situated on Deck 9 with panoramic windows all around, is a room called the Windjammer on all the *Vision* ships. Here, those who prefer an informal setting and casual dress can enjoy breakfast, lunch and dinner with open seating, self service and beautiful views. The nautical/maritime décor fits the room perfectly.

Tillberg Design AB shaped the Windjammers on the *Grandeur* and the *Enchantment* and has experience from similar projects from the *Sovereign* series. The high glass dome creates an interesting room for the Windjammer on the *Grandeur*. It is decorated with fine wood paneling and bird carvings. The Windjammer on the *Enchantment* is of a similar design.

Wall ceramic panels by Nini Anker Dessen and Magne Aurstad (cv p 283). From Rhapsody of the Seas, *Windjammer.*

Jason Moul, b. 1968, British: "Fish". Metal. Grandeur of the Seas.

Due to the great number of passengers onboard the *Voyager*, where the café is located aft, a new way of approaching the design was necessary.

The room was divided in two; one half being the Windjammer and the other the Island Grill. RCI wanted a light, fun, tropical décor. Tilberg launched two concepts. One relates to the islands for the Island Grill, as the ship was to sail in the Caribbean. For the Windjammer, a little Miami Beach and seaside beach motif along with touch of water was used to tie in the Pool Deck. The mosaic wall behind the serving counter is a cheerful splash of the 1930's and 1940's, featuring women in bathing suits, palm trees and beach umbrellas. The artist also included the characteristic lifeguard towers which have stood on Miami Beach since the 1940's, no two of which are alike. ■

*Page 74:
Tanya Kuiters,
b. 1964, Norwegian:
"Where the Sea
Meets the Sky".
Ceramic and porcelain murals.
Windjammer Café,
Deck 9.
Tanya Kuiters uses
high-temperature
stoneware and
porcelain as her
medium. The sails,
waves and elements
of sand and shells
symbolize a journey
on the sea and
arrival on the shores
of an undiscovered
country where anything can happen.*

Windjammer,
Legend of the Seas.

Windjammer,
Voyager of the Seas.

Solarium

When the Swedish firm Arkitektbyrån AB received its first contract for a solarium on the *Legend of the Seas*, there was nothing like it on any cruise ship. They created an entirely new area: an upgraded deck with an elegant swimming pool and sliding glass roof. In the end they came upon the name: Solarium. The firm's previous experience was in designing bathing areas and shops for children on Finnish ferries, as well as houses on land and cars for Volvo.

The idea was to create an "outdoor" room indoors with emphasis on art and an air of serenity - in contrast to the lively outdoor deck with the big swimming pool. "We achieved this in the *Vision Series* where we made six solariums and two children's areas," says architect Lars Iwdal. "In addition, both the *Legend* and the *Splendour* have Health Spas done in a Roman style with a massage room, aerobics and artistic decoration. The whole time we emphasized that the space should have an air of serenity."

Helaine Blumenfeld (cv p 265): "Seated Mayan Figure in red Persian Travertine". Vision of the Seas.

For the Solariums, the architects chose the theme "a trip around the world". This has resulted in each Solarium taking a theme from the great ancient cultures: Greek, Roman, Egyptian, Indian, Mayan and Byzantine. For each theme London Contemporary Art found antique urns, wall-paintings, stone slabs, entire floor inlays and an array of castings. Mosaic inlays were made in the ceilings. Pillars in the form of Egyptian women support the entire roof of the Egyptian Solarium on *Grandeur* and *Enchantment*, making it particularly distinctive. Much of the Egyptian artwork is composed of replicas of artifacts from the British Museum.

It was also here that Helaine Blumenfeld got her first commission for RCI. She did two sculptures, which architect Lars Iwdal calls "fantastically beautiful," adding: "She is very skillful and she always does first-class work. She did the large sculptures which are in the Solariums on the first four Vision ships; we are extremely pleased with them." ■

Stephen Knapp, American: Feature in marble and glass. Splendour of the Seas.

Helaine Blumenfeld: "Moorish Sculpture". Grandeur of the Seas.

Open decks – sport decks and pools

"The architects can sometimes be a little modest," says Gjert Wilhelmsen. "One example is the late Per Høydahl, who created a special quality in the outdoor areas of the upper decks. He was a former colleague of architect Geir Grung, who participated in forming the exteriors of the first ships. His strength was in the overview and greater vision. He always had a number of skillful young architects on his team, as they wanted to learn from him.

"Høydahl was also highly creative, thanks in part to spending so many of his holidays in France and Greece. He began by making large sun-sails for the *Nordic Empress*. He strung them up as he had seen this done in the Greek Islands. This created a beautiful kind of light. He also introduced green elements in the form of plants in our pool areas, and had a great eye for quality in tile work and other details. The collective impression he created worked very well."

Jens Petter Askim took over the Vision ships after Høydal. He created a lovely exterior for the *Radiance of the Seas*, the first ship in the Radiance series – perhaps the finest exterior ever made. "Per Høydahl and Jens Petter Askim began working under Geir Grung. When they parted ways, Per took the commissions for RCI with him: the profile of the ships and the open upper-decks. Askim joined after he finished a commission to design the national Stiklestad Center in central Norway.

Høydal and Askim have put their hallmark on the top decks of the *Vision Class* ships. *Legend's* Sun Deck was the work of Høydahl. John Maxtone Graham writes in his book about the *Legend of the Seas*: "The Roman Pool within the Solarium is only the smaller of two up on *Legend's* Sun Deck. The second lies forward of the funnel, framed within Royal Caribbean's traditional swimming-sunning area, a deck that is the work of Norwegian architect Per Høydahl. Within the space separating the funnel from the mast, he fashioned a structure that is sun bowl by day and, equally useful, a nocturnal amphitheater equipped with a dance floor forward of the pool and ringed with attractive conical lamp fixtures suspended from each sun-walk facing.

"But the pool is, as always, the principal focus: it is complete with a waterfall and flanked by twin whirlpools, each shaded by an elegant scallop-shaped awning. In fact, five similar awnings are featured prominently within this upper-deck complex. In addition to the two mentioned, there is a third pool in the forward starboard corner that serves as a bandstand. One level higher up on Compass Deck but within participatory reach of the pool are two larger awnings, shaped again like giant sheltering scallop shells. Soaring out from either side of the mast base, they provide shaded elevated oases for deck chairs.

"Høydahl clearly still admired the awning, a predilection first exhibited throughout his upper-deck design for the *Nordic Empress* back in 1990. His awning inspiration dates from a walk along the curving beach at La Baule, that stylish resort north of St. Nazaire where rows of white canvas cabanas line the sand. The practicality of *Legend's* shipboard awnings is buttressed by their aesthetics: With pleasing design synchronicity, Høydahl's five vinyl scallop shells echo the dominant steel scallop shell of the Viking Crown Lounge looming overhead.

"One level higher than Compass Deck, a crescent of forward balcony has been devoted to an observatory – a boon for passenger stargazers. Sheltered from the deck lights aft and sharing the bridge's darkened perspective, amateur astronomers revel in this unique feature. Høydahl and Eide collaborated to ensure that

Bruce McLean: "Sun, Sky, Sea, Sand, Shimmer". Paint on Steel Panels. Voyager of the Seas.

Architect Geir Grung did the exteriors of the first RCI ships. Here with a model of Song of America.

The Pool Deck on the 142 000 gros tons Voyager of the Seas *has impressive dimensions. The statues are copies from British Museum.*

Windjammer's uppermost skylight directly behind the stargazers could be suitably darkened."

Høydahl was charged with shaping not only the vessel's open upper decks but the character of her profile as well. He wrote: "It has been a challenge to shape the different volumes, trying to make a balance between the elements where they play up in harmony with each other."

"Of all the creativity required to produce the *Legend of the Seas*, Høydahl's is literally the most far-reaching. What he created in this and other *Vision Class* ships has been seen by millions of passengers and spectators alike, either in actuality or via circulation of cruise brochures," says Maxton-Graham.

Jens Petter Askim took over the job and the legacy from his colleague: "The main task has been the shaping of the entire exterior based on a 'general arrangement,'' says Askim. "It is not like it was in the old days, when one first designed the ship and then the rooms." He has mainly created exteriors for the *Vision series*, including the Promenade Deck and the top deck, entailing furnishing the Sundeck and Sunwalk with bars and adjacent pools.

The ships Askim is most fond of are *Grandeur* and *Enchantment*: "There is harmony in their forms; they are spacious, lovely and open. The 400-square-meter sliding roof above the Solarium was constructed as a unit that ties the whole area together. It was a bold idea and it worked better on the last four ships, where the funnel was drawn back. *Splendour* does not use the Solarium without the roof because of the smoke from the funnel.

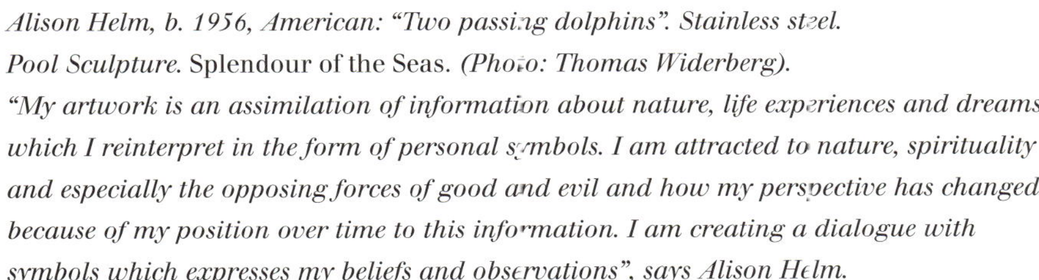

Alison Helm, b. 1956, American: "Two passing dolphins". Stainless steel. Pool Sculpture. Splendour of the Seas. *(Photo: Thomas Widerberg).*
"My artwork is an assimilation of information about nature, life experiences and dreams which I reinterpret in the form of personal symbols. I am attracted to nature, spirituality and especially the opposing forces of good and evil and how my perspective has changed because of my position over time to this information. I am creating a dialogue with symbols which expresses my beliefs and observations", says Alison Helm.

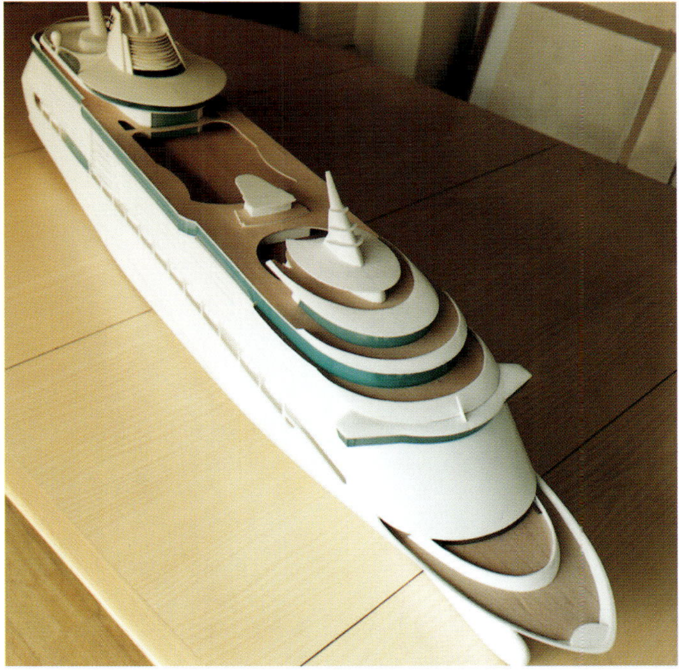

Model for Grandeur of the Seas *made by Per Høydal and Jens Petter Askim.*

"Open space and elegance are the key words to describe the exterior decks in the *Vision series*. We start with the general arrangement and attempt to get it to be as maritime and elegant as possible. RCI has a maritime tradition that goes all the way back to 1970, but as the dimensions increase, one has to break down the elements to create a more human scale. The ships have become so huge that one can make an entire climbing wall as a feature. On the whole, one is left in peace to work on the design. Fewer people have an opinion about the exterior than those who have something to say about what's inside the ship. With the interiors, there are phases by which different things must be finished. There are many meetings with the Steering Committee and changes are made. The financial framework becomes much more important with the interior than it does with the exterior decks," says Askim.

"The funnels are among the elements that can be pretty freely designed. The Viking Crown is a given. The same is true of the radar mast and partly also the forward section with the bridge. The design for that is somewhat inspired by Njål Eide's ideas of light shafts and the like.

"The task for the Viking Crown's exterior was to design it so that the glass panes were arranged in a geometric system using very few differently shaped parts. The materials were predetermined. Powerful drawings resulted from such tasks – and all was drawn by hand. We found solutions in collaboration with the shipyard, solutions that integrated form and aesthetics. But today there is no choice but to use computers if one is to work with the new ships in the *Voyager* and *Radiance series*." ■

Part II

Onboard

"A ship this size has all the opportunities that you would experience in a small town."

Fred de Cosse,
Hotel Director, Legend of the Seas

Legend of the Seas

"The art combines visual and legendary themes,
illustrating old myths,
birds in flight,
the sparkling crests of the waves
and the power and grace of Viking Ships."

Peter Layton
British sculptor

David Smith, "Harlequin", Card Room.

Hilde Vemren, b. 1953, Norwegian: "Morning Light". Acrylic on canvas. Detail. Main Stairs, Deck 8-9.

Travelogue

A brisk sea wind is blowing, the sun is setting. The air is charged with excitement. A majestic ocean liner pulls away from the dock in Olbia Harbor, Sardinia.

The port is full of all types of ferries, some worn out, others gleaming as if they came straight from the shipyard. "Beware of Propellers - Attenti alle Elice," warns a rusty sign astern on the Calabria of Napoli. Through a thick coat of paint, we can see that she has sailed under the name Pireus Express in a previous life.

The bridge of the *Legend of the Seas* is bustling with activity. Captain Wildung and his officers are on full alert every time the vessel is maneuvered in or out of harbor. This is a 279-meter-long ship with 70,000 tons of steel we're talking about. The harbor pilot rolls himself a cigarette. It's a major operation releasing the moorings: on the foredeck we count five men in blue overalls and hard hats, plus an officer in white. "Let all go fore." Full power to the bow and side propellers, and we glide sideways out of the dock in very slow motion; with all our tonnage, we move with more ease and elegance than the small ferries far below. But all the real power is on the bridge. We are witnessing a minor miracle. The mammoth ship is maneuvered with one hand and a joystick from the bridge wing. It is a matter of great pride to command such a magnificent vessel, built to cruise the world and able to sail in all kinds of conditions.

Captain Thomas Wildung steers Legend of the Seas *out of Olbia, Sardinia. The heavy traffic demands full alertness.*

Legend glides slowly out of the harbor, headed north along the beautiful northeast coast of Sardinia: past Aga Khan's Costa Smeralda; into the sunset and through the straits between Sardinia and Corsica, passing Bonifacio, the old Genoese fortress city on Corsica's southern tip. These are waters steeped in myths and legends from Ulysses' journeys to Aga Khan's playground for the wealthy at Cala del Volpe and Porto Cervo on the northern part of the island. Sunset over the Mediterranean and a glass of dry champagne await us.

Mike Newby, Glassworks "Hommage to SS France"

Legend of the Seas

The nearly identical sister ships, *Legend* and *Splendour*, are fast ships with a top speed of 24 knots. They can cover great distances and visit many harbors, e.g. in the Mediterranean, in the course of a single cruise. Moreover, *Splendour* and *Legend*, which each can carry 1,800-2,000 passengers, will soon be the shipping company's smallest vessels. It's a good size for capturing new markets, where it would not be wise to begin with larger ships. What's more, these ships are beautiful; they make a good impression in the harbors.

Captain Thomas Wildung recalls his experiences with new markets. RCI sailed for 2–3 seasons in the Orient with *Sun Viking* in its day without any notable success. In those days everyone was buzzing about the construction of the six big ships in the *Vision Class*, so a relatively small vessel in the Orient didn't attract much attention. However, a great deal of effort went into marketing *Legend of the Seas'* "Royal Journeys", which became a success with 17–21 day cruises to the Middle East, Southeast Asia, New Zealand and Australia in Oceania. *Legend's* itinerary has also included ports in Israel, Egypt, Jordan, the United Arab Emirates, Oman, India, Singapore, Thailand, Malaysia, Indonesia, Vietnam, Brunei, the Philippines and China.

The Baltic cruises have featured the Scandinavian capitals and Tallinn, Estonia, and a two-day stay in St. Petersburg, Russia. The Baltic Isles/Norwegian fjords itinerary has featured stops at ports in the Netherlands, France, England, Ireland, Scotland and the Norwegian fjords.

Mediterranian ports of call have been Barcelona, Monte Carlo/Cannes and Marseilles in France and Viareggio (for Florence and Pisa), Naples, Capri, Civitavecchia (for Rome) and Venice in Italy, with other cruises to Heraklion, Santorini, Rhodes and Athens in Greece, Kusadasi (Ephesos) and Messina in Turkey and Valletta in Malta. ■

The Legend of the Seas *is the first of the* Vision Class *ships. She was built at Chantiers de l'Atlantique in St. Nazaire, France in 1996.*
Gross Tons: 70,000.
Length: 264 m/867 ft.
Beam: 32 m/105 ft.
Draft: 7.5 m/24 ft.
Cruising speed: 24 knots.,
Passengers: capacity of 1,800 (double occupancy).
Crew: 723.

The Captain:

A life in ships and at sea

"They have been exciting years. Each year brought something new: new vessels, new routes, new concepts. It's a privilege to sail as a captain for RCI.

"The flip side of the coin is that you become somewhat less of a seaman and more of a managing director with each passing year. Life at sea used to be more varied and perhaps more fun. Even though we're given plenty of time off with three months ashore for every three on board, we work under tremendous pressure so that three months on board today take a lot more out of us than eight months did ten years ago. Everything we do is monitored and checked, and the passengers just get more and more demanding. I've seen big changes just in the last five years. Some people have learned the advantage of complaining the moment they come on board – the more they complain, the more they get. Unfortunately, many people have systematized this habit, and the word "no" is becoming more and more difficult to say."

Captain Thomas Wildung, born in Sweden in 1945, has spent his entire life around ships and sea. His father, a sea captain, exposed him to shipboard life at a very early age. This naturally enticed him to seek a life at sea. After graduating from college in 1965, he hired on as a sailor aboard a freighter bound for South America. After three carefree but eventful years along the shores of North and South America, he decided to pursue a maritime career, joined the Swedish Merchant Marine Academy and graduated three years later. With a new licence in his pocket, he joined one of Sweden's largest shipping companies, the "Johnson Line" and stayed there for 14 years. During those years he plied the Seven Seas gathering vast experience on all kinds of vessels as he moved up the ranks. He joined the cruise industry in 1985 and was appointed Master at Royal Caribbean in 1987. ■

The Hotel Director:

Like a small town

"My responsibilities are not just limited to the satisfaction of our guests; I've got to look after the well-being of the crew as well. A ship this size has all the situations that you would experience in a small town. So it's very rewarding."

Back in the good old days of the sixties, when he was with Cunard, liners were a means of transportation, taking passengers from one port to another. "Forty years ago we regarded a 20,000 ton ship with 800 passengers as a big ship. Now we have 140,000 ton ships with 3,600 guests, and they are more demanding. These days cruise is something almost anyone can afford; it used to be for the well-to-do."

When airplanes captured passenger transport, a lot of shipping companies went out of business. Now the industry has been revitalized.

"Good staff are the key to success. Our employees learn an awful lot when they come on board this ship. Whether they are waiters or cabin stewards, we polish up their skills. The company encourages promotions according to the RCI-system. Promotion is not just based on length of service, but on merit and attitude, so there is a lot of motivation for young crew members to improve themselves and advance through the hierarchy. And they stay with the company.

"It's a challenge for everyone on board. You can't go home after work. Your job is not just a job you do – it's a way of life."

Legend's Hotel Director, Fred de Cosse, has been in the business for more than 40 years, ever since 1959 when he went to sea on the old *Queen Mary* as a 16-year-old bell boy. Born in England and raised in Ireland and Canada, he worked for several cruise companies in patisseries, dining rooms and bars and in the administrative and housekeeping departments. He held various positions, including Night Services Manager, Bar Manager, Dining Room Manager, Crew Purser, Chief Steward, Chief Purser and Food & Beverage Manager. In 1977 he was promoted to Hotel Director aboard the *Monarch of the Seas*. Since then he has served as Hotel Director aboard several cruise vessels throughtout the world. ■

Captain Thomas Wildung was born in Sweden 1945, and has spent his entire life around ships and sea. He joined the cruise industry in 1985 and was appointed Master at Royal Caribbean in 1987.

Legend's Hotel Director, Fred de Cosse, was born in England 1943. Since 1977 he has served as Hotel Director aboard several grand cruise vessels throughout the world.

The Centrum Sculpture:

Janus, the God of Light and Lord of the Voyage

Entering the Ship on Deck 4, passengers emerge into the magnificent Centrum designed by Njål Eide. Suspended between the lift shafts in this soaring space is a sculpture that spans three decks. Entitled *"Janus"* and constructed from stainless steel, polished glass and fibre optics, this glittering work is by British artist Peter Layton. According to legend, Janus was the god of light, opening the sky at daybreak and closing it at sunset. In time, he also became the patron deity of voyage and presided over all beginnings and endings and all entrances and exits. The artist says, "I offer this theme as a good and relevant omen in celebration of *Legend of the Seas*. The sculpture combines visual and mythical themes, illustrating the power and grace of Viking Ships, birds in flight and the rippling movements and sparkling crests of the waves." Through the imaginative choice of materials, a light, elegant structure has been created, with a stepped canopy-like design bestowing a sense of intimacy on the grand scale of the Centrum. By reflecting the ambient light and color, the glass elements are imbued with mysterious depths and magical qualities." ■

Peter Layton (cv p 302):
"Janus".
Steel, polished glass, fiber-optics.
Centrum, Deck 4-7.
Peter Layton says: "It was very interesting when we actually were putting this sculpture up, and it was sheer magic when the scaffolding came down. We had never seen the piece assembled before and it was worth all the problems and pain during the installation. It was one of those peak moments – on top of the mountain – there are few of those in one's life. It had worked – it looked fantastic." (See also page 301).

The Stairs:

Legends from various regions of Europe

The artwork on the forward stairway links the public areas with the cabin corridors. Each corridor takes a European country as its theme, and their relative locations are loosely related to the map of Europe. Northern nations like Norway are displayed on the upper decks and southern countries such as Italy and Greece are placed on lower decks. The "Nile Painting" by British artist Jane Thomson, which depicts a journey down the Nile to the Mediterranean, links the corridor themes of Italy and Spain. Its motifs of music and dance allude to the Egyptian-influenced Art Deco Show Lounges. The stylistic link is affirmed by two Art Deco Erte sculptures situated outside the "That's Entertainment" Theater. ■

Nicholas Verall, b. 1945, British: "Green Shutters, Provence". Oil on canvas. "House with painted walls". Main Stairs, Deck 6-7.

Bernie Fuchs, b. 1933, American: "The Merchant of Venice". Oil on canvas. Main Stairs, Deck 5-4.

Brigid Collins, b. 1963, British: "Bering". Oil on canvas. The explorer Vitus Bering 1681–1741. Forward Stairs, Deck 8-9.

The Solarium:

"Not just hanging some pictures on the walls"

Nichola, "Nicky", Elstone of London Contemporary Art on procuring the art for *Legend of the Seas:*
"We had a lot of fun and headaches. In the shipyard we had these huge crates with all the art still in them - they were all over the place and it was a complete mess. Two hours before the ship was to sail, this man came up and said, 'These cases have to be strapped down.' How was I supposed to do that? He said that we were going to hit a storm and that it was my responsibility to strap them down. Actually, my job was to say, 'That looks nice, but if you can move it a little bit to the right, it will be even nicer.'

"Almost everywhere we turned, there were battles with the yard during *Legend's* installation. The yard was actually contracted to install all of the artwork, I don't think they realized how much art RCI had actually ordered – no other ship had ever had that much art on board. They must have thought that we were just going to hang some pictures on the walls.

"With the Nicolas Phillips panels in the Solarium it was us or them. Richard D. Fain, the almighty CEO of RCI, said, 'This won't work', he looked at the sketch on the board. I said, 'Believe me, it will work, and it will look beautiful.' He said, 'OK, convince me.' We had one of the pieces made to full scale. Two of the architects came to London to approve it before we sent it to the Steering Committee meeting. We lit it from the edge and underneath, just to see how it was going to look.

"Everything was going swimmingly, and everybody thought it was great, no problem, and we went off to a nice lunch. When we came back, the whole piece had cracked. We had forgotten to switch the lights off, and the heat from the lamps cracked it. We had to ship this cracked piece to the Steering Committee meeting in Miami because Fain hadn't seen it. We weren't looking forward to that.

"Before it came to that, however, we got the message that Fain wanted to reverse the etching of the glass. Originally, the etching was on the face, but he wanted it on the back because the grease on people's fingers would get into the etching and change the coating. So we had to have another piece made anyway, and our day was saved. And this time we made sure it was done perfectly. We were installing artwork up to the very last minute.

"The last thing we did was to hoist the pool sculpture onboard in Brooklyn. It was midnight and I had organized a huge crane and persuaded the French workers who had been working around the clock during the whole crossing to return to work after their meal to help us install the sculpture. It was very dark, and the lighting was poor. Ben Jenkins was sitting inside the head of the sculpture, guiding pins into position and fastening screws. Somehow it worked, and the sculpture is still there."

"Coming into Miami was amazing. I don't think I've been quite so emotional in my life. ■

Nicolas Phillips, British: Etched glass relief. Solarium, Deck 9.

Victor Lind on his collapsible painting:

"The theme had been specified in advance: the Age of the Vikings. "It extends more than five meters on each side of the Centrum – all-in-all, nearly a 20-meter-long frieze.

"It was supposed to be possible to fold the walls together to make room for the camera shop's daily exhibition of snapshots. That was difficult. I had to imagine a design that could work as a kind of series. I thought of the Bayeux tapestry, which is like a comic strip from the year 1066 – a narrative about what happened when William the Conqueror invaded England with his long boats from Normandy in France.

"We took a field trip to Bayeux in France to study the tapestry," recalls Lind. "The solution was to divide the frieze into sections; it just wouldn't do to paint a long frieze that would have to be broken into pieces whenever the camera shop needed space. We designed it in sections like a filmstrip. It is much easier to justify folding up a number of discreet compositions.

"After trying several options, Njål Eide showed the rough drafts to the other architects and to the artistic consultants at LCA. The response was unanimous: 'We like it.' The RCI Steering Committee agreed. What they were shown was the result of a long process. You wouldn't go to them with something you hadn't thought out properly." ■

Victor Lind (cv p 305): "The Voyage". Acrylic and metal leaf on aluminum. Main Stair Lobby, Deck 6. Based on the Bayeux tapestry, a woven "comic strip" from 1066 that chronicles William the Conqueror's invasion of England from the coast of Normandy in France.

The Dining Room:

Romeo and Juliet

Nini Anker Dessen:
"I made the Romeo and Juliet tapestries for the two floors of architect Njål Eide's splendid Dining Room on *Legend of the Seas*. The result was beautiful, and that definitely had something to do with Eide's color scheme.

You learn a lot from a job this large. You have to get used to big dimensions, which are ten times more difficult than small formats. That's especially true of the composition; you can't just make a drawing and trust that it can be blown up.

The wall hangings in the Dining Room were woven by the world's most skilled craftsmen in Aubusson, France, where they have a centuries-old tradition in this field." ■

Nini Anker Dessen (cv p 283):
"Romeo and Juliet".
Tapestry. Dining Room, Deck 4-5.

The craftsmen in Aubusson can weave an enormous work in three months' time. As a rule, the weavers are men, and they have often learned the trade from their fathers. They know all of the techniques, and they work rapidly and beautifully. If the wall hanging is large, four men may sit next to each other at the loom. The biggest projects for the cruise ships could never have been finished in time without professional weaving assistance in the final phase.

Nini Anker Dessen (cv p 283): "Romeo and Juliet". Tapestry, detail. Dining Room, Deck 4-5.

The *Curved Art* in Windjammer

Nini Anker Dessen:
"Together with Magne Austad I did a work that we called *"Curved Art"*, a collage with a free-standing sail for the mid-section of Windjammer Café.

Nini Anker Dessen and Magne Austad (cv p 283): "Sea and Shore". Ceramic decoration.

"The work is a combination of Magne Austad's painting in the upper part of the picture and my collage done with paper appliqué and textiles in the lower part.

"The rest of the room is decorated with large ceramic reliefs featuring Windjammer motifs on the walls. It began when Njål Eide asked whether we could do something in ceramics. I had never worked with ceramics, but we began to work on the project, and we learned a lot as we went along. Tommerup Tegelverk on the isle of Fyn in Denmark produced the ceramics. It's a place where "foreign" artists are welcomed. It helped that they also produced the table tops so that the color scheme could be harmonized with the rest of the room." ■

"Curved Art". Painting and Collage.

"That's Entertainment" Theater

Romain de Tirtoff (1892–1990), Russian: "Zobeide" (large picture) and "Erte" (small picture). Bronze. Forward Lobby, Deck 4. These sculptures are situated at the entrance of the "That's Entertainment" Theater.

"That's Entertainment" Theater.
Architect Howard Snoweiss.
Stage curtain by Paramount Parks.
Glass sculpture by Italian artist Gianni Arico, b. 1941.

Splendour of the Seas

This ship's unique art
creates an atmosphere of
classic elegance
that lives up to the ship's name.

Larry Kirkland
(cv p 299):
"Celestium".

Thai artifact.

Travelogue

The Windjammer Café is a lovely restaurant with a spectacular view of Miami's skyline and the intense speedboat traffic below. Here we can enjoy the finest service in a beautiful maritime setting; huge glasses filled with exotic drinks garnished with umbrellas and blue straws. The passengers have boarded for their first day of an 11-day cruise to Mexico, Grand Cayman, Jamaica, Aruba, and Curacao, and they are familiarizing themselves with the beautiful ship.

Judith Poxon Fawkes, American: "Compass Roses 4". Tapestry woven of linen which was grown in Scotland, France and Lithuania. Purser's Desk, Deck 5.

Outside the Dining Room, we lose ourselves in the breakfast menu: Chilled juices – orange, tomato, grape, prune, pineapple, cranberry, grapefruit, apple and pear nectar; Fruit – all you can eat; 10 different kinds of cereal; 10 varieties of baked bread; Danish pastry, croissants, doughnuts, brioches, toast and eggs; fish and meat in every variation you could desire; tea and coffee, a bounty of alternatives.

In the Boutiques of the Centrum, we find creams and perfumes, teddy bears, ceramic dogs, and Marco Polo's Store. There is a 30 % sale on Lladro figurines this week; gold items from 99 dollars, and thermoses that keep their contents cold.

Elin Sjøen works at the Purser's Desk. She has six years of experience on cruise ships and can handle almost anything. She tried the life of a landlubber for a few years but found that she is happiest at sea: She explains: "The *Splendour* is a ship with soul. Among the passengers there are approximately 900 'repeaters'. These are people who have traveled with the ship before. The guests are for the most part pleasant. On our last cruise a huge South American party almost took over the whole ship, dancing and singing."

Splendour of the Seas

Splendour of the Seas is the second ship in the RCI fleet built especially to cater to an international clientele. Like *Legend of the Seas, Splendour* has a higher service speed than later vessels in the *Vision Class,* which allows for more varied itineraries. In fact, *Splendour* has cruised more different itineraries than any other ship in the fleet: The eastern coast of South America, different seven-day itineraries in the Mediterranian Sea, including ports of call at Piraeus (Athens), Rhodes, and Mykonos in Greece, as well as Dubrovnik in Croatia. The *Splendour of the Seas* is also the ship in the RCI fleet with the highest proportion of elderly passengers. This is because *Splendour* has sailed on relatively long cruises, from 10 days in the Caribbean to 12 days in Europe. Young people don't want to use their entire vacation time on one trip. "Mature passengers tend to complain a little more, but they don't break anything," comments the Captain. Northern European cruises focus on the ports of call and sightseeing excursions for the passengers. In the Caribbean, sunshine, calypso music and coconut drinks attract a younger crowd. ■

The Splendour of the Seas *was built in 1996 at the Chantiers de l'Atlantique yard in France. Gross Tons: 70,000. Length: 264.4 m/867 ft. Beam: 32 m/105 ft. Draft: 7.5 m/24.5 ft. Cruising speed: 24 knots. Passengers: 1,804 (double occupancy). Crew: 723.*

The captain:

Mariner, administrator, and a little bit circus director

"It's important that people know our name," remarks Captain Olsen. "When I first started working here, in 1987, I had barely heard of Royal Caribbean.

"When we build several ships that look alike, the décor contributes to the vessel's identity. All the ships are beautiful; they each have their own theme and personality. For example, the *Splendour of the Seas* sails to Europe and has a classic elegance."

The ship has more than 2,000 works of art onboard and Captain Olsen says that many passengers take the time to walk around and view the artwork, appreciating the experience. "They feel the interior is interesting and diverse," he says. "Some individuals have even tried to steal some of the art. But they can't take Larry Kirkland's Centrum sculpture with them. It extends over six decks and is so big that an experienced climber really should do the vacuuming," laughs Olsen.

"The King and I" Dining Room is dominated by Thai artifacts.

Captain Tor Olsen was the Master of Splendour of the Seas *when this interview was conducted. He became later one of the Captains on* Voyager of the Seas.

"The sculpture on the pool deck has been called a lot of names – none of them suitable for print," he adds, "especially when we repaired the deck around it and put it back in place. The crew couldn't remember how it was fitted. They were looking for the right angle so the artist wouldn't get mad," the Captain recalls.

"The art probably doesn't mean so much to the crew; most have little time to enjoy art," says Olsen. "But what the passengers appreciate, we appreciate. You can't help but feel a sense of pride when the passengers boast about the surroundings. We feel that attractive surroundings are important."

Over time, Olsen has become as much an administrator as a seaman. "There are many situations that require follow-up. What's more, the Captain is always a bit of a circus director for the passengers. In Europe, one is more of a seaman than in the Caribbean. European seas offer greater challenges, both in traffic and weather; we can experience fog and other ugly things that we don't have to deal with between Miami and Mexico," he explains.

"For me personally, it is a special pleasure as a Norwegian

Captain to take the Norwegian-registered *Splendour* up the Oslo Fjord to her home port of Oslo on a beautiful summer day and moor beneath the ancient walls of the Akershus Fortress," concludes Captain Olsen. ■

The Hotel Director:

Enjoy your meals and you will enjoy the cruise

James Spencer hails from Lancashire in northwest England. The first Royal Caribbean ship he served on was the *Nordic Prince*. Since then, he has worked stints as Food and Beverage Manager and Hotel Manager on several of the company's ships.

"We get a lot of comments on the art onboard," says Spencer. "The Thai artifacts in the Dining Room are popular, with the two original Temple Dogs by the entrance as the most impressive. So is Larry Kirkland's magnificent Centrum sculpture."

The Thai Temple Dogs have a special story behind them, says Spencer: "They contained more than we knew about when they were put onboard. After two years, the ship was put in dry dock for maintenance. During dry dock work, the air conditioning is turned off and it gets hot. In the morning, I went past the dogs and everything was normal; in the afternoon, it was getting hotter and suddenly there were mushrooms growing, and little worms coming out of the figures.

"I told the Captain, and he said: 'Have you been drinking or something?' He came down to see and couldn't believe his eyes. White mushrooms right on the front of the statue. The spores must have been in the wood for at least three or four years – it was amazing. But we got rid of it with chemical and powerful cleaners."

Spencer also points to some of the paintings, and the beautiful bronzes and marble onboard. "I myself am specially fond of the pieces by the entrance to the Theater," he says, "and the glass sculptures in the lounges are absolutely incredible."

Spencer observes that the Centrum works well as a meeting place, with the Champagne Bar as "the extra elegant little something," while the Purser's and Excursion Desks function as an efficient hotel lobby. "It's a focal point for the whole ship," he says. "The two glass elevators give a good view over the huge atrium and its Sun Disc sculpture. However, glass and brass are always a maintenance headache," he adds.

Spencer says the greatest challenge under his responsibility is producing quality meals for so many people, all to be served at the right moment: "If you enjoy the meals, you enjoy the cruise."

It's also important to keep the crew happy, he adds: "We have a staff of 740 people. It's a tough job to keep them all motivated, but without people this ship would just be a large piece of steel." ■

James Spencer, Hotel Director, Splendour of the Seas.

Centrum celebrates the Cosmos

"Kirkland is professional and skilled at presenting art. He made a model and took photographs that were dramatic, giving the Steering Committee the feeling of actually seeing the sculpture in the space. They fell for it completely. Then we were allowed to complete the project in peace," says architect Njål Eide.

"We developed a good relationship. Njål was not afraid that I was going to create something that was contrary to his aesthetics. His willingness to let me explore has been important because Njål is a fellow who likes to control the design of everything down to the doorknobs!", says Kirkland.

"I spent two days in Oslo at Eide's office. They had a large model of the Centrum. It was a huge space, 8 decks high and serves many functions. The ships interiors are visually very complicated with lots of materials, forms and details. My idea was to find a simple, elegant but bold form that would become the central icon of the space. The first day at the office I just looked at the model and asked questions. That night I drew up the idea and the next day we made a crude model out of strings, cardboard, tape and the top of a slide projector for the structural ring. The form of the work is a huge sun form, and captures the natural light streaming in through the atrium skylight."

"The most important thing for Njål Eide was to have something hanging within the space to create visual interest within the atrium. For me it was to create a unique icon on board the ship, something of memorable simplicity. Interestingly, the form was adapted as a motif on elements and surfaces throughout the ship. As well as being a beautiful design, the sculpture had to have at the essence of the concept the engineering to keep it securely suspended in the atrium. The entire sculpture is like a tension spring. There are an equal number of stainless steel cables pulling up from the inside and down from the outside of the Sun Disc. Each of the sixty sun rays acts like a small structural beam that gives the exact tension needed to keep the entire ring rigid in the space. The Sun Disc is slightly cone-shaped to give it extra strength to resist the forces upward and downward.

"From the first Oslo model, we made our own scale model of the atrium with the sculpture, and immediately started working with an engineer. Often engineers can scare off an idea as being impossible to build. An important factor for the success of the RCI project was to bring in a brilliant structural engineer, Charles Keyes, from Martin and Martin in Denver, Colorado. Charles is one of the foremost tensile structural engineers in the world. He understands the complexities of forces and is dedicated to enhancing the aesthetics of the sculptural form. Many structural engineers will say: 'You need bolts that are really big and even bigger beams because of the fear the work might fall apart'. Charles carefully blends structural strength and artistic vision. I hire Charles as a consultant to engineer all my projects with RCI. He really knows what is going on in ships and the construction language. But because he works with art, he makes sure that aesthetics are the key. It has been a close and unique partnership and a wonderful collaboration." ■

Larry Kirkland, (cv p 299): "Celestium". Champagne Bar, Centrum, Deck 4-9. This environmental artwork in the Centrum celebrates the Cosmos. The sun disc of golden aluminum occupies the central space with its glowing presence.

A complex structure system with an array of stainless steel cables from the top deck helps to suspend the main Sun structure. These many cables gather at the atrium floor into the Earth's sphere of tooled aluminum.

On the walls of deck 7 and 8, are figures of the Celestial sky, made from aluminum covered with oxidized silver leaf. These images are taken from the first printed star map by the famed German engraver Albrecht Dürer in 1515. The work pays homage to our universal quest: to explore and discover. As our ancestors ventured across seas to unknown lands, future generations will reveal the mysteries below the oceans and above this Earth in the worlds beyond.

Stairs

Geoffrey Pagan, American: "Untitled". Ceramic wall relief, Forward Stairs, Deck 2-3.

Lawrence Mathis, American: "Line of Oaks". Oil on canvas 19A. Main Stair Lobby. Deck 10.

Gregg Lefevre, American: "Sea".
Mixed media on canvas. Main Stairs,
Deck 3-4.
Panel of the stairway mural tryptych,
encompassing unique instruments
of navigation, including astrolabes, sextants,
compasses and sun dials suspended
in time and space.

Upper decks, Pool and Solarium

The solarium is an upgraded deck with an elegant swimming pool and sliding glass roof, as an 'outdoor' room indoors with emphasis on art and an air of serenity – in contrast to the lively outdoor deck with the big swimming pool.

All photos show the Solarium on board Splendour of the Seas.

A large, beautiful bowl, inspired by traditional Greek ceramic design, hangs by the entrance to the Beauty Salon & Spa.

"Fisherman from Santorini". Painted wood. Replica. Fitness Center/Spa, Deck 9.

Alison Helm,
b. 1956, American:
"Two passing dolphins".
Stainless steel.
Pool sculpture. Deck 9.

Viking Crown

Maria Veronica L. Solem (cv p 323) and Halfdan Greve: "Viking Landscape". Acrylic painting with ship's bow. Mixed media. Ship's bow by Halfdan Greve. All furniture is designed by the room's architect, Njål Eide.

Inger Sitter (cv p 316) had the idea for the dancing floor on Splendour of the Seas, *designed by architect Njål Eide and executed by Hamy Sveis of Norway.*

Grandeur of the Seas

The ship embodies the elegance of the grand epochs of world art – but also the carefree style of the 1920's.

Alice Kettle: "Answers". Tapestry (detail).

Phillip Jackson (cv p 295): "Don Giovanni". Bronze, resin.

Travelogue

It's hot and damp on the sun deck in San Juan, Puerto Rico. Rain and sunshine alternate. We are not far from the equator; the contrast from our last week in Alaska is striking. The passengers are also different. Here, there are families with small children, many young people, and partying on deck at night, with dancing, joking and true romance.

Suddenly, a heavy thunderstorm lets loose; blankets of water pour down as the packed deck clears in half-a-minute. Three minutes later, the sun is shining again, and the deck is full of happy people. It's 86 °F in the air and 88 °F in the pool. A moderate breeze blows from starboard.

Air-conditioning is a blessing; it's nice and cool. It seems almost surreal to sit by the Purser's Desk in the beautiful Centrum created by the architect Njål Eide, and look at the huge brass and glass elevators gliding silently up to deck 10. Inside the elevator, the rug indicates that it is Wednesday and a woman's voice says: "Going up." Otherwise, the only sound is the trickling of running water from the fountain.

The next port, home of luxury boutiques, fish and shellfish, is Charlotte Amalie on St. Thomas, in the US Virgin Islands, with Magens Bay, palm trees, clear green water, turtles and white sandy beaches. The town is chock-full of tax-free shops, and the floating establishments are marked with large signs reading: "Bar". In there, the mood ranges from wild and upwards.

Knut Steen: "Centrum Sculpture".

> *"She is definitely a good ambassador for the company."*
>
> *– Captain James McDonald*

Grandeur of the Seas

The *Grandeur* has been sailing in the Mediterranean from Barcelona and Rome in the summertime, with autumn cruises to Canada/New England from Boston, before setting course for the cruise season in the Caribbean.

Her traditional 7 night cruises in the southern Caribbean leave from San Juan, Puerto Rico to exotic ports such as Oranjestad on Aruba, Willemstad on Curacao, Philipsburg on St. Maarten, and Charlotte Amalie on St. Thomas in the Virgin Islands. It is a cruise that offers colonial Spanish fortresses, tropical rain forests, the world's most beautiful beaches, wildlife reserves and picturesque fishing villages. ■

Grandeur *at the quay. The* Grandeur of the Seas *was built in 1996 at Kværner Masa Yards in Helsinki. Gross tons: 74,000. Length: 279 m /916 ft. Beam: 32.3 m /106 ft. Draft: 7.6 m /25 ft. Cruising speed: 22 knots. Passengers: 1,950 (double occupancy). Crew: 760. Photo: Knut Vadseth.*

The Captain:

Safety is number one

Captain James McDonald was dedicated to the *Grandeur* from the building stage. He supervised construction of the ship at Kværner Masa Yards in Helsinki. Construction of a ship this size is a long and complicated process, as is the selection of art.

"You don't build a ship, then go out to buy the art afterwards," smiles Captain James McDonald. "It is decided by the architects and art consultants a long time in advance. They did a nice job with the *Grandeur*. The passengers like the art.

Captain James McDona was born in Canada. Danish heritage may ha influenced his decision t navigate the courses of h Viking ancestors. At age 15, McDonald set sail as an ordinary seaman during summer vacatior while attending military boarding school. After graduation, he was dra back to the merchant marine on a more perma nent basis, outward bou on various types of carg ships. He earned his Master Mariner's certific tion in Canada in 1987. McDonald joined Royal Caribbean in 1990.

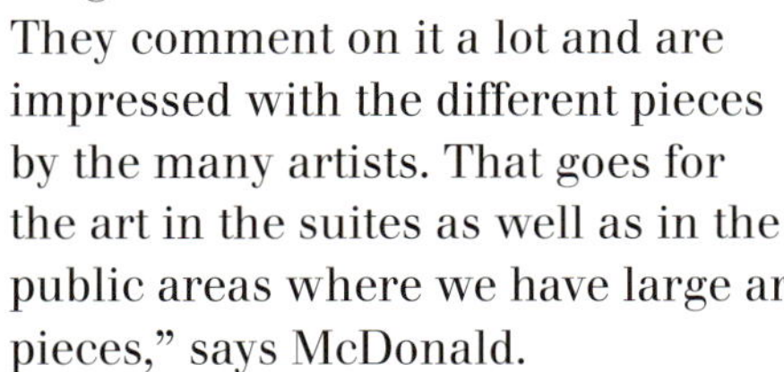

They comment on it a lot and are impressed with the different pieces by the many artists. That goes for the art in the suites as well as in the public areas where we have large art pieces," says McDonald.

But besides maintaining a beautiful ship, the Captain has his priorities. "The Captain's main duty is to ensure the safety of the passengers, the crew and the vessel itself," he asserts. "There are a lot of administrative duties, but safety is number one. Still, I spend a lot of time with the guests certain nights of the week. I roam the ship, meet them on the open deck, by the gangway, and if I get the opportunity to be ashore, I meet them on the dock and they visit the bridge. They are curious about many things: the ship, me. And I am of course interested in all their comments, good or bad." ■

Steve Keller, purser on Grandeur of the Seas, *has been sailing for 10 years with RCI on various ships, including the* Sun Viking, Song of Norway, Nordic Empress, *and* Monarch of the Seas.

Each guest is number one

Steve Keller, purser on *Grandeur of the Seas* understands his responsibility well: "The mariners are important to security, to the running of the ship, the maintenance and navigation. But the hotel department deals with the guests, the most important factor onboard," he says. "We interact with the guests in all ways."

He continues: "The guests come here to feel very special and to be well taken care of. Our goal is that each and every passenger feels that he or she is the number-one guest onboard. They could have chosen to stay at a resort ashore, but instead they come onboard, unpack, while the hotel moves day by day to new ports of call. You go to bed at night and the next day you wake up in a beautiful new place. On shore you wake up in the same place every morning," comments Keller.

The hotel director also puts emphasis on the ship's surroundings: "Most of our guests are overwhelmed when they see all these beautiful works of art as they walk around the ship. And every piece features a plaque which tells about the artist and the piece. This enhances their time on the ship, and makes our hotel classier," he points out.

"This is also *our* home," Keller continues. "The people who run this hotel work for four to eight months straight. We are here more than we are at our actual homes. So we take pride in this being our home, and all the art and beautiful design enhances that. And it enhances our pride. It gives the crew a sense of identity. Each ship is our home, and we identify strongly with it." ■

The Centrum Sculpture:

A floating construction in a closed world

Knut Steen created the beautiful floating Centrum sculpture onboard the *Grandeur of the Seas*:

"It was Gro Nesjar of London Contemporary Art who wanted sculptures for a few small and exclusive ships," recalls sculptor Knut Steen. "Suddenly, I was involved. Then the shipping company went bankrupt and I thought that would be the end of it. But she turned up again with RCI, and we were able to use one of the models we had lying around."

The first work Steen did was a hanging sculpture for the Centrum of the *Grandeur of the Seas*. "I did it together with Halfdan Greve, who worked for Njål Eide and is a great guy. It was fun to be a part of all that. I had only a vague and uncertain idea, and we made a model that we placed inside a model of the ship itself. Halfdan is amazing with his fingers and got the small fragile components to stick together. Eventually, we managed to construct it, and it now hangs from four wires. It looks great," he says.

"Over the years, there have been many jobs for the RCI fleet – there have been many fun things to do," Steen continues. "This art is robust and unsnobbish. It strikes a chord with all kinds of people, and of course they remain onboard for a week or two. The passengers walk around surrounded by the art every day, which is a fine thing. Many of them do not frequent galleries; some have scarcely been in a museum and may never find their way there."

Steen points out that creating art for ships requires artists to take into consideration certain technical requirements that are of no consequence on land. "Your relief must remain securely fastened to

the wall even in heavy seas," he explains. "You must anticipate dangers related to sharp corners and edges." But he feels he had good support from the others involved. "Cooperation with the architects and London Contemporary Art has been characterized by a generosity of thought seldom met in other contexts," he says.

"I am preoccupied with ships," admits Steen. "It's just amazing that such things can float. A ship is a project that is clearly well thought out. It is a closed world. It is inspiring to know that it sails to many different places. An atmosphere has been created where things just glide together to form a whole, which is the ship, a whole that travels around. It's a strange concept." ■

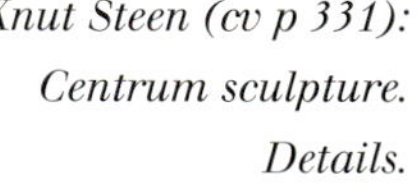

Knut Steen (cv p 331): Centrum sculpture. Details.

A South Pacific Journey

Maria Veronica L. Solem (cv p 323): "The Spirit of Happy Islands. An ode to the people of the South Pacific". Acrylic painting on canvas.

"My biggest project aboard the *Grandeur of the Seas* was based on a South Pacific theme," says painter Veronica Solem. "The assignment was to decorate a large lounge all the way aft. As it happened, I traveled to Bali and Micronesia and around to small islands to get some inspiration. Nicki, from London Contemporary Art, joined me. She was to buy artifacts for display in the lounge and a huge model of an outrigger.

"Andreas has to come along," I said at the meeting with the architect. My son was five years old and we were going to be away for many weeks. So, we were off, and Nicki organized everything. She didn't like cockroaches though, so we never made it to New Guinea. I insisted that we go to Micronesia to avoid tourists. We ended up in a little village where we found a room in a cottage and got fresh lobster from the fisherman each day. Andreas played with the children and I was inspired. It was a nice time, off the Philippines, where they have such beautiful sails, and in Micronesia, where they have such beautiful outriggers," reminisces Solem.

"After a few weeks, we proceeded to a new island, on a mission to find the perfect boat. On this island, there was only one hotel, installed in an abandoned Japanese field hospital from World War II. It rained buckets for five days and we just barely managed to get by," Solem remembers, adding: "It was difficult."

But the travelers found a guide who took them to an old castle: "A notched stone castle that looked like a Norwegian Viking house," recalls Solem. "A mystical kingdom from 2000 years ago. It is said that there was an Indonesian prince who journeyed to this island and built a city on the land and another on the water, then disappeared again. That got our imaginations going. But we still needed to find the perfect outrigger."

They eventually found a boat builder who built lovely miniature boats. "We wanted one in half-size. 'Yes, that would be okay', he said. Payment was adequate by any standard. The boat builder had never seen so much money in his life. He lived in a mudhole at the end of the road, literally in a container. He sat and made miniatures of boats that must have been the pride of the island in a distant past. A wonderful man, just lovely, with twelve children in the container and pigs walking around outside. 'We would like you to make us a boat that is two meters long,' we said. He didn't have a

Model of outrigger built in Micronesia for the South Pacific Lounge.

Maria Veronica L. Solem: Paintings, South Pacific Lounge.

measuring tape, so it turned out a bit smaller.

"He got his money and the first thing he did was buy a huge television set and invite the entire neighborhood into the container. We felt that they should start building huts again. We explained that containers were dangerous, as they were airtight. 'Ah,' said the man, 'that's perhaps why our blood pressure is so low.' But the boat was nice and now it's sailing around the Caribbean together with my wall paintings aboard the *Grandeur*."

Solem returned home, and started to work with "calm and discipline, and my own feelings regarding what the Pacific Islands are really all about. I managed to avoid the film 'South Pacific' and painted my own experiences. The result was huge paintings for the Aft Lounge. I simply had to include the mountain Bali Hai and I wanted to include a respect for the Pacific culture which the film didn't have. Everyone was satisfied, but I thought it came out a bit overdone when I saw the paintings installed.

"Is this art or decoration? If I am to have fun and want to look forward to doing the work then I have to be involved. Otherwise, I simply become a decorator. That's why it's dangerous to expose artists to such projects; they can so easily slide into a decorative mode without ever capturing the spirit which brings it to life. Either you become a decorator and make palm trees and hula girls for 'South Pacific,' or you have to find the essence of the thing," says Solem decisively. ■

The Stairs

Yolanda Sonnabend (cv p 325): "Swan Lake". Mixed media. The panel shows the evil von Rotbart being disguised as an owl. Odette descends in a cascade of swans.

Yolanda Sonnabend: The panel represents the ballroom with Odette's swan apparition, and Odile below in black. The warm opulence of the interior contrasts with the panels below, which are silvery and watery. Images of guests are indicated at the foot and sides of the grand staircase. The red curtain lends an air of theatricality to the scene. Forward Stairs, Deck 5-6.

Helaine Blumenfeld (cv p 265): "Shadow Figure". White Staturario marble. Main Stairs, Deck 9.

Robert Heindel, b. 1938, American: "Abstract Dance". Oil on board. Main Stairs, Deck 9-10.

Alice Kettle: "Answers". Tapestry. Main Stairs, Deck 1-2.

Jack McCarthy: "The Gypsy from Bizet's Opera Carmen". Oil on canvas. Main Stairs, Deck 7-8. Carmen is a passionate free spirit, a gypsy with only one fear: her destiny in the cards. She dances with arrogance to overcome that fear.

Casino Royale

Alex Ryman, British: "Sphinx".

Peter Zsiba – Maura Smolover (cv p 319): "A Royal Flush". Art glass, crystal and jeweled playing cards. Casino, Deck 5.

Zsiba – Smolover: "Wheel of Fortune". Mixed media.

Las Vegas

The Solarium:

Helaine Blumenfeld and her Moorish figures

"Grandeur was Helaine Blumenfeld's first ship. I asked Helaine if she knew somebody in Pietrasanta who could make some figures with a Moorish flavor in marble. Helaine suggested another artist - a girl who was frightened to death to do this project - and then she said 'Maybe I should try'. Then she came up with one of the figures, the figure "Ami" for the Solarium - actually my favorite. The architect was sold on the idea. That was the first of many projects that we did together."

Gro Nesjar, LCA

Helaine Blumenfeld, (cv p 265): "Creation". Marble. This sculpture brings together all the elements: Earth, Fire, Air and Water, which make up the creation myth. Relaxation Room aft, Deck 9, Spa.

"They said they wanted a figurative sculpture in the Solarium, and I ended up with four Moorish figures," recounts Helaine Blumenfeld. "They were beautifully placed. I did a lot of Moorish figures that they didn't use. As I made them better and better I started to eliminate other models. The exciting thing in this job is that you make such a lot of different pieces - they lead you in different directions.

"RCI has really done something amazing. They give you that chance to grow, to extend yourself. The kinds of things they have let me do have been really groundbreaking. To do wall reliefs on the scale I have done for the ships had been my dream. And you learn so much and you expand yourself so much. To be able to do this and have a place for it is like fulfilling that dream.

"I have always, like all other artists, been divided between what I call 'my work' and my commissions. But with this there is no distinction. When I am doing it, it is my work– and I'm lucky it's a commission.

"One other really important thing about working for RCI or with commissions –is that I'm given a deadline. I used to take so much time to do things, but suddenly I saw I could work in another way. I really could do it. I could come up with a major piece in a few weeks. The first Moorish figures I did were done so fast; nobody could believe you could work that fast. In a way, I learned to follow in marble the spontaneity that I usually have in clay – to work rougher, faster. The deadline forces your inspiration to come more quickly. Your doubts disappear, and then the work is out of the studio instead of living with you for months and months, and may be holding you back. It's important to have time enough for a major work, but it is also important that you don't have too much time," says Blumenfeld. ■

Top: "Stars" by Rebecca Newham. Mosaic by Jesmonite Technologies.

The four large Moorish sculptures for the Solarium on Grandeur *was Helaine Blumenfeld's first of a long series of commissions for Royal Caribbean.*

Upper Decks

John Ashworth (cv p 257): "Propulsion". Pool sculpture. Reinforced stainless steel. Deck 9.

Helaine Blumenfeld (cv p 263): "Waves". Patinated bronze. Beauty Salon, Deck 9, aft. The artist has tried to capture the mystery, the power and the beauty of water. For her, water is the symbol of life. In its flow it mirrors the energy and the unpredictability of life. In its continuity it represents the enduring quality of life, constantly striving for purification and renewal.

Sarah Galloway, b. 1963, British: "Sandblasted and slumped". Glass panel, Deck 9.

Enchantment of the Seas

The ship's theme is Festivals – transforming the ordinary, creating a world of fantasy: enchantment, allure, celebration, charm, delight, fascination, conjuration, magic, witchcraft and wizardry.

George Cutts (cv p 279): "Reflections". Detail.

"Venetian mask".

Travelogue

On our way from Haiti to Miami we pass Cuba, so close yet so far away. Large container ships pass numerous low coral reefs that seem to jump out from the evening haze. And just as suddenly disappear as the sea gets rougher. We are sailing between three hurricanes, and may catch a bit of one tonight, even though we changed course and called at Labadee, Haiti, instead of the Bahamas in order to avoid heavy seas.

Mike Newby (cv p 310): "Festival". Stained glass panel. Main Stairs, Deck 5-4.

"What will happen if we get hit by the storm?" a passenger asks during a tour of the bridge. "Nothing, even if we sail straight through it, except that some of you might get a bit seasick," replies an unruffled Captain Per Arne Kjønsø. He grew up in Folla, home of some of the roughest waters on the Norwegian coast, so he knows what he's talking about.

We continue our routine onboard. During the evening there is an all-out party on the pool deck with tall umbrella drinks, an energetic Caribbean band, and local folk singers accompanied by a synthesizer booming out convincing drum rhythms. Later, up in the Viking Crown it's not even close to full in here although the hour is past midnight.

The ship seems to have a life of its own. The Purser's Desk is the ship's heart and soul, also for the more nocturnal among the guests. The restaurant is the stomach, while the bridge is the head. The Champagne Bar is blonde and seductive and arouses other desires than the wily Casino Royale, which surfs on dreams of wealth and happiness.

Enchantment of the Seas

The *Enchantment of the Seas* has been sailing in the Eastern and Western Caribbean featuring ports of call as different as the "Dutch" village of Philipsburg, St. Maarten, "Danish" Charlotte Amalie of St. Thomas, the US Virgin Islands, and Nassau in the Bahamas in the Eastern Caribbean. In the Western Caribbean, the *Enchantment* has been calling at Key West, Florida, which hosts Hemingway's home and the only living coral reef in the continental USA, and Playa de Carmen and Cozumel in Mexico, with its hand-crafted articles, sandy beaches, and riding tours through the Mayan jungles. Georgetown on Grand Cayman, with its famous Seven Mile Beach and Ochos Rios in Jamaica, with its beautiful gardens and lush tropical landscape. ■

Conspicuous art

Enchantment is a magnificent ship, featuring more conspicuous art than that of the more refined *Rhapsody* and *Vision of the Seas*; here, the art is brazen and aggressive in its effect.

Throughout history, people have celebrated special occasions such as the changing of the seasons and the summer solstice. Ancient cultures honored their gods through rituals, processions, music, dancing and singing. Carnival was originally held on Shrove Tuesday, the final feast before the 40-day fast of Lent. Brightening up the winter months, Carnival incorporates elements of pagan festivals, such as the Roman "Saturnalia," named for Saturn, the god of harvest.

The artwork commissioned for the ship was intended to reflect the ship's theme of festivals and celebrations from around the world. The art also enhances the themed main public areas, such as the Centrum, the My Fair Lady Dining Room, the Orpheum Theater, the Carousel Lounge, and the Fascinating Rhythm Lounge.

In addition to the primary theme pieces, other items were acquired for spaces throughout the ship, ranging from the smaller public rooms and the circulation areas to individual passenger cabins and some crew areas. Among these are the themes chosen for the cabins corridors: Sun, Air, Water, Fire and Earth.

Some of the items are ancient artifacts, such as the 8th century sandstone relief of a male deity from central India, while others, such as the kinetic stainless steel sculpture by British artist George Cutts, titled "Reflections", were created especially for the vessel. ■

Enchantment of the Seas *was built in 1997 at Kværner Masa Yards in Helsinki, Finland.*
Gross tons: 74,170.
Length: 279 m/916 ft.
Beam: 32.3 m/105 ft.
Draft: 7.6 m/24 ft.
Cruising speed: 22 knots.
Passengers: 1,950 (double occupancy).
Crew: 760.

The Captain:

Between hurricanes and paperwork

"I am proud when I can show off a ship adorned with high-quality art," says Captain Kjønsø. "Appearance is important for our passengers. The refrain I hear goes: 'It's a beautiful ship, Captain, it's a beautiful ship.' Just look at the Centrum, with Carl Nesjar's "Northern Lights." RCI is among the world's foremost art purchasers, an expense that is well worth the cost."

The office work steadily increases for the modern day ship's Master. "We are becoming more and more computerized. We're supposed to become paperless, but we're drowning in paper." Captain Kjønsø points at a long series of manuals on a shelf in his spacious office. "Here is our 'Bible': You can't memorize everything, but the most important things are in these manuals and are a part of how we run a big passenger ship. Quality assurance is in accordance with the ISO 9000 rules. Now we need to learn ISO 140001," sighs the Captain, with a hint of longing for deepwater sailing in his eyes.

Captain Kjønsø is not only the administrative director, he is also a veteran seaman: The *Enchantment* is suddenly caught between three hurricanes. One of the three storms came out of nowhere, quickly developed into a tropical storm, and then a full-blown hurricane.

The Master plans an alternative route, but because of the passengers' flight connections, it would not be a good idea to arrive in Miami late. The solution is to change course to Labadee, Haiti. The *Enchantment* arrives in Labadee rather late in the day; it's raining lightly as a result of Hurricane Dennis. Kjønsø then weighs anchor at eight o'clock that evening and heads full speed for Miami. "This is why we have a helm on the ship," remarks Kjønsø "It's fun when something out of the ordinary happens, but you can get a bit stressed." ■

Captain Kjønsø was born on the Island of Vikna, north of Trondheim on the west coast of Norway. He went to sea in 1964, at the age of 15, and sailed on cargo ships until 1969, when Norwegian shipowners Skaugen, Gotaas-Larsen and Anders Wilhelmsen started Royal Caribbean Cruise Lines. Kjønsø has now been with RCI for over 30 years and has sailed as Chief Officer or Staff Captain on most of the ships in the RCI fleet.

The Hotel Director:

The race is largely on the culinary side

"Part of the secret of success is to hire experienced staff for all leading positions," says Hotel Director Siegfried Kontzny. The soul of the cruise ship is in the hotel: "It's the expectation of our guests – to get good food and good accommodations. Everything else comes onboard with the passengers, making up the ambience.

"The bigger ships are getting more popular," he continues. "That's one of the reasons why there is now a race between the major players in the industry to build the biggest and best ships. The smaller companies will not be able to survive. Our merger with Celebrity gave size and diversity.

"The race is also on the culinary side. We are always looking at what our competitors are doing. The guests want lighter food and more variety," explains Kontzny, who also believes the artwork plays a major role. "The art makes a visual difference between *Enchantment of the Seas* and our twin ships. People expect art on board this class of ship today. The architects and designers know what they are doing, and their work enhances the ambience considerably."

Kontzny admits, however, that cleaning the Centrum sculpture is a big headache. "It's nice, especially at night when it reflects the lights," he says, "but I doubt if anybody thought about who was going to clean it when they designed it. That was probably not their first priority. A couple of times a year we have to bite the bullet and get somebody to hang down in the boatman's chair from deck 10 to deck 4 to clean it." ■

Siegfried Kontzny was born in Munich, Germany. He began his career with a four-year apprenticeship at the famous Hotel Vier Jahrezeiten in Munich. In the 1960's, he sailed with Holland-America and Swedish-American Line until he went to Bermuda as a sommelier. He spent 18 years with Holiday Inn, 13 of them in the world-wide headquarters as a member of the corporate management staff. He was then recruited by RCI as Hotel Manager. He has sailed on most of the company's mega-ships.

Carl Nesjar and his *Northern Lights*

The large prism sculpture floating in the air has its roots in Nesjar's fascination with ice crystals and prisms. "I was at MIT's Center for Advanced Visual Studies working with ice sculptures when I got interested in prisms, and made a proposal for a chapel, or meditation room, with sketches and models," recalls Nesjar. "Large prisms would be built into the ceiling and four or five huge prisms in the walls. They could be oriented towards the south and would refract and scatter the light."

The sculptures onboard the *Enchantment* are in acrylic – an expensive material. "It took us a long time to find prisms of that size," recounts Nesjar. "They hang and glitter because of the way they are positioned and refract the light. The German poet/philosopher Goethe was very preoccupied with prisms and colors. Towards the end of his life he said he would rather be remembered as a scientist than a poet. He conducted studies on the interplay in the edges of prisms, where light refraction is most intense."

Nesjar states that he has also found a prism-like effect in other media: "I've taken color photographs of frost in the sun and underexposed them so that everything around is black, while the small frost particles look like color-shining prisms," he explains. "If you under-expose with the camera, you see them as red, blue, orange, and green. It looks like a starry sky in many colors." ■

Acrylic prisms capture the light in Carl Nesjar's sculpture "Northern Lights". Centrum, Deck 4-9.

David Buckland and his three canvases on the Main Stairs

David Buckland (cv p 274): "From Festival in Mysore, India". Photography and oil on canvas.

"For the *Enchantment of the Seas*, I was commissioned to make three large works based on the Festival of Light in Mysore, southern India," says photographic artist David Buckland. "When working from a photographic starting point, you are almost forced to visit the place upon which the work is based. In other words, to get started, you have to be able to point the camera at something real to make pictures. You have to be there, where it is happening, the light, the smells, the whole ambience. And Mysore was extraordinary. I have never experienced anything like it. There was an all-day parade of elephants, dancers, acrobats, music and always flowers, and more flowers, and colors and noise and people. The job for me was to distill it all somehow, the religion, the reason for the Festival of Light, the culture, into art works that managed to convey all this wonder.

"Giving the sense of Mysore with its incredible festival, in one work of art is like trying to condense three days into one single slice of time. One photograph would only give you one slice of time from the three days; by combining several images on a single canvas, you have the chance to address several slices of time; by combining paint into the equation, paint that is the color of the sunlight, the kind of ochre color that was the sandstone, you add a feeling of languor. The painting now has the chance to stretch its

own time, and say, 'This is my passage through that whole wonder of three or four days'. This is the reason I work in this way, combining physical paint and fragments of photographs.

"This is my perspective on how photography can work. It really is the most extraordinary medium. I can show a photograph to anybody, anywhere in the world and they can understand it. Pictures of politicians, pop stars, war, advertising, cultures, sexy women/men, everyone understands them, they represent a vision, a way of communicating worldwide. Photography really is the universal language. But if you now take its potential and put it into an art form, stretching its capability so that it's not just locked into that split second, you have the chance to reconstruct a whole festival on three canvases.

"When I arrived back to my studio in London, I converted all the essential photographs into digital data so that I could begin the process of electronic editing.

"All this electronic information is converted into minute squirts of colored dye, and you can literally print onto anything; art paper,

David Buckland: "The Maharaja's Palace". Photography and oil on canvas.

canvas, or even glass. It's all very physical and almost full circle back to the early days of photography, with the wonder and possibility of the photographic image." ■

The Stairs

Gianni Arico, b. 1941, Italian: "Orfeus, the God of Music, Theater and Dance". Bronze relief. Forward Stairs, Deck 5-6. Gianni Arico is a sculptor, architect and metal engraver, living in Venice. He has created numerous public works, including the great sculpture "Joy", located at the gates of Venice; and a monument to Christopher Columbus at the Sea, Air and Space Museum in New York.

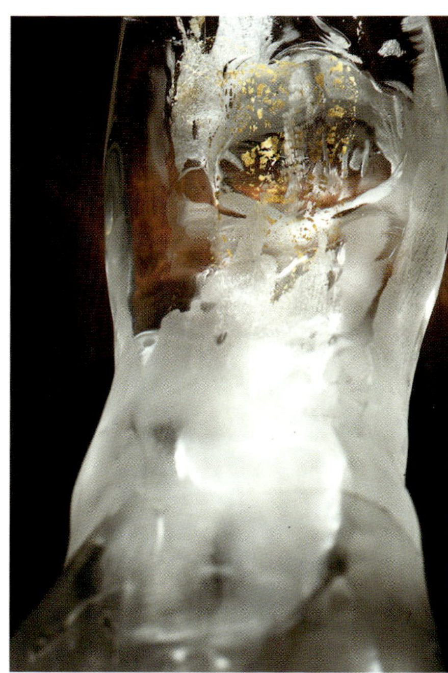

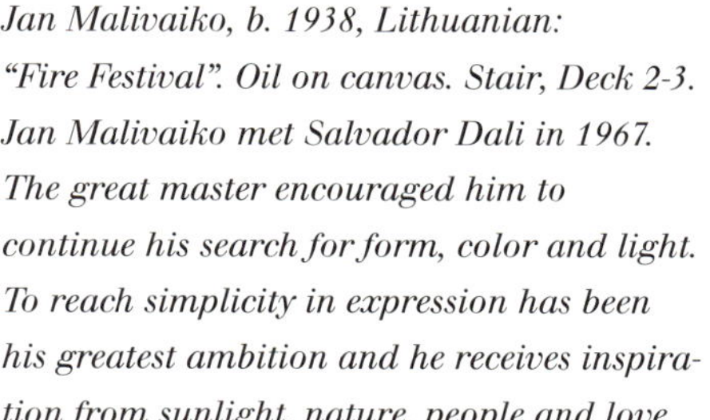

Jan Malivaiko, b. 1938, Lithuanian: "Fire Festival". Oil on canvas. Stair, Deck 2-3. Jan Malivaiko met Salvador Dali in 1967. The great master encouraged him to continue his search for form, color and light. To reach simplicity in expression has been his greatest ambition and he receives inspiration from sunlight, nature, people and love.

Gianni Arico: "Two Glass Blowers". Cast glass sculpture. Niche. Forward Stairs, Deck 3-4.

Gianni Arico: "Candlelight Festival, Fireglass Blowing". Bronze relief. Forward Stairs, Deck 3-4.

Viking Crown Lounge

On the *Enchantment of the Seas*, Kyrre Andersen and Liv Anne Lundberg made a relief in the Viking Crown for the architects Yran and Storbraaten. It is made of arched brass and depicts a modern Viking voyage. It was based on photos that man had taken of the earth from the moon, put together in a Viking pattern. The design is about man´s journey on earth and in space, from Viking times to the first century of the space age. ■

Jonathan Clark: "Ship with quarn". Cast aluminium.

Casino Royale

In the public areas onboard *Enchantment of the Seas* there are numerous artworks of great interest. On the following pages a few such pieces are highlighted. ■

Maura Smolover and Peter Zsiba (cv p 319) designed the artwork installations in the Casino on the Enhantment of the Seas *as well as in the casinos for several other RCI ships. The theme of one of these installations is the strange legends being told of the numerous tall ships with their treasures sunken in the Triangle of Bermuda. Here water blends with fish, seashells and jewels to create an underwater fantasy dream.*

Orpheum Theatre, Library and Bars

Melanie Boone/Paramount Parks, Stage Curtain. Orpheum Theater, Deck 5.

Anthony Stones, b. 1934, British: "Orfeus". Bronze sculpture. The Library, Deck 7. Anthony Stones works in the figurative humanist tradition. He is influenced by the Italian figurative sculptors Marini, Manzu and Messina. His main aim in his art work is to give pleasure.

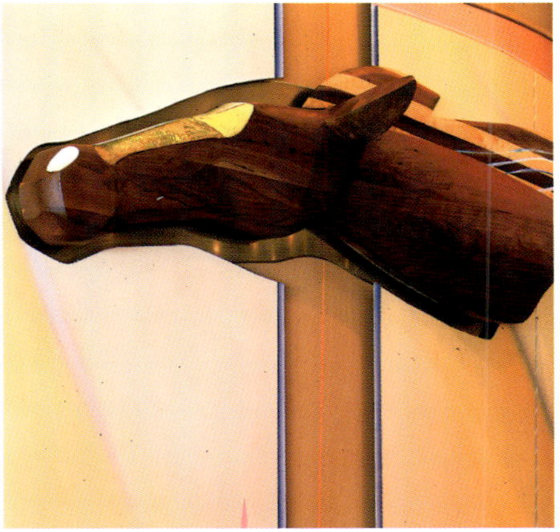

Maria Veronica L. Solem (cv p 323), acrylic painting and Peter Esdaile (cv p 289), sculpture. Above: Detail. Horse's head by Peter Esdaile. Carousel Lounge, Deck 6.

William Palmer: Four-masted Schooner built in Bathmain in 1896 and lost off Nantucket in 1912. Model built in 1902. Schooner Bar, Deck 6.

Maria Veronica L. Solem (cv p 323): Mixed media, Centrum, Deck 5-6.

Upper Decks

Helaine Blumenfeld, (cv p 265): "Creation". Cast bronze wall reliefs. Solarium, Deck 9. "Creation" was inspired by the variety and richness of Indian mythology, particularly myths of creation; the origin of the world, continuity of life, spirituality of love, and the human capacity for joy. One of the panels shows the mother of Buddah. She is supported by a branch from the tree of life. It also portrays the joyousness and religious fervor of her son who symbolizes the relationship between the spirit and the human soul.

The Solarium

George Cutts (cv p 279): "Reflections". Pool Sculpture, Stainless steel. Deck 9.

Rhapsody of the Seas

The ship features music as its main artistic theme in the Broadway Melodies Lounge, the Edelweiss Dining Room, the Shall We Dance Lounge and the Moonlight Bay Lounge, while the corridor themes include Classical, Folk, Popular, Jazz and Rock'n Roll.

Larry Kirkland (cv p 296): "Soul Boat". Metal and glass.

Richard Erman, b. 1952, American: "Pinvare". White Carrara marble.

Travelogue

It's high noon on a Sunday in August. We're headed north towards Alaska. There is thick fog at the entrance to the Inside Passage and the Master has two choices: "Either I go in, or I go to sea," he says.

He chose to go in, and it was a good choice. It's pleasant in the sun on the pool deck, with the jacuzzi and the pool bar. There are a lot of people sitting here, sunning themselves and enjoying the view of the heavily forested Alaskan coastline.

Also on deck are our dining companions: a dotcom gentleman from the U.K. who resides in Silicon Valley, and his wife, who works with goats, horses and dogs. The cruise is her gift to him for their silver wedding anniversary. She doesn't know it yet, but he will get her a huge diamond ring in Juneau, at a reduced tax rate.

Atle Ellefsen, Norwegian: "Regatta". Pool sculpture. Stainless steel. Deck 9.

And we are finding out that art can have so many functions aboard a cruise ship: A woman just announced over the loudspeaker that tickets for tomorrow's excursion will be handed out by the Fred and Ginger sculpture. That can only be called integrated art.

A quartet is playing a beautiful and timeless minuet by Buccherini in the Centrum near the Champagne Bar. The room invites you to let loose and indulge yourself. And there is plenty of elegance here: There's no harm in showing off a beautiful dress or a handsome husband. In the Schooner Bar there's piano music, Errol Garner style, into the wee hours of the night.

We are sitting on deck in Haines when we are cast in shadow as P&O's *Dawn Princess* glides into the fjord in the twilight, heading toward the little fishing camp. The vessel appears small against the enormous mountains, but beautiful, lit up like a town at sunset. Is the *Princess* waiting for us to leave the dock, we wonder? But then she turns and continues slowly out of the fjord into the sunset. There is something magical about a ship setting out on the ocean – what will be her next port of call?

Rhapsody of the Seas

The Alaskan cruises normally last from May to September between Vancouver, on Canada's west coast, and Seward in Alaska. A week's cruise up north is enough time to experience harsh gold-mining ports such as Ketchikan, Juneau, Skagway and Sitka, and nature's gems, such as the Inside Passage, Misty Fjords, Glacier Bay and the Hubbard Glacier.

In the spring and fall, the *Rhapsody* has been sailing to Hawaii, calling at Honolulu, Kailua Kona, Hilo, Nawiliwili, Kauai, Lahaina, and Maui. During the winter, the vessel has been cruising the western Caribbean. ■

The Rhapsody of the Seas *was built in 1997 at Chantiers Naval, St. Nazaire, France.*
Gross tons: 75,000.
Length: 279 m/892 ft.
Beam: 3.2 m/106 ft.
Draft: 7.6 m/25 ft.
Cruising speed: 22.3 knots.
Passengers: 1,998 (double occupancy).
Crew: 765.

The Captain:

A tight ship in challenging seas

"Here in Alaska, we encounter challenges all the time," says Captain Arnolf Remø. "Ocean fog can be wicked. There are fishing boats in the fairway and poor visibility, and we need to stay on schedule so that the passengers can catch their flights home, even if the weather is against us the entire trip.

"Alaska is a challenge for a seaman," he continues. "You need to be alert at all times. Navigation must be exact; we are sailing through narrow passages with many skerries. On parts of the voyage we use a pilot. On occasion, the pilot does not arrive due to the weather, and then we need to go and pick him up. In the Caribbean, the voyages are more routine. Once you clear the breakwater, you have a couple of thousand meters under you."

Captain Remø followed the installation of the artwork when the Rhapsody was built in St. Nazaire. "People notice art," he says. "Some 100,000 passengers pass through this ship each year. Many are interested in art. It is important that we have art onboard. The environment would be sterile without it."

"Beauty has its price," he adds, "but the ship looks beautiful and the guests are happy. The Centrum sculpture is impressive and there is a lot of well-placed art in the corridors and stairwells. Even the rest rooms are decorated with colorful contemporary art."

Cruise ship traffic is important for the local population in Alaska, explains the captain. "Small ports such as Skagway, Juneau, and Haines earn 69 dollars per person who comes ashore. Having four large cruise ships docked in Skagway makes a difference to the village with a winter population of 800. The entire town gears up for cruise ship tourism in the summer. In the winter, the temperatures drop to minus 40 °C, and the population tries to keep warm inside while they wait for next summer."

Remø has been five cable lengths from the large glacier in Glacier Bay, but large ice blocks often break off, so it is essential to exercise caution. On occasion, the *Rhapsody* must circumvent the ice when it can't sail between the icebergs. Conditions vary greatly from week to week.

"A 'tight ship' is a necessity for operating the way we do," says Captain Remø. "We have a small crew for so many passengers. Everyone must give their all; we have no room for slackers. We need to move on to the next port, and you can't leave a dining room filled with 1,100 passengers waiting for their food." ■

Arnolf Remø, one of the two captains of the Rhapsody of the Seas, *taking the ship into an Alaskan fjord. Remø grew up in the town of Ålesund on the western coast of Norway. In 1967, he set out to sea, working as a seaman on bulk carriers and container ships that sailed worldwide. In 1977, he began his career with RCI onboard the* Nordic Prince. *In 1989, he was appointed supervisor for the construction of the company's new mega-ships, the* Monarch of the Seas *and* Majesty of the Seas, *at the shipyard in St. Nazaire, France. Remø is now Master of* Adventure of the Seas. *(Photo: Jon Lie)*

"Even in the rest rooms ..." Ceramics by Nini Anker Dessen and Magne Austad (cv p 283).

Elevator areas are richly decorated. Instruments by Marc Berlet (cv p 259).

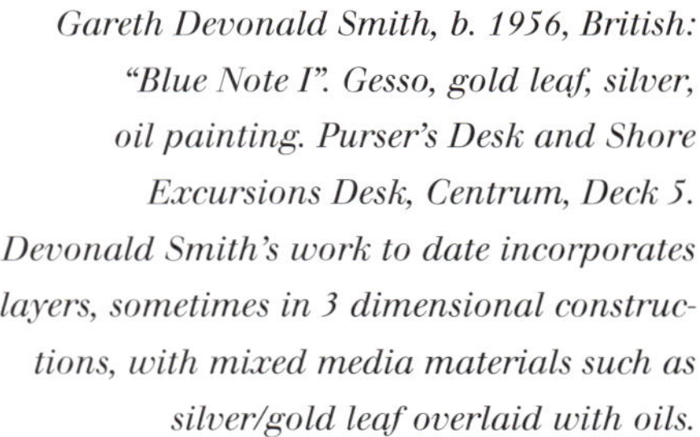

Gareth Devonald Smith, b. 1956, British: "Blue Note I". Gesso, gold leaf, silver, oil painting. Purser's Desk and Shore Excursions Desk, Centrum, Deck 5. Devonald Smith's work to date incorporates layers, sometimes in 3 dimensional constructions, with mixed media materials such as silver/gold leaf overlaid with oils.

The Hotel Director:

We look at the big picture

Hotel Director Behram Tavadia says he receives many comments about the artwork on the ship, especially on some of the sculptures, the paintings, the Carrara marble sculptures, and the Egyptian artwork in the solarium. "The art is what amplifies the ship's beauty," he says. "The Diadem" (Centrum sculpture), expresses the theme of the ship. The history of the suspended sculpture is the combined Rhapsody of the waves and music.

"The best thing about this hotel is that our guests don't have to pack and unpack to go from one place to another," adds Tavadia. "And they don't have to plan what they want to do. We plan a huge selection of activities for them. Within that framework, they can choose shore excursions or the activities onboard. It's a complete vacation."

However, Tavadia admits that the task of ensuring passenger satisfaction is hard work. The machinery has to run smoothly. "It's based on people from more than 50 nations with different cultures and backgrounds," he explains, "providing service for a multi-national audience.

"Generally speaking, crew members stay with RCI for many years, continues Tavadia. You live in an environment where you also work. Onshore, when you leave the office you leave your colleagues behind. Here they are with you 24 hours a day. And some people can't deal with that. But once they've crossed that first barrier, it's a great career." ■

Behram Tavadia, popularly nicknamed "Bob" by his colleagues, was born in Bombay, India. After earning a degree in Business Management and Business Law in 1980, his thirst for travel took him to the Middle East, where he started his career with the Sheraton Hotel Group. In 1986, Tavadia joined RCI as a Purser Officer onboard the Song of America. *As Hotel Director on the* Rhapsody of the Seas, *Behram welcomes all guests onboard and wishes them a pleasant voyage.*

Jonathan Clowes

on his sculpture *"Diadem"*

"We built the 'Diadem' on a fast track as time was short from our introduction to the project," recalls Jonathan Clowes. "We were pressed for time throughout the whole process. Most of our children helped us in order to finish on time. Daniel signed on to the veneering crew, while Douglas did courier service for the project. Lynn, who had just finished her Master's Degree in Management, ran the veneering crew. My wife Evelyn had to keep focused on painting the 'Rolling Wave', the centerpiece of the 'Diadem' sculpture. I had every imaginable detail coming my way, all critical, all urgent."

There are seven individual pieces in the model and Clowes says: "The shape is almost generated by the arrangement of those seven pieces. We built the piece

as a whole shape when we did the original fiberglass in Maine. The cradles held it in the right position, and the steel was bent in there. We worked with the steel workers eight weekends in a row for 10 hours a day to bend the steel that holds the piece together. It was then cut apart to be veneered and shipped.

Jonathan J. Clowes (cv p 277): "Diadem", Centrum sculpture. Wood, glass and bronze. Jonathan Clowes' work has been characterized as quiet and contemplative. He feels that a piece of fine sculpture should communicate the artist's love of relationships – extending the gifts of one to meet the needs of another. As the work evolves, aesthetics and function interact to create a uniquely balanced whole and, on a deeper level, each piece engages the viewer's spirit.

So we had seen the pieces together, but never hung up in the air as a single entity.

"We met the shipping deadline and left for France where *Rhapsody* awaited the installation of her Centrum sculpture. The sculpture went up the night before the ship sailed. It was so incredible to see it go up, hanging as intended! It looked wonderful," beams Clowes, adding: "Assembly was a tense process. We went out on sea trials for three days right after the pieces arrived so that we could work the whole time. The alpinists who helped us get everything right in the rigging worked until the ship left the harbor. They were tightening trim buckles for an hour after she sailed, and we actually got off the *Rhapsody of the Seas* with the pilot.

"Then we went onboard again in New York to pick up our tools and sailed on to Miami. That gave us an opportunity to observe how the sculpture behaved at sea, and adjust the rigging, do some cleaning and other final details. So we were dangling from boatman's chairs in the middle of the sculpture on the passage to Miami. And the Captain put the ship through a set of exercises to show us how the sculpture moved with the ship. That made it possible to trim the wires and the connectors to a standard that satisfied the engineers on the *Rhapsody*." ■

Jonathan J. Clowes: "Diadem," Centrum sculpture. Wood, glass and bronze. Details.

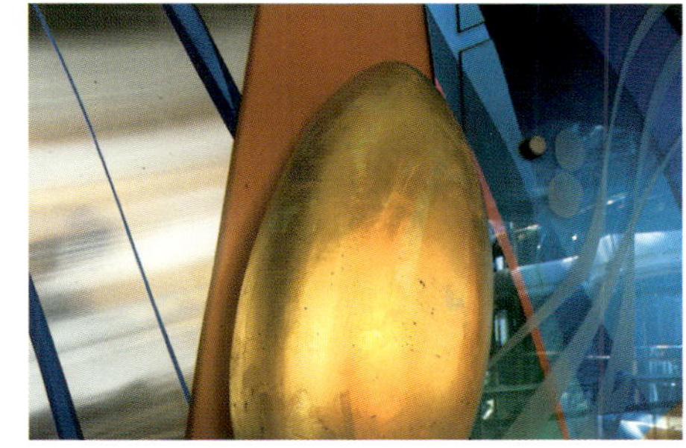

Maria Veronica L. Solem, (cv p 323): "A Moment of Eternity". Metal and oil on canvas. Centrum, Deck 7.

Maria Veronica Solem's relief in the Centrum, stretching over three decks – of glass, painting and stainless steel, was a technical departure for her and a challenge completely different from any she had ever encountered before. The glorious artwork is visible from everywhere in the Centrum. When she started doing her first piece for RCI, on the Legend, *she says she never would have considered doing a thing like this. "I was a painter," says Solem. "I could make a six-meter painting, but make such a relief? Not in my wildest fantasy!"*

Stairs

Niches:
Giovanni Balderi, b. 1970, Italian: "Air" and "Icaro". White Carrara marble. Main Stairs, Deck 9-10. Balderi studied with Ledo Tartarelli, one of the most famous marble carvers of Pietrasanta. Ledo's mastery inspired the artist's passion for marble and in particular the pure white statuary marble of the Italian Alps.
Middle: One of Åse Frøyshov's (cv p 292) tapestries, "Rhapsody in Blue".

Raymond Karpuska, b. 1952, American: Niche sculpture. Steel and brass. Main Stairs, Starboard, Deck 3-4. For more than 20 years, Ray Karpuska has been expressing his view of the world through an interplay of energy, fluidity and hue which is his signature.
The tapestry detail is from Åse Frøyshov's "Rhapsody in Blue".

Louise Sheridan b. 1955, British: "Blue Moon". Acrylic and collage on canvas. Forward Stairs, Deck 6-5. Louise Sheridan's paintings are like treasure maps with clues and occasional glimpses of other worlds.

Luca Dall'Olio, b. 1958, Italian: Untitled. Oil on canvas. Forward stairs, Deck 10.

Roland Piche, b. 1938, British: "Bird of Transformation". Cast bronze. Main Stair Lobby, Deck 9. In Piche's sculptures the simplicity of the form masks the complexity of intent.

Windjammer

Nini Anker Dessen and Magne Austad (cv p 283) have made some impressive ceramic panels with a distinctive maritime feel in Windjammer Cafe, Deck 9.

Bars and lounges

Janet Stayton's (cv p 327) paintings dominate the "Moonlight Bay Lounge". Deck 6.

Gustav Lochstoer, b. 1919, Norwegian: "Sovereign of the Seas". Ship Model. Schooner Bar, Deck 6. Gustav Lochstoer and his ancestors have all played an active part in the Navy. Studying the ships and the building of models started as a hobby but quickly became his full time occupation.

Rig made by Lyngør Seilmakerverksted, Norway. Schooner Bar.

Queen Mary,
Ship model.
"Shall We Dance".
Lounge Deck 6.

Broadway Melodies Theater

Paramount Parks (see also p 252) produced the beautiful stage curtains for the theater onboard Rhapsody of the Seas.
Stan Morrell, director of the division in charge of the works for the cruise industry, explains:

"We work with an artist we feel is best suited to translate the desired concept, or an artist recommended by the architects or LCA."
These pieces are truly works of art – layer upon layer of painting, printing, appliques, embellishments – all hand done.

Stage Curtain artist Steven Rundle, based on a concept by Howard Snoweiss Design Group.

Casino Royale

The Casino on Deck 5 is designed by architect Howard Snoweiss. ■

Jane Skeeter, b. 1950, American: "Galactic Panoramas". Glass. Jane Skeeter and her team of glass artisans, designers and old-school craftspeople are committed to expanding the familiar look and use of glass as an artistic medium, as well as it's contribution as an architectural component.

Floor feature by Interior Design and Procurement Services.

Solarium

The Solarium, Deck 9 is designed by Arkitektbyrån of Gothenburg, Sweden. All the Solariums on the *Vision Class* ships are heavily themed. For the Rhapsody Solarium the overall theme is "Ancient Egypt". The calmness of the Solarium invites one to a relaxed day by the pool, even in port. ■

Motives from Egyptian mythology. Replicas. Carved stone.

"Sphinx" by Stephen Knapp, American.

Sirkka Ahlin, b. 1947, Finnish, and Brigitta Lehtonen, b. 1947, Swedish: "Mirage". Wall decoration. Fused glass panels with themes from the Nile, the Pyramids of the Giza Plateau, detail of the Temple at Karnak, the temple of Horus at Edfu and Ramses II at Abu Simbel and fragments of papyri. These two artists and designers have worked together for 17 years, mostly with integrating glass in architecture.

Vision of the Seas

The ship celebrates the power of the artist's imagination. Its themes include Mayan and Aztec culture in the Solarium, mythology in the Casino Royale, and Egyptian heritage in the Health Spa.

Helaine Blumenfeld, (cv p 265): "Seated Mayan Figure". Red Persian Travertine. Solarium.

Knut Steen (cv p 331) "Fire." Red Persian travertine, marble relief.

Travelogue

The Solarium is one of the finest rooms on the *Vision of the Seas.* It's peaceful and quiet in here, with comfortable seating, and service from the crew that seems to take place effortlessly. The room and its sculptures by Helaine Blumenfeld, together with the generously large reclining chairs and sumptuous stacks of terrycloth towels, create a relaxing atmosphere. Outside, the blue sea glistens, seemingly to infinity. Mighty Alaska is aft, with glaciers, seals, whales, brown bears, endless woods, American Eagles and millions of salmon. It's another day of luxury on the *Vision of the Seas.*

The *Vision*'s restaurants serve the best of fresh foods; Alaskan salmon and lobster tantalize our taste buds, as well they should in these waters. Vegetables, meats, fish and shellfish are loaded on board from local sources and kept in special storage rooms that maintain just the right temperature and humidity to preserve freshness. Restaurants on land might well learn from the service on this ship. Each evening, the *Vision* serves four-course dinners to 2,000 passengers in two sittings, and there are always two choices each of warm and cold entrees. The service and quality are impeccable, and warm dishes are presented piping hot. Within an hour after the first sitting, the hall has been cleared, the tables reset, and the smiling staff open the doors again, precisely at 8:30 p.m.

Over the PA system, Captain Bang's voice resounds: "North 51 degrees, 11 minutes, west 28 degrees and 20 minutes." We are just 26 nautical miles northwest of the Pine Island entrance to Queen Charlotte Strait, he informs us. That's where we will begin sailing between the islands again. Our average speed since we left Ketchikan has been 16 knots. We have sailed 1,898 nautical miles or 3,500 kilometers. The remaining distance to Vancouver is 247 nautical miles or 444 kilometers. The speed required to reach Vancouver tomorrow morning is 13 knots, but due to the tide and the Simon Narrows, we have to speed up a bit.

Like no vacation on earth ...

Raymond Karpuska, b. 1952, American: "Dive to the Max". Brushed and mirrored stainless steel sculpture. Having lived and worked in Florida for more than 20 years, Karpuschka has always felt a strong urge to create works that are a celebration of nature and man's place in it. His poolside sculpture "Dive to the Max" is a marriage of sky and sea, united by graceful figures who seem to dive directly from the sun into the water below.

Vision of the Seas

The Vision of the Seas *was built in 1998 at the Chantiers de l'Atlantique yard in Saint-Nazaire, France. Gross tons: 75,000. Length: 279 m/915 ft. Beam: 32 m/105 ft. Draft: 7.5 m/25 ft. Cruising speed: 22 knots. Passengers: 2,000 (double occupancy). Crew: 765.*

Vision of the Seas is the namesake and the capstone of the very successful *Vision Class* series of vessels.

For several years now, during the summer seasons she has been sailing to Alaska on seven-day cruises from Vancouver. The cruise program has featured ports of call that echo the goldrush: Skagway, Juneau and Ketchikan, and the striking scenery of Misty Fjords National Park, Glacier Bay and Hubbard Glacier.

Vision has also been sailing to Hawaii, and between Mexico and San Diego, with several calls along the Mexican Riviera and Acapulco. She has also been crossing between Seattle, Vancouver and Victoria as well as sailing from San Juan, Puerto Rico to Charlotte Amalie, in the Virgin Islands, to Willemstad in Curacao, via the Panama Canal to Puntarenas and Caldera in Costa Rica, on her way to Acapulco. ■

Captain Leif Otto Bang:

"Expect the unexpected"

"The *Vision* sails with some 3,000 people onboard, about the population of many small towns," says Captain Bang. "The evolution has been astounding, in ships, facilities and art."

He says the art attracts many passengers. "Some go around and view it carefully. Others know little about art and ask me about it, and that's amusing. Passengers who know art tell me that the scope and variety of works on board *Vision* amazes them. Much relates to travel, to being in motion. The investment in art is considerable," he adds. The captain enjoys being surrounded by beauty – both onboard and by wonderous scenery.

Seamanship is essential in Alaskan waters. Here a skipper has to steer, chart courses and ensure safety constantly; navigation can be a full-time job, up to 24 hours a day, which doesn't leave much time for the cruise Captain's role of socializing with the passengers.

"In Alaska you have to expect the unexpected," explains Bang. "Fog or drift ice – it keeps you on the bridge. At Simon Narrows on the Inside Passage in northern British Columbia, the tidal current can run at 15 knots. So the skipper is constantly on the bridge when *Vision* sails these Narrows on its way northward, because there's only one time of day it can get through, and sometimes that may be two o'clock in the morning."

Captain Bang last sailed to Alaska in 1992, and observes: "The biggest change since then is that the piers are better; there were lots of rotten pilings the first time we were here. But nature remains unchanged. The tides are just as strong as ever. At Skagway, the Gold Rush Capital, there's a 30-foot difference between high and low tides, and the current is always strong in Tracey Arm Fjord on the way northward from Ketchikan to Juneau, Haines and Skagway."

The *Vision of the Seas* was built in 18 months at the Chantiers de l'Atlantique yard on the southwest coast of France. "Construction went smoothly," recalls Captain Bang, "and the ship was one hundred percent finished when we first set sail with 573 invited guests on board. That was a result of competence," he acknowledges, but adds: "There was also a bit of luck. *Vision* is a lucky ship.

"You have to run a tight ship to make it all work," remarks Bang; "We take that for granted, but nonetheless it's remarkable that everything runs so smoothly. Ships are often said to have their own souls. Indeed, there are differences from ship to ship, but a ship in itself is inanimate. It's the passengers and crew who create its atmosphere. So there's some individuality, even though RCI ships share a common character and style." ■

Leif Otto Bang went to sea at the age of 16 from Ålesund, Norway, sailing on tankers and freighters alike. With more than 30 years of experience at RCI, he recalls the times of smaller cruise ships, like the ships that carried around 700 passengers.

Hotel Director:

The ship with an open space

"We have a most beautiful ship, with some of the finest artwork on any ship in the fleet," says Hotel Director Malcolm Chapple. "The Centrum area featuring the main stairs is superb. We get quite a bit of positive feedback. Our ship is still almost new, and I'm sure the other *Vision Class* ships elicit the same reaction. The Centrum area with the open atrium, the Masquerade Theater, the Aquarius Dining Room, the large glass areas, and the artworks evoke striking reactions from our guests," he says.

"The experience of the open space on this ship is quite real," continues Chapple. "You never feel claustrophobic. If you tour some of the ships built in the 1980's, you never have the feeling of open spaces and light, and the uplifting experience that comes with them. You walk down corridors with dark carpets and dark paneling; they look nice, but feel a little bit confining.

"By comparison, we feel proud when we're docked alongside two or three liners from other companies. Perhaps I shouldn't say it, but their ships look like floating high-rise apartment buildings," he observes.

"When I discuss the art with the crew, (after all, they clean the pieces), they all say how striking the works are. They like the masks on decks 7 and 8, but they don't like the sculpture in the Centrum when it comes to cleaning. We usually find someone with climbing experience and we rig up proper tackle for them to work around the sculpture. That's a two-day event and it's done once every three months. But we must be careful that it's switched off. There are 3,000 volts running through it!"

The Hotel Director points out that art is everywhere, not just where it gets a lot of attention: "In the accommodation area in the forward section of Deck 2, the lobbies have striking pieces of art, but the 100 people who live in that area are the only ones to see it. You turn a corner in some remote corridor of the ship and boom – you see a stunning work of art." ■

Hotel Director Malcolm Chapple: "The artworks evoke striking reactions from our guests".

Centrum: Scale and details

Peter Layton and Simon Moss have made several important works of art for the RCI fleet. Among them are two large Centrum sculptures in stainless steel, "Janus" for *Legend of the Seas* and "Ariel" for *Vision of the Seas.* ■

Peter Layton and Simon Moss (cv p 302): "Ariel" from "The Tempest" by Shakespeare. Suspended sculpture in float glass, stainless steel, gold plated brass and acrylic. Centrum.
The main centrum sculpture is a visual fantasy representing a dancing spirit-like figure. In Shakespeare's "The Tempest", Ariel is described as an airy will-of-the-wisp, invisible at will, all light and spirit, symbolizing man's imagination and vision. In his final speech, Prospero entreats Ariel to ensure "calm seas, auspicious gales and sail so expeditious that shall catch the Royal Fleet far off". The sculptures' jewel-like shapes combine scale with delicate detailing. The polished surfaces absorb and reflect a myriad of colors and sparkling highlights. Soaring, elegant forms and graceful flowing movement enhance and focus the drama of the magnificent Centrum space.

Peter Layton and Simon Moss (cv p 300): "Gate of Dreams". Stainless steel, gold-plated brass, float glass and acrylic. Centrum, Champagne Plaza fountain pool sculpture. This sculpture is constructed from layers of float glass and laser-cut stainless steel shapes. Its title, "Gate of Dreams", alludes to the mythological gates through which dreams pass – some to delude and some to be fulfilled.

Varied artistic expressions

Throughout the ship there are a variety of artistic styles and expressions. However, only a limited number can be shown in this book. On these pages we show an example of how differently the individual artists work, and how the pieces of art, after all, contribute to "one picture" – the soul of the ship. For the guests, an "art study tour" of the ship can be a rewarding activity in itself. ■

Christiane Pettersen, b. 1943 French: "Show Boat", Acrylic and silkscreen. Showboat Lounge.
In her early years as an artist Christiane Pettersen was influenced by the "Constructivists", in the Russian spirit, with a passion for the "mise en scene". She sees herself as a story teller in a journalistic manner. She feels that color is like music and so should be sensitively used.

Maria Veronica L. Solem (cv p 323): "An Odysee", Painted metal and Canvas. Centrum.

John Ashworth, (cv p 257): "Cross Section III". Wood, bronze and other metals. Library, Starboard, Deck 7. John Ashworth likes to explore the aesthetics and principles of engineering in his sculptures. The controlling factor is his sense of wonder at the magic of fundamental things; space, time, infinity, energy, tension, mass balance and the qualities inherent in materials. This sculpture has its main concern in the area of gravity, the sweeping move of the planets, held firm in the embrace of gravity.

Nini Anker Dessen and Magne Austad (cv p 283): Mixed media (ceramics, metal and canvas). Forward Stairs, Deck 8-9.

Anne Hathaway, b. 1954, American: Watercolor. Library, Deck 7. Although she never received formal art training, Anne Hathaway has been painting since she was a child in Rome.

Masquerade Theater and Casino Royale

Stage curtain by Miguel Condé, executed by Paramount Parks. The Masquerade Theater, Deck 5. A central theme in Miguel Condé's works of art is relationships in our day-to-day lives. What exactly is it that leads one to embark on a relationship with a certain person, then to continue on without a second thought about another? Condé feels that the viewer of his art will relate to this piece based on his or her life experiences, and what people see in his art often has much more meaning than what motivated him to create it. Condé started drawing as a young child in New York. At the age of 24, he was awarded a grant by the French government to study at the Bourse d'Etudes Libres. He is now a permanent resident of Spain.

Casino floor feature by Interior Design and Procurement Services.

Detail from Casino ceiling.

Janet Stayton:
"You can't be timid"

Janet Stayton, an American painter who lives in Italy, has completed several large commissions for RCI. Her personal favorite is a series of paintings 11 meters long, made for the Some Enchanted Evening Lounge on the *Vision of the Seas*.

"I listened to Shostakovich constantly while I was doing the paintings for *Vision of the Seas*," recalls Stayton. "He's such a good companion for an artist, grabbing from the future and the past, bringing humor and tragedy all together. He keeps you from letting your shoes get glued to the floor. There's a lot of Shostakovich in that Some Enchanted Evening Lounge. Maybe I found a new direction in myself with these paintings," muses Stayton.

"Working on a ship you have to ask: Who is the viewer? What do people do on a ship? They walk around, they keep seeing the same things over and over again. And they stroll by the paintings. In a museum, you sit back and you look directly at the art, and then you go home, meaning your experience is short," says Stayton.

"But the paintings on a ship are multi-experiential in terms of time. I always thought about the paintings as having a passage in them; as people walk by, they can discover something new every time. The idea of the painting is not always in looking at it; it can be in walking by it. It's like reading – as you walk by, you gather experience about the painting. The next time you come, you will see something new. Then you add that to having seen it before and you have a different visual experience.

"Certain paintings have to be seen from a very long distance," Stayton continues. "I did this ballroom for Vision of the Seas, and I had seen the same project on the Rhapsody before, but the room obliterated it. This presents a problem for the painter. I had to pump it up since you are almost 100 feet away as you look at the painting and it has to hold the entire room. And it works. That's its job.

"You can't just make a painting on a wall, you have to melt with the architecture and make it sing through the whole room. You can't be timid." ■

Janet Stayton (cv p 327): "Painting". Oil on linen. Some Enchanted Evening Lounge. Aft. Starboard, Deck 6.
The name of the ship Vision of the Seas *and of the room Some Enchanted Evening offered the artist an array of possible themes and variations. In her paintings here, Stayton uses recurring passages, in various juxtapositions, painting-to-painting. There is color, line and form, rather than sound. The huge room itself reverberates with a visual music, and the thematic images are stretched to the far edge of abstraction, so that all is not quite as it appears.*

EXIT

Helaine Blumenfeld, (cv p 265): "Dream II". White Statutorio marble, in combination with red travertine and rosa portugale. Main Stairs, Deck 6-7.

Helaine Blumenfeld:

The magic of the sea, the mystery of old myths

Blumenfeld's three groups of wall reliefs for the stairways attempt to explore the mystery and power of the sea. She feels that water is the purest and most enduring of all the elements. With their flowing forms and dream-like images, these reliefs are intended to convey the beauty and magic of the sea.

The two seated Mayan figures in the Solarium were inspired by the Hero Twins who are so important to the creation mythologies of both the Aztec and the Mayan peoples. These twins were depicted as being responsible for creating the resources necessary for human life. One of the twins provided order and the other change. These sculptures resonate with the visual themes that Blumenfeld uses when working with mythological figures. They have the characteristic layering, breaking up of surfaces, and drapery. The decorative patterning, textures and mystery are also very typical of Mayan stone carvings.

For the Aztec columns, the artist was inspired by the rectangular blocks of stone that were opened and used in Aztec and Central American art to "contain" the body of a god or goddess. The palm shape, rounded on top (coming from the volcanic palmate stone) was used in Central American art to encompass the body of the God of the Games (Macuilxochitl), who was frequently shown wearing a feathered headdress. Blumenfeld feels that the depth and layering, as well as the abstraction that characterizes her sculptures, bring these columns to life. When she was carving them, she says she felt as though she was working with ancient artifacts. ■

"Hero Twins One and Two". Mayan seated figures in red Persian travertine with inlaid colored marble. Solarium, Deck 9.

Aztec column in red travertine. Solarium, Deck 9.

Knut Steen:

The four Elements

Knut Steen (cv p 328) observes that from the time of the Greeks, man has been fascinated with the four elements: water, fire, earth and air. In his eyes, these formed the basis for all philosophical reflections about nature. To him, they are the foundations of our existence, so he has symbolized them in these sculptural reliefs. ■

Large photo below: "Earth". White Carrara marble. Niche. Main Stairs, Deck 8-9

Niche sculpture: "Water". Black Belgian marble. Large wall relief: "Earth". Black Belgian marble. Main Stairs Deck 7-8.

Right, middle: "Water", white veined marble relief.

Right, bottom: "Fire". Red Persian travertine marble. Main Stairs Deck 9-10, Niche Port side.

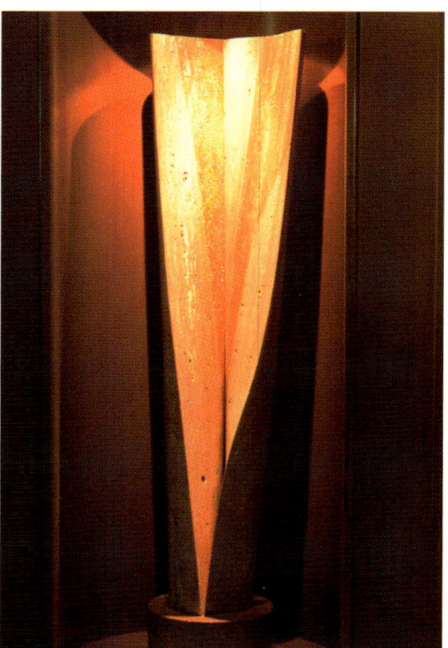

Inger Sitter (cv p 314): "Underwater Landscape". Reliefs in marble. Main Stairs Deck 2-3.

Inger Sitter:

A play of forces

Inger Sitter (cv p 314) portrays reefs and large rock formations that meet and struggle for power. She tries to show points of gravity that are displaced and currents that press between the big blocks of rock. Her art symbolizes cosmic struggle, and she feels that the human element is a part of this cosmic whole. ■

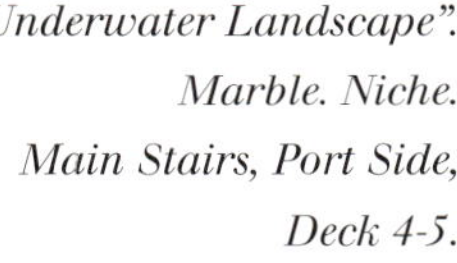

"Underwater Landscape". Marble. Niche. Main Stairs, Port Side, Deck 4-5.

"Between Sand and Stone". Colored marble. Main Stairs, Deck 3-4.

Dining Room and Viking Crown

Gunhild Strømnes (cv p 333): Resin sculptures in the Viking Crown. The objects which decorate the elevator walls consist of large leg-shaped amulets. These amulets were used by the vikings as magic objects believed to protect one from all evil. The shapes are beautiful and the symbolic meaning is obvious. The size of the amulets, their rhythm, the space in between and the repetition are all important effects. In each of the resin amulets Gunhild has cast different objects which have an ornamental quality. The shape of the legs speaks of their geographical movements then and now.

Aquarius Dining Room, designed by Robert Tillberg Design AB, Sweden. The architects chose a "Nordic look" for this room, with light birch panels and a dark blue base, giving it a little more spacey feel – a hint of astronomy and outer space.

Mike Newby (cv p 310): "Aurora Borealis". Glass sculpture. Viking Crown.

When Michael Newby was invited to design a piece for the Viking Crown Lounge, images of northern landscapes came to mind. Viking longboats, broken ice, high seas and the northern lights – the stuff of legends. These elements have excited Newby since he was a boy, and he enjoyed using them in the design and creation of The Ice Ship/ Aurora Borealis. The sculpture is a marvel with 350 individual pieces of glass extending up to 2.5 meters above deck level.

Ships onboard the ship

Ship model by Per Storm Iversen in the Schooner Bar, Deck 6.

Paul Wendling b. 1968, American: "SS United States". Brass ship model. Crown and Anchor Study. Deck 8 aft, starboard.

Bill Owens: "Captain Nemo's Submarine". Ship model. Explorer's Club, Deck 8. Jules Verne (1828–1905) was a lawyer, notary and stockbroker when he started writing in 1863. The most translated French writer, his work has been described as visionary. In 1870, Verne wrote "20,000 Leagues Under the Sea," featuring Captain Nemo and his submarine Nautilus. This model, built by Bill Owens, was used in the Hollywood movie based on the novel.

Ship model: "Gloucester Fishing Schooner", circa 1900. Windjammer Café, Deck 9. These "sharp-shooters", as they were called, were used in the early 1800's and during the war of 1812 as privateers, as were hundreds of fishing schooners off the Atlantic coast. In 1848, a new type of vessel, now known as the "Romp" model, was launched in Gloucester. This ship was much sharper and more finely lined. At the time, its innovative design created a sensation, marking the beginning of a new era in fishing schooners. The fishermen were proud of the superiority of their new craft and they sailed them with great daring. The fame of the Gloucester sailors spread throughout the world.

Pool deck and Solarium

Laurence Broderick, (cv p 269): "Tortoise". Porstoy marble. Solarium. When working on this commission, the word "tortoise" conjured up many thoughts for the artist Laurence Broderick. It is a creature from our past, prehistoric, powerful and long-lived. Broderick says man has always marveled at this slow-moving animal that just gets on with living. For him, this creature will always be reminiscent of warm climates.

Rebecca Newnham, b. 1967, British: "Serpents Mosaics". Solarium. The two-headed serpent was a symbol of the sky in Mesoamerica and is linked with Regal and Priestly office. The symmetry of the two heads suggests equilibrium or the balance of opposite forces.

Ralph Young, b. 1950, American and Melissa Mueller, b. 1960, American: "Hermanas de las Olas", broken tiles and hand-made ceramic mosaics. Pool deck, Deck 9.

Mueller and Young wanted these murals to be vibrant and flowing, infused with color. They naturally drifted toward a nautical theme, portraying a stylized image of grand ocean liners upon a swirling ocean. These mosaics embody the mystique that has always been associated with cruise ships – a larger-than-life quality, a dreamlike escape. The ships are huge, partially out of their frame, giving an image of vastness and forward motion. The viewer feels as if the ships are literally bursting forth from the murals.

"Snake Head". Fountains, terracotta finish. Jesmonite Technologies.

Voyager of the Seas

The ship sails her guests on a voyage through history into a new millennium. Lobbies and corridors are themed by centuries, from the 21st century, featuring futuristic science fiction, the 20th century with Art Deco and Modernism, the 19th century with Impressionism, through Empire, Neo-Classical, Renaissance and Gothic to Classic Roman, Greek and Egyptian art.

Larry Kirkland (cv p 299): "Oculus". Dichroic glass pyramid with steel and aluminium. The "Beacon" on the Pool Deck and the "Oculus" beneath it, running down to the Royal Promenade Ceiling, are at the heart of the ship.

Michele Benedetto, b. 1941, Italian: "Reflection (male)". Sculpture. Black Belgian marble.

Travelogue

Kvaerner Masa Yard, Turku, Finland, August 1999. Report from a different world.

The ship looks like Hamburg in 1945. It's hot on top of this huge collection of steel, but we find some shade for our lunch break and there's a slight breeze. Veronica Solem passes around some morsels she got at the colorful Turku marketplace. We take the construction elevator up 11 decks on the outside of the huge hull. A man from RCCL is talking at the top of his voice into his cell phone, an essential tool for maintaining contact with colleagues on board. The distances are enormous – 300 meters from prow to stern. The ship has two thousand workers on board, but will it ever sail?

Above: From Voyager *in August. Supervisor Chris Gottelier (to the right) with his indispensable phone, and a more relaxed Morten Jensen. They are having lunch on the deck outside the Golf Bar – pasties, strawberries and sandwiches. To accompany the food, cold "Aqua" packed in ice. The temperature is 30 °C (90 °F) in Turku, Finland.*

Right: Kyrre Andersen works in tight conditions.

Kvaerner Masa Yard, October 1999. Do we dare to believe it?

10 weeks have passed since we last were here. In three weeks, she is to leave Turku. Veronica Solem's huge wall paintings in the Golf Bar have survived under a heavy layer of plastic.

Here we are onboard 142,000 tons of steel, glass, cables, cabins, one-armed bandits, rolls of carpeting, cardboard boxes and garbage containers, while the Finnish and Italian shipyard workers are sweating away: welding, hammering and screwing together what is to be the largest cruise ship in the world. It is so big that there's no use writing home about it. No one would believe it anyway. Can we believe that this very ugly duckling will be transformed in just a few weeks into a swan, sailing the deep-blue Caribbean while champagne flows and the band plays "Moonlight Serenade" or "Strangers in the Night"? The fire alarm is tested five times an hour. It works. Every time.

Very few of the shipyard workers will see the vessel completed. She will sail from Turku on Sunday, October 31, 1999 with scaffoldings and a couple of hundred Finnish shipyard workers still onboard.

Captain Svein Pettersen sounds the foghorn loudly, causing everything not welded down to shake, as the *Voyager* disappears like a glittering castle of lights into the fall evening, out into the Bay of Finland, on course for Miami.

From Kvaerner Masa Yard: Voyager of the Seas *is scheduled to leave the shipyard soon. Her sister ship is already being outfitted.*

Miami, November 1999. Nothing is impossible.

The metamorphosis took place somewhere in the Atlantic. The miracle has happened. Like an imposing queen, she lays there in the middle of the Port of Miami.

In the open Solarium, the passengers are snoozing lightly in the sunshine. It is November 18th and 25 °C (80 °F) in the Port of Miami.

Here we are, sailing out into a tropical Caribbean night on a sea full of fish, with some sharks up on the dance floor, and lobster tails on dinner plates, accompanied by a chilled Chablis. It's sunset on Deck 12 and a steaming night in Dorothea Volkart Nordahl's installation of plastic, rubber and aluminium known as The Vault Nightclub. We may not be on our own balcony to enjoy the sunrise, but then again we might ... Nothing seems impossible aboard the *Voyager of the Seas.*

From Vision to Voyager

Realizing the vision of a cruise fleet for a new century

RCI's CEO Richard D. Fain: "When we embarked on the *Voyager Class* ships, it was clear that the industry had moved to yet another stage. Until that point there was no technical reason or design advantage to building a ship larger than the *Vision Class* ships. Those ships were basically large enough to reach full economies of scale and they had every kind of activity anyone would want. And they were easy to get around on.

"As we finished the *Vision series*, we realized that people really enjoyed this large number of choices of where to go and what to do. This was a much bigger success than we expected it to be. What is more, passengers wanted even more choices if we could find a way to provide them.

"But our passengers don't want to get lost. They need to feel that this is their ship, not a city. So we found ways to make this kind of a ship; large, but user-friendly, easy to find your way around, easy to get around, but still offering a wide range of choices.

"And we also found new focuses: The children's area was something that had traditionally been an afterthought on cruise ships. On the *Voyager Class*, it plays a crucial role."

In this way, RCI worked to create the ideal ship for the Caribbean cruise market. But there was a growing need for ships to sail in other waters. The *Vision Class* ships are better suited for these markets: fast, beautiful vessels of a reasonable size, and with a size that makes it possible to pass through the Panama Canal. These ships laid the foundation for yet another series of innovations, culminating in the *Radiance Class*, which further develops the *Vision* model. ■

A huge Pool Deck on Voyager of the Seas. *It's main artistic feature is Larry Kirkland's Glass Pyramid, "The Beacon".*

Victor Lind (cv p 305): Etched and painted aluminium relief. The artist has exhibited widely in Europe and has undertaken many monumental commissions for artworks in banks, factories, schools and several cruise ships. In the making of these works, he was inspired by the beautiful patterns that develop in the process of working on graphic metal plates.
Victor Lind's large metal work streches from the Royal Promenade on Deck 5 to Deck 9. Forward Centrum Wall.

Like no other ship ever

3,800 architects
Richard D. Fain does not merely think financing, ports of call and the look of the ship. He asks: "How do we solve the logistics for the passengers, the luggage and all the garbage produced onboard?" You have to keep on top of things when dealing with 28 architectural firms and 3,800 architects and designers. It took a total of 10,000 hours of work in 15 countries to plan and design the world's largest cruise ship. In the course of the three-year planning period prior to the actual building, a form of collective intelligence evolved. Fain says that while a Steering Committee may not be the most efficient design process, it preserves innovation and creativity. Everybody can have their say before decisions are made, and the architects compete with one another. That is what has brought forth dining rooms with balconies, giving guests a grand view, the Royal Promenade that serves as a town center, ice skating rink and a TV studio, in addition to such extravagances as outdoor roller blading facilities, golf simulators, a basketball court and climbing wall.

"We make several mock-ups during the process. The idea is to provide input for making timely decisions. Voyager is a good example," explains Kelly Gonzales, Manager, Newbuilding Design. "With the Royal Promenade as a unique feature, we built a one-to-one scale mock-up of the Promenade in Turku. A lot of people went over to see it. It was the first real idea we had of what the Promenade was going to feel like. It was a good working tool, and we used it to change things, technically and in terms of design. shapes, likes and dislikes. And seating has a big impact on the overall experience."

Installation of Casino Floor Feature is always a complicated job.

Good planning is essential. If you put 10 kilos too much in each of the 2,200 passenger and crew cabins, you end up with a ship that is 2.2 tons too heavy when it is finished. It is good to have some leeway when you know that the ice for the Ice Skating Rink alone weighs eight tons and the special floor for the ice weighs five tons. Not to mention 56 tons of art worth USD 12 million.

"We had chair shows, that is, presentations of the furniture and seating for the large areas like the Dining Room, the Show Theater and the Windjammer. We went through and kicked tires to make sure that everything worked. Richard D. Fain sat in all the chairs. It was a good test because we had, as we would have onboard the ship, a variety of sizes and

The Project Leader:
Gunnar Bjørn has been with RCI for 10 years and has been involved in building vessels the entire time. As Senior Supervisor, he headed up the Site Inspection Team in Turku. He has supervised the construction of the *Voyager*, *Explorer* and *Adventure of the Seas*.

"Building three cruise ships simultaneously is no nine-to-five job," says Gunnar Bjørn. "I started on the *Voyager* already in 1994. We sat up in Lapland, Finland with people from the shipyard, the architect Njål Eide and some people from RCI. We kicked around ideas and brainstormed.

"I had my hands full with managing the construction of two Vision ships, the Grandeur and the Enchantment, which were built

One of Larry Kirkland's complicated models for his huge installation in the Main Centrum, "The Dancer and the Tutu".

Scaffoldings are plentiful – and very high. Main Centrum – the last days before delivery of the ship.

in Helsinki. The latter was finished in July of 1997 and the contract for the Voyager was signed the same year. The last of the five ships in the Voyager series will be delivered in the fall of 2003; nine years after the first ideas were aired in Lapland."

The organization at RCI's office in Turku expanded tremendously in the course of building the Voyager and now has about 100 people. "We've never had so many people in an Inspection Office before," says Bjørn. "We have had two captains and two chief engineers who will take over the ship once she is finished. They have had the opportunity to be here and follow the finishing process, gaining detailed knowledge about all the systems onboard. Their knowledge is not limited to the last phase. They have been here for a year or so.

"One of the reasons why we are so many is that we want as many as possible of those who are to take over the ship in a relatively short while, to have the opportunity to get to know her in advance. The first team of officers will stay onboard for a few months after she enters the market. Then they will be replaced rather quickly.

"I can understand that way of thinking very well: Taking over a vessel like this one is such a big responsibility that it would not be a good idea for the leading officers to come onboard "cold" just before departure. This ship is very different from anything we have built to date. The next time around it will be much easier; then we will have a ship already sailing which can serve as a 'training vessel' for the next batch of officers," says Bjørn.

Project Leader Gunnar Bjørn.

"*Voyager* has been an incredibly complex technical job and an enormous challenge, but it is also quite an emotional business. I went down into the shipyard last night. It was dark and she laid there, cabins flooded with lights, almost ready to sail. I just stood there alone and looked at the ship.

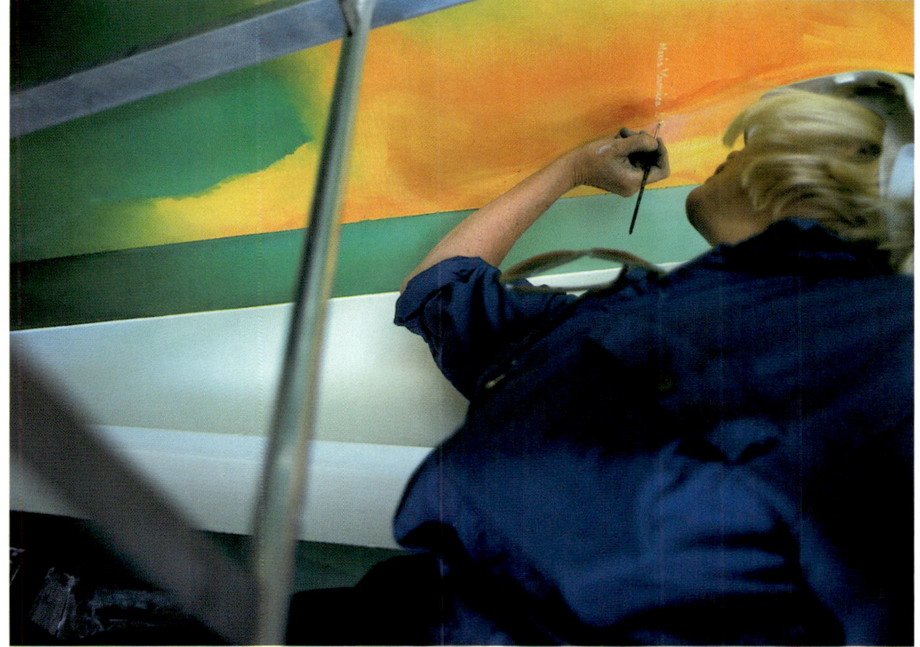

Maria Veronica L. Solem was told that the wall was 4.1 meters high, but it turned out to be 4.3 meters. Such circumstances call for improvisation and a certain amount of on-the-spot painting. The huge golf painting had to be given a "frame," which was painted around it after the scene was mounted. Solem primed the wall before she could start to paint the extra frame around the original picture – in a slightly different color. No one would guess that the artwork wasn't conceived exactly like that from the very beginning.

It was a great moment, and very emotional. You are part of creating something very few have the privilege to participate in during the course of their professional career. Building a tanker is very different, completely different from seeing how a vessel like this one comes to life. Building a ship like this can't be compared with anything else, not even with building a hotel. This is a huge, very complex society – on a keel." ■

This interview took place a month before the Voyager of the Seas *left the shipyard in Finland.*

The *Voyager of the Seas*

Itineraries
The *Voyager* has made round trips from Miami all year round to Labadee, the private beach paradise reserved exclusively for Royal Caribbean guests on the mountainous and secluded north coast of Hispaniola, Haiti. Also on the itinerary: Ochos Rios, Jamaica, with the lush, green tropical countryside spotted with waterfalls and winding rivers; Grand Cayman with its turquoise waters and sun-drenched beaches, ideal for snorkeling and all kinds of water sports; Cozumel, Mexico with the golden shops of San Miguel, its world-renowned coral reef, and its famous Mayan temple ruins on the mainland.

***Voyager* in figures**:

- As long as a 17-car freight train
- Longer than four 747 jets
- Twice as wide as Broadway in New York
- More than 10,000 persons worked 41,600,000 hours to complete the ship
- 1,864 miles of electrical cable run through the ship, a distance longer than from San Francisco to Chicago
- 65,331,779 cubic feet of air is transported and handled by air conditioning every hour on the ship
- Contains the largest investment in artwork by a cruise company, valued at USD 12 million
- The Dining Room seats 1,919 people; the La Scala Theater seats 1,362 people. ■

Voyager of the Seas *leaves the shipyard for the first sea trials with the assistance of tugboats.* *The* Voyager of the Seas, *the world's largest cruise ship, was built in 1999 at the Kvaerner Masa Yard in Turku, Finland.* *Gross tons: 142,000. Length: 311 m/1,021 ft. Beam: 48 m/157.5 ft. Draft: 8.8 m/29 ft. Cruising speed. 22 knots. Passengers: 3,114 (double occupancy). Crew: 1,176.* *The* Voyager *has 14 passenger decks, 14 passenger elevators, 4 bow thrusters, and 2 stern thrusters. (Photo: Jouni Saaristo)*

The Captain:
A smooth-sailing ship

"Since we first embarked on November 21st 1999, the ship has received a strong and positive response from our guests" says Captain Pettersen. "The Royal Promenade and the Dining Room have received the most praise. Whoever thinks that our passengers are uninterested in beautiful interiors and good art is mistaken. On the contrary, it is something which engages them very strongly."

Pettersen observes that RCI has expanded tremendously since 1990, with many new ships being built. "Every time we have a series of new ships, we all wonder whether they will be able to fill them, but so far they always have," he says. "We have pretty much been filled to capacity on *Voyager*'s cruises. That is partly because they're new and interesting, but it's also because of a growing market. As time passes, you gain a reputation in the market and people return. It's fun for us to get to know people as they return again and again," he continues. "Some of the waiters remember the guests by name and remember the ship they sailed on their last cruise. That never fails to impress people."

Pettersen calls the ship "a city at sea," saying: "I come from a little village in Norway, and we could fit everyone in the whole municipality onto one of our cruise ships. It's a whole society, and we use a lot of electricity! Not counting what is used to operate the ship, we use about 12 megawatts. That's enough power to run my entire village for the winter – with plenty to spare.

"When we weigh anchor and leave the dock, we must be completely self-sufficient. The same applies if we have an accident," explains Pettersen. "A lot of work goes into preparing for contingencies that will hopefully never happen. Routines must be drilled and tested and maintained. We have 1,200 crew members and a turnover of about 80 crew per week. Many hours every day are spent on drills alone."

The Captain emphasizes that safety is the most important thing, "but comfort is also crucial," he says. "We have advanced stabilizer systems. Everything we can do to limit unwanted motion is a good thing. We have done everything that is technically possible to make sure that our ships move as little as possible. However, if you have a full-blown storm, it's impossible to prevent some motion. With normal weather, the vessel feels like a hotel on land – you notice practically no difference at all. We are, and try to be at all times, a smooth-sailing ship," remarks Pettersen.

Captain Svein Pettersen (left) began his career as a seafarer in 1955 and joined RCI in 1970 as Chief Officer for the Nordic Prince, *which he assisted in bringing to Miami as a brand new ship from the shipyard. Since then, Pettersen has served on all of RCI's ships and has been a captain since 1975. He was also site manager for all the Mega-class ships and a senior supervisor for the Vision Class ships built in Finland. Now Captain Pettersen is the master of the largest cruise ship in the world, the* Voyager of the Seas. *Mexican harbour pilot to the right.*

Captain Pettersen reflects on the changes he has seen in the industry over the years: "Of course sailors are at least as good today as they were when I started out in 1955, but now they follow a different path to higher positions," he observes. "In my day, we started at the bottom, and many years of sea duty were required before you could get your first certificate. Today, the years spent in school are counted as sea duty and sailors get their certificates without much sailing experience. That's how the company can meet today's requirements for, among other things, electronics expertise among the crew. But when you are the Captain of a large ship, it is good to have experience with the various tasks and types of people for whom you are responsible." ■

The Hotel Director:

Sun makes people feel happy

"We started in January 1999," recalls Hotel Director Tony O'Prey, "when we brought the senior management team for Hotel Cruise Director, Chief Purser, Food and Beverage Manager and Chief Housekeeper, into Miami. We spent a week in the office, meeting with every department involved with the *Voyager of the Seas*. Then in May, we brought 26 of the middle management and supervisors into Miami for a week. We spent a week teambuilding and we did that again in August, so when we boarded the ship, we all knew each other. We had worked together, played together, and we were a very close-knit team."

O'Prey says his ambition was to pass this sense of team spirit all the way down, through all the crew. "With nearly 1,100 employees in the hotel department, teambuilding was a major factor in the success of this ship," he asserts.

O'Prey says the art on the ship serves more than a decorative purpose. "We make activities based on the art collection," he explains. "We place a nice art catalogue in each cabin, and the Art Auctioneer does an art tour every Monday morning."

In fact, O'Prey thinks the art on the ship is indispensable. "The art makes a big difference; it is necessary," he says. "Imagine coming down these stairs and looking at a blank wall. There are huge sums invested in building a ship like this, and art should be a major part of it. We would all miss it if it was not there. We can't imagine the Royal Promenade without the sculptures and the other artworks."

However, like his colleagues on other ships, O'Prey faces some difficulties in keeping the artwork maintained: "The art and its complicated lighting require maintenance and attention from the staff. With the very high Centrum sculpture, you have to rig up a chair so that they can get to it. The same goes for the chandelier in the Theater. To change some lights up there they have to rig up a walkway to get across. It can get quite complicated." ■

Tony O'Prey started his career as a mariner in 1960, when he joined Shaw Savill Line as a junior purser. After 16 years sailing around the world on passenger vessels and cargo carriers, in 1983 Tony went ashore and joined the management team of the Sheraton Hotel in Auckland. However, the sea was in his blood. When Royal Caribbean called him in 1985, he didn't think twice. Since then, Tony has sailed on most of RCI's ships. In October 1998, Tony was appointed Hotel Director of the Voyager of the Seas. *For more than a year, he was involved in the planning and preparation for the operation of the ship.*

Like no previous Art Program

"Selecting art and decorative elements for the *Voyager of the Seas* has been an extremely challenging and exciting task," says Gro Nesjar, partner and head of London Contemporary Art's (LCA) Oslo Office. "Given the enormous size of the ship, and the fact that no yard, cruise line or architects have ever built a ship of this magnitude, it must be said that we and the others involved in the project have really navigated uncharted territory."

The architects assigned for ships in the *Voyager Class* were divided geographically among LCA's three offices, located in London, Miami and Oslo.

"As always, we want to create a vacation environment that is interesting, appealing, and accessible for the passengers," says Joan Blackman, partner and head of the LCA Miami Office. "We begin by creating a unifying 'red thread' or theme which act as a framework for the artwork for the entire ship. As *Voyager of the Seas* was truly the first Millennium cruise vessel, LCA developed the concept of history leading up to the Millennium as the 'Ariadne's or red thread'. The art from nearly all centuries and cultural periods are explored. The art is meant to be bold, unconventional and, above all, memorable, creating an attractive yet provocative environment for the passengers." ■

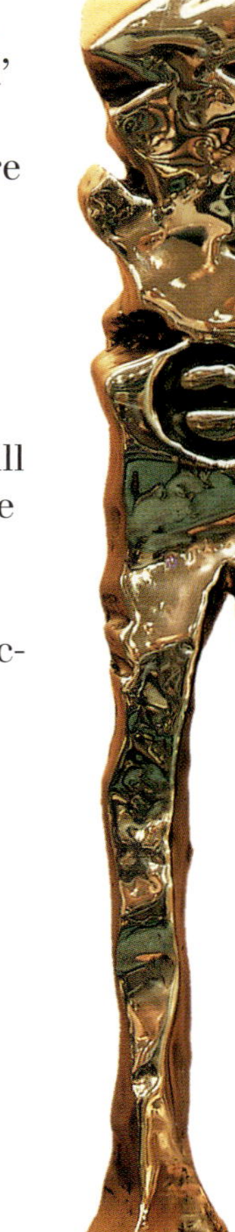

Inger Sitter (cv p 316): "Glacier". Marble relief. Main Stair, Starboard, Deck 8-9.

Åse Frøyshov (cv p 292): Wool and nylon tapestry. Main Stairs, Port Side, Deck 13-14.

Marc Berlet (cv p 259): "Jumeaux I". Nautical stainless steel sculpture. Forward Stairs Lobby, Port Side, Deck 5.

The Royal Promenade

The Royal Promenade, essentially a street within the ship, is an entirely new concept for cruise vessels. *Voyager's* Promenade has several whimsical and playful artistic elements for passengers to discover during their stay onboard: A small-scale interpretation of the Statute of Liberty by Arman; a vintage Morgan automobile that was a gift to the ship from Royal Caribbean's Chairman Richard D. Fain; an authentic English telephone booth; realistic sculptures from daily life by the sculptor Mirabelle. ■

Larry Kirkland (cv p 299):
Sculptures "The Dancer and the Tutu".
Stainless steel, aluminium, cable, acrylic, glass, gold and silver leaf.
The two sculptures interact with projected and transmitted light to suggest effervescent and ephemeral movement. They are the visual terminus for the Royal Promenade.

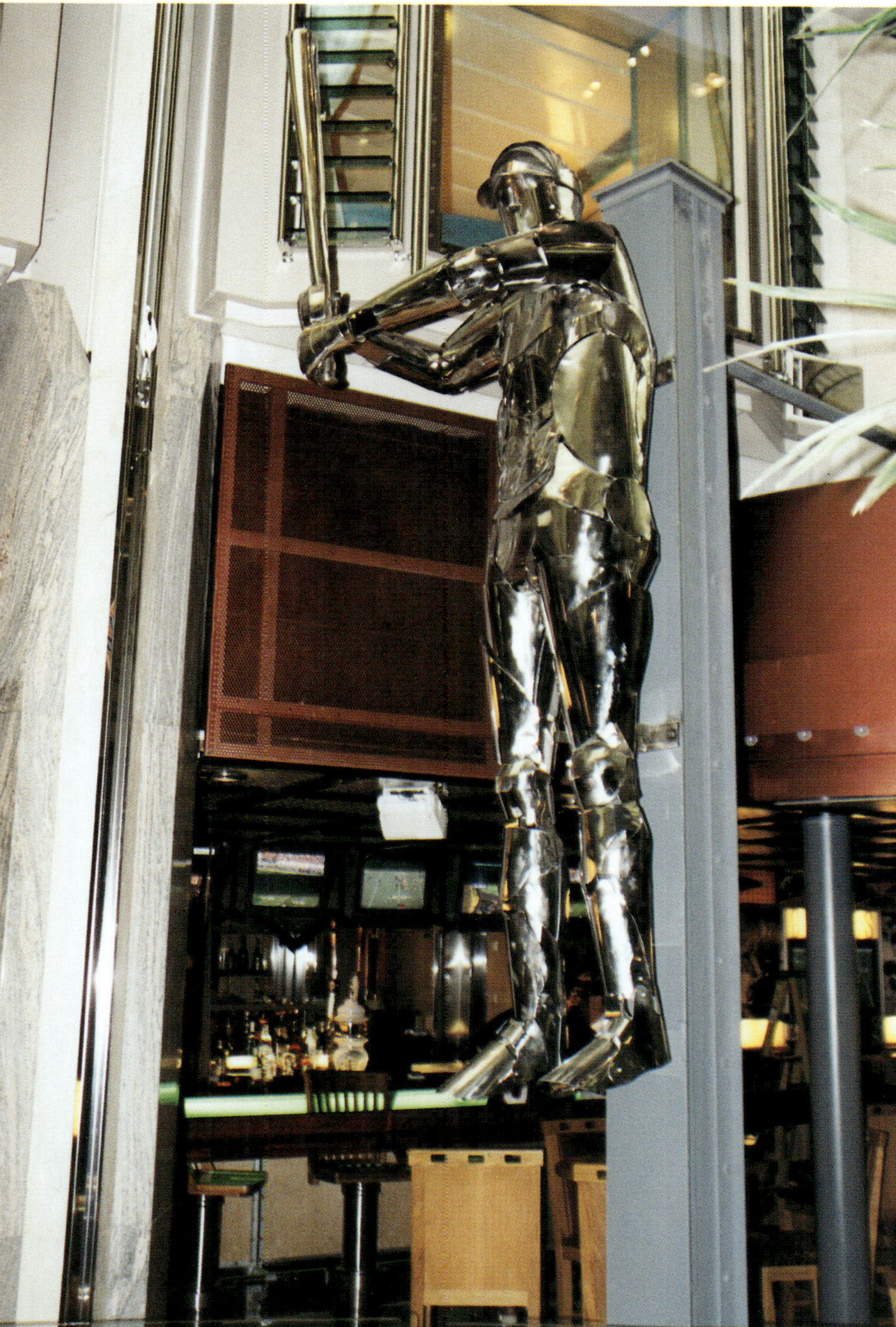

Luis E. Brieva (cv p 266): Sheet metal sculpture, "Baseball Player". Sports Bar, Deck 5. The artist thinks of sportsmen as "super beings," who reach a superior mental and physical state through their practice and discipline. Their quest for perfection, "Altus Situs, Fortis" … the highest, the fastest, the strongest, was inspiration for using the various polished metals to reflect their goals. (Photo: Jon Lie).

Royal Caribbean's CEO, Richard D. Fain donated his Morgan car. Royal Promenade, Deck 5.

The stairs

The Main and Forward Stairways feature art combining production techniques used 5,000 years ago with those used today, reproduced in media as diverse as marble and photography. ■

Knut Steen (cv p 331): "Sun". White Carrara marble. Main Stairs.

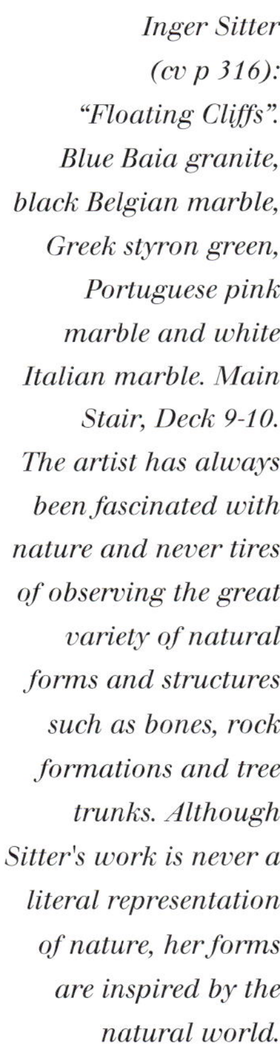

Inger Sitter (cv p 316): "Floating Cliffs". Blue Baia granite, black Belgian marble, Greek styron green, Portuguese pink marble and white Italian marble. Main Stair, Deck 9-10. The artist has always been fascinated with nature and never tires of observing the great variety of natural forms and structures such as bones, rock formations and tree trunks. Although Sitter's work is never a literal representation of nature, her forms are inspired by the natural world.

Helaine Blumenfeld (cv p 265): "Angel in Flight I". Relief, White marble angels have appeared to man, from the time of the Old Testament, as creatures of unparalleled beauty. They are the closest representation of pure spirit that man is capable of seeing. They are our spiritual messengers. The artist has used them as a metaphor to remind us that as long as we can "see" angels, we shall continue to be connected to the life of the spirit that lies at our center.

Helaine Blumenfeld: "Wrapped Female Figure II", White Macedonian marble. Niche. Main Stairs, Starboard, Deck 3-4. This sculpture is from a series called "Souls" which represent the spirituality and mystery that give us meaning. The artist has tried to show the soul as something that illuminates our physical presence. The human form is abstracted and simplified, and it is clothed in drapery that seems to emphazise its transcendent qualities. This figure portrays the feminine soul, imbued with calm, waiting to be discovered.

Top:
Tertit Prestegaard. "Sky". Hand woven tapestry. Main Stairs, Port Side, Deck 2-3.

Above:
Nini Anker Dessen (cv p 283): "Golden Dream". Hand-woven tapestry. Main Stairs, Deck 6-7. The artist's tapestries are inspired by glimpses of, or moments in nature, which remain imprinted on one's mind. They are composed mainly using "clean" colours and reflect the clean light of the North.

Above: Fin Serck-Hanssen (cv p 313): "Glacier". Photography. Forward Stairs, Starboard, Deck 5-6.

Niche left: Michele Benedetto, b. 1988, Italian: "Reflection (male)".

Right: Nini Bjønness, Norwegian: Glass mosaic.
On the rear wall: Robert O'Dea, British: Forward Stairs Lobby, by elevators. Deck 10.

Left: Barry Rowe, British: "Relaxing after Dinner". Acrylic on canvas. Cigar Club, Deck 5.

Bars and Cafes

Right: Maria Veronica L. Solem (cv p 323): "Over the Rainbow" and "The Morning Light". Oil on canvas. 19th Hole Golf Bar, Viking Crown, Starboard, Deck 14. "Golf" is the focal reference of this painting. The artist has used form and color to achieve the feeling of air and silence associated with playing golf.

Far left: Fredrik Brodersen, Lyngør Seilmakeri (see p 270): "Motive from traditional rigging". Schooner Bar, Deck 3.

Left: Ship Model, "Johanne Karine". Schooner Bar.

Right: Maria Veronica L. Solem (cv p. 323): "Il Grotto". Oil on canvas and imitated sandstone. Aquarium Bar, Aft, Deck 4. The Southern Islands of Norway inspired this painting with their round, ice-polished forms and the summer light of Scandinavia. The furniture is designed by Njål Eide (see p 44–49).

Top: Harald Egede Nissen, b. 1950, Norwegian: "Porthole with Sailboat at Sunset, Marine 1". Oil acrylic on canvas. Schooner Bar. Deck 4.

Lionard Slate: "From Nicaragua". The painting was awarded first prize in a RCI fleet crew competition for artistic contributions to the Voyager of the Seas. *Two of his pieces are hanging in the crew's "Silent Room". (Reading Room)*

The Dining Room was designed by Architect Robert Tillberg, Design AB, Sweden.

The Dining Room

The Dining Room, its three decks themed around three famous operas (The Magic Flute, La Boheme, and Carmen), features stage sets, fantastic costumes, and original memorabilia, as well as a tremendous trompe l'oeil opera scene painted mural that extends through three decks. ■

The impressive chandelier was made by Kalmar, Vienna, Austria.

Deirdre Clancy, b. 1943, British: "Pappagena" Costume. Magic Flute Dining Room, Deck 5. This artist's work is inspired by her experience as a stage and film designer. The costume is 'timeless" with 18th-century influences, as Mozart's opera "The Magic Flute" deals with the transcendental nature of trials and transformation as seen through 18th-century eyes.

Edward Burra, 1905–1976, British: Theater Model Original Design for "Carmen". This theater model was realized from the original design by Burra and constructed by Tim Blazdell and Alan Bain in the Royal Opera House Model Room, London. It depicts Act I of the opera "Carmen" by Georges Bizet, as performed by the newly founded Covent Garden Opera Company at the Royal Opera House, Covent Garden on 14th January 1947. Carmen Dining Room. Entrance, Deck 3.

Robert Morley & Co. Ltd. (est. 1881): Metal and wood with gilding, Antique Erard 46 String Gothic Concert Harp No. 5134. Sebastian Erard, b. 1752, Strasbourg, started making harps and pianos in Paris and moved to London in 1796 at the time of the Revolution. His contribution to the modern piano and harp can hardly be exaggerated because the design of the mechanism of modern grand piano and harps are derived from his inventions.

Casino Royale

There are two Casinos on the Voyager. The main Casino Royale offers a glamorous stroll through the 1930's. Busby Berkley-style features are designed to dazzle the passengers, created from combinations of glass, brass, fiber optics and sound effects.

The Spinners Casino on the Royal Promenade houses the largest roulette wheel and game on any vessel in the world. Here the

Treasure Floor by Zsiba/Smolover. The main Casino offers a glamorous stroll through the 1930's with combinations of glass, brass, fiber optics and sound effects.

entire casino is one big interactive roulette game, complete with a 23-foot high kinetic ball tower which feeds the balls to the wheel. The sound and light effects are a technical feat in themselves.

The American artist pair Zsiba/Smolover created the Casino Royale art features.

Says Maura Smolover: "We gave the casino a thematic identity. What we needed to do was to be an entertainment feature and attraction above and beyond the movements and lights that are already there. When someone comes into this ambience, they should see our work. But to be in focus is not to be in focus against a white wall. It's a focus in a context with a lot of competition. That's the job, and the fun."

The "Chorus Line" is an art deco musical from the 1930's. As you walk in, the song "We're in the Money" plays and the lights move. It's is a four-minute event with tap dancing.

Another feature is from "Pennies from Heaven", showcasing a different set of figures, a rainbow, a different soundtrack – and it rains money. There's a

Peter Zsiba and Maura Smolover (cv p 319): "Pennies from Heaven", Multimedia.

... "Now from clouds with silver linings
Angels toss their coins. What timing!
Pennies from heaven twirl and gleam
Pots of gold spill in a stream
Life's a glitter, spinning round ..."

rainbow stack of coins and each girl has a spray of pennies that changes colors. The Rainbow falls: the magenta, the blue, the green – the lights go into amber as they travel up the stack. And the sky goes from sunburst to darkness.

"When the Casino is not operating, we want to make it an inviting space for people to walk through," says Smolover.

"Peter Zsiba and I were both trained as theatrical designers," adds Smolover. "So as in a theater production, you will find light, sound, costumes, and actors." In fact, the Casino installations required so much electrical equipment that the artists had to build a separate space for the wires. ■

Cleopatra's Needle

The Secondary Lounge (Cleopatra's Needle) is filled with atmospheric Egyptian art and artifacts, while the main show lounge, the La Scala Theater, celebrates the grand Italian theater, but with a modern interpretation. The main art-works are life-sized marionettes designed by one of Italy's fore-most theater set designers and artists. ■

Copy of Ancient Egyptian Ship delivered by Steve Johnson. Entrance vestibule to Cleopatra's Needle. Secondary Lounge, Deck 5.

Copy of the "Cleopatra's Needle", the famous Egyptian obelisque supplied by Novidis, London. The original was taken to London in 1877. At the entrance of the Secondary Lounge, Forward Centrum, Deck 5.

La Scala Theater

All stage curtains for the Voyager Class are made by Paramount Parks Global Entertainment, Charlotte, NC.

Piero Lorenzini, b. 1965, Italian: "The Opera Singers". Wood, paper-mâché, epoxy resin, styrofoam, fabric and beads. Deck 3, inside La Scala Theater. The artist is one of Italy's most famous scenographers. Here he wanted to emphasise the sumptuousness of opera and its strictly theatrical aspect by which the characters are defined.

The Vault

The artwork and decoration for the Night Club consist of black and fluorescent colored rubber, that glow in the dark. ■

Dorothea Volkart Nordahl, b. 1947, Swiss: "Scuttlebutt". Plastic, rubber and aluminium.
The Vault Night Club, Deck 3-4.
On old American naval ships, the "scuttlebutt" was a cask, barrel or fountain of water where the sailors could easily drink. On larger ships, the "scuttlebutt" was the place where sailors with different tasks from different parts of the ship met not only for drinking, but also to get the latest news and gossip from different levels on the ship. The American word "scuttlebutt" has become a word for gossip or rumor, officially used for the first time in "Night Game" (1988 American film): "I hear some scuttlebutt says he likes to kick the ladies around."
As the disco area looks like a large barrel where passengers will undoubtedly be playing "night games" of their own, the artist thought this would make an appropriate title for the very contemporary and exciting artwork.

The Library and the Champagne Bar

Jay Pritzker-Library, Deck 7 with photographic portrait of Jay Pritzker, mounted onto a glass wall designed by Mike Newby (cv p 310).

Helaine Blumenfeld (cv p 265): "Angel of Life". Marble sculpture. Champagne Bar, Deck 5.

The artist has carved this sculpture out of Macedonian marble, which is highly crystalline, so that the piece seems to radiate its own inner light. The angel is a metaphor for man's spiritual existence, and is closely associated with the myth of creation. The different sides of the sculpture portray the order and chaos that suggest creation, the tenderness of love and the power of the spirit. The outer shape of the piece, starting from a small base and rising upward and outward, accentuates its ascending spirituality.

The Viking Crown and the Chapel

The Viking Crown area has always been RCI's trademark. On this vessel, the Viking Crown area, which incorporates a multi-denominational wedding chapel, is a more subtle and elegant space, featuring bronze inlaid terrazzo feature floors.

In this first cruise chapel in the world, Graham Jones made the glass skylight panels and Susan Klebanoff created the tapestry. Michele Oka Doner created the beautiful floor. It is a calm space, with 60 seats. ■

Michele Oka Doner (cv p 286): "Jazz". Floor medallions. Bronze, terrazzo, mother-of-pearl. Viking Crown Jazz Club, High Notes Bar, Deck 14.
The artist hoped to create a special site with a visual language: chords, notations, notes, rhythms, beat, pitch, instrumentation, and lots of energy.

Graham Jones, b. 1958, British: "Veil". Stained glass ceiling. The artist's works reflect the natural world. They are abstract images that aim to evoke feeling. They convey duality; paradoxes of tension and harmony. The Chapel Ceiling suggests a parting in the veil that separates man from the sight of God. It is designed to evoke the sense of awe that is universal and innate to the human experience of God.

Above: Susan Klebanoff, b. 1955, American: "Seven Days of Creation". Tapestry. This artwork symbolizes the energy present at the beginning of any new endeavour, passage or creation. Energy, as it radiates out from its central source, creates a universal light that illuminates all that it touches. Chapel, Deck 15.

Upper Decks

The Solarium and Health Spa create an environment that is peaceful and luxurious, akin to an ancient Roman bath. The art comprises a collection of antiques and replicas of original works characteristic of ancient times.

The Windjammer Café and Island Grill offer an informal and light setting as an alternative to the grand Dining Room. A Basketball Court and Rock Climbing Wall are popular with the younger clientele. ■

Fleur de Marie Kelly, British: "Constatine Bath Scene". Fresco. Shipshape Center, Deck 11.

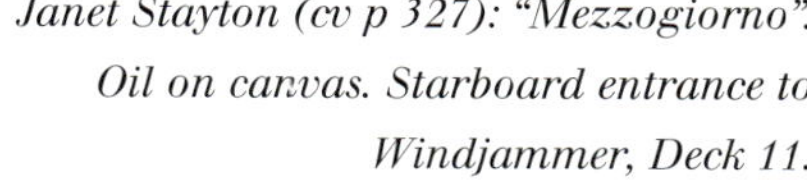

Janet Stayton (cv p 327): "Mezzogiorno". Oil on canvas. Starboard entrance to Windjammer, Deck 11.

Rebecca Aird, b. 1970, British: Mosaic. Windjammer Cafe, Deck 11.
Aird has translated the traditional art of mosaic to give a more modern feel, making use of the new colors and materials available today. She has designed this piece in the Art Deco style of the Miami sea scene paintings by artist Barry Rowe.

Barsanti Marble-Bronze-Mosaic (Italy). Solarium.

Kyrre Andersen and Liv Anne Lundberg (cv p 255): "Spin". Stainless steel illuminated by colored light. Outside the Windjammer Cafe, Deck 9-10-11.
The artists' interpretation of the curved wall as a sail has inspired them to fill this sail with wind and light. They want this artwork to express movement and lightness.

The Basketball Court and Rock Climbing Wall are popular features onboard Voyager.

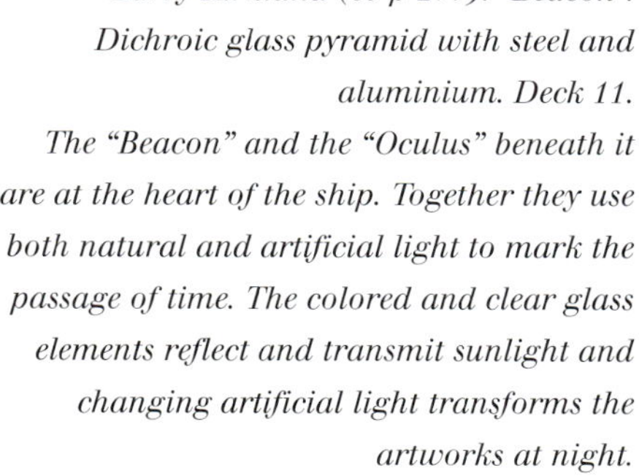

Larry Kirkland (cv p 299): "Beacon". Dichroic glass pyramid with steel and aluminium. Deck 11.
The "Beacon" and the "Oculus" beneath it are at the heart of the ship. Together they use both natural and artificial light to mark the passage of time. The colored and clear glass elements reflect and transmit sunlight and changing artificial light transforms the artworks at night.

Replicas of famous Roman marble sculptures circle the top of the colonnade above the Solarium on Deck 11.

Barsanti Marble-Bronze-Mosaic (est. 1897, Italy): Reconstituted Marble Figure, replica of "Hercules Farnese". Museo Nazionale di Napoli. Health Spa, Deck 11.

Bruce McLean b. 1944, British: "Sun, Sky, Sea, Sand, Shimmer". Powder coated paint on steel panels. Sky Bar, Deck 12.

Part III
Artists and Artisans

"I love the fact that ideas can live in materials."

Michele Oka Doner
American artist

Travelogue

Studio Sem, Scultori SRR, Via Piro Assegno 4, 55045 Pietrasanta, Lucca, Italy, is the inscription on the box down by the iron gate. It is a scorchingly hot July day, and the area is crowded with a fascinating array of white marble and wonderful figures, jagged old fragments of stone, some old bicycles, Madonnas and figures of Christ. Studio Sem is not large, perhaps 100 meters long and 40 to 50 meters wide. The machines drone away and the marble dust billows as blocks are cut and sculptures are made for cemeteries, collectors, sculptors and vessels that cruise the seven seas.

Gro Nesjar talking to London.

Aqua Potabile, "potable water", proclaims the sign over a marble sink. The artisans are in their undershirts. The youngest are wearing masks over their noses and eyes. The old-timers are not concerned with such newfangled inventions. The stone comes clean-cut in three- and four-sided blocks. In the midst of all this industrial clutter, the ever-elegant Gro Nesjar stands in a doorway, talking to London on the mobile telephone. Everything is completely natural and unaffected. No one pays any attention to anyone else; everyone is working on his or her own sculpture, with his or her own block of stone. The head of this goal-oriented chaos, American Keara McMartin, is usually to be found in her office, but occasionally comes out into the yard to inspect some stone or solve a practical problem.

This is a rough-and-tumble, non-picturesque industrial environment - a stone workshop. Everyone smokes. Classic marble sculptures dot the clutter. A pallet of stone comes toward us on an express truck; we jump out of the way. Life at Studio Sem seems to have its dangers. Keara discusses stone quality with a young Korean woman who later walks around with an eagle eye, examining the blocks of stone for hours.

This creative, dusty, sweltering workshop is the birthplace of the lovely marble works made by eminent artists such as Helaine Blumenfeld, Inger Sitter and Knut Steen that ornament RCI's luxurious air-conditioned cruise vessels, but a first-time visitor would certainly never suspect it.

Knut Steen (cv p 331): "Pantomime". Marble. Entrance Palladium Theater, Deck 6, Grandeur of the Seas.

Keara McMartin and Studio Sem

"Sem taught me about the quarries, cutting the blocks and making enlargements, as well as about the history of sculpture first hand. He was like a living encyclopedia with the exception that he was passionate about anything you might ask him. My own curiosity led me to pick his brain at every opportunity."

– Keara McMartin

Pietrasanta is a small town of 20,000 nestled up against the foothills of the Apuan Alps in Tuscany. With the Alps behind it and the Riviera just a couple of miles away, it is a natural attraction for tourists and artists alike. For centuries the town made a name for itself producing some of the most beautiful classical statues in the world. At the turn of the 20th century, it was home to numerous studios, employing as many as 100 artisans each to meet the tremendous demand for marble statuary. Sem Ghelardini began working in one of the large studios as a teenager, then later established his own studio together with his mentor Niccolai.

For 15 years, the studio continued to produce classical and religious works. Then the synod, under Pope John XXIII, brought an end to high ornamentation in favor of austerity. By the early 1960's, work had dried up for Pietrasanta's artisans, who found themselves in a crisis that would endure for many years to come. What saved the artisans and the town was the arrival of modern masters like Henry Moore, Isamu Noguchi and Juan Miro. But many artisans rejected outright the idea that they could make a living producing modern sculpture. Sem was alone in his enthusiasm for the new opportunities. It was his excitement that helped cultivate the new modern sculptors and changed the face of Pietrasanta. Through his enormous generosity and sense of humor, as well as his natural talent for sculpture, he became an icon in the world of sculpture who rivalled the fame of some of the sculptors he worked for.

Since Sem's death in 1997, Keara McMartin has been running the studio as sole administrator, with the help of her partners, the head foreman, Sergio Benedetti, and one of Sem's sons, Massimiliano Ghelardini. How did a young American woman come to run this world-famous studio in a country known for its macho men?

McMartin arrived in Pietrasanta in 1980 to study carving techniques and stayed for several years, returning to her home in Annapolis, Maryland from time to time. "In 1983, I decided to stop carving and return to making wall hangings in fabric. I wanted to stay in Pietrasanta because I had fallen in love with the district: the colors of Italy, the climate and most of all, the people," reminiscences McMartin.

Her studio was directly across the street from the Bar Igea, a famous

Hard and dangerous work in the Carrara marble quarry. (Photo: Romano Cagnoni)

watering hole for all the sculptors and Sem's favorite bar. It was there that McMartin met Sem, sitting at his usual table at the bar and wondering out loud what a young woman lacking the requisite coating of marble dust was doing in a town of stone carvers. As she explained her circumstances, Sem whipped his little corduroy hat off his head and asked if she could produce another just like it.

McMartin was not a seamstress, but she accepted the challenge anyway and made him a hat. That was the first of dozens of hats that she would make for him over the next 15 years. Several months later, Sem asked her to come and join the studio as an assistant in the office and she accepted the job. She accompanied him to the quarries and began to understand the different characteristics of the local marble. She became well acquainted with the workers in the quarries and the activities of the studio on a day-to-day basis. At Sem's suggestion, she began making marble inlays instead of working with fabric. Because of the diversity of the stones employed in inlay she learned the colors, properties and faults of just about every type of marble in the world in a short time.

Manager Keara McMartin and Norwegian Sculptor Knut Steen with proud Studio Sem craftsmen. The white marble sculpture was made for Grandeur of the Seas. *(Photo: Morten Krogvold)*

Over the years, McMartin became Sem's right hand, but she says it wasn't easy stepping into his shoes. "Being an artist in my own right I feel that I have a good sense of aesthetics and quality, both of which are imperative in the decision-making process at the studio and in collaboration with the artists. However, it took years for the artisans at the studio to trust me with a decision. This was a man's world and none of them were willing to take direction from a woman, let alone an American. There was a thick climate of nationalism and that, coupled with Italian machismo, made my job frustrating and sometimes nearly impossible. I had to prove myself every step of the way and hope that Sem would back my decisions. Most of the time he did, and it happened often enough that they gained confidence in my abilities to direct them," she says.

Even so, it was never McMartin's ambition to run the studio, but as she explains, the turning point came when Sem suffered a series of minor strokes that incapacitated him. "All of a sudden I found myself alone facing the artisans with their daily problems and having to take the ultimate responsibility for the decisions. Inevitably, working with a natural material, you get cracks, or holes or a little accident happening like an edge chipping. Somebody has to step forward to make the decision when the artisan asks, 'What do we do here?' Abandon the work, or get another block? Perhaps we could talk to the artist? If nobody steps forward, the artisans simply lay their tools down and go home. They are employees, the implication being that decisions of that nature are not part of the job," continues McMartin.

Technology is rapidly developing to the point where simple works of a geometric nature can be made by machine with little or no finishing touches required. McMartin speculates that the day will probably come when almost all the work is made by machine with a minimum of manual labor. For now, however, the studio remains a very human and vibrant place. "All kinds of sculptors come to the studio, either to have the work produced for them or to rent one of the few available spaces to create and produce their own work," explains McMartin. "The younger people who rent space don't have a teacher – the whole studio is their school. They can learn an enormous amount just by watching the craftsmen work; learning what tool to use for what job, and about all the possibilities for getting the most out of any given stone. I consider the younger sculptors to be an investment in that way. All the help we give them will eventually come back to us if they ever become successful. It's nice to be in the midst of a constant exchange of ideas and cooperation."

McMartin explains that making sculptures and reliefs in marble for RCI is different from what the studio was used to. With other big commissions, she says, there is always a certain amount of flexibility. The material and the size can be changed even at the last minute, and weight is not generally a consideration. "Working for the ships, we have to consider an array of things like complex fixings to fit upright struts inside the walls, sometimes planning with the builders where the supports have to be to take the weight," she says. "Mounting huge reliefs on the side of a building, you don't have a problem with the weight, but on the ships you have to make quite advanced systems to mount things and keep them as light as possible. All of Helaine Blumenfeld's reliefs are painstakingly hollowed out to save on weight. For every 100 kilos you put on a wall on a high deck you have to pour 1000 kilos of steel below the waterline to compensate for the balance.

"The visual aspect of working for a ship is completely different," says McMartin, "because the spaces are very tight and the lighting is somewhat low. For instance, for the important works we have made for the main stairs, you can't get much distance away from the art to look at the whole thing, so the artwork has to render its content from very close up. Sometimes we even have to coach the artist and say 'this is too high' or 'this is going to be much too dark, because the light is low.' We have to explain to them how they must modify the work to be fixed to a wall permanently. It's difficult for an artist to work

The giant stones are cut out of the mountains in Carrara. (Photo: Romano Cagnoni)

like that. He has a vision of what he wants the work to be and then he has go back and change it to make it fit that specific ambience."

McMartin gives a lot of the credit for the ultimate success to London Contemporary Art: "They make the modifications to the work to meet the regulations long before the work is presented to me in model form – screening out the problems before they become our nightmare. Somebody has to be responsible and London Contemporary Art has a huge capacity to do that," she says.

"Looking over the images, in cooperation with LCA, we have to see if they are going to be suitable even with respect to safety. And aesthetically if they are going to work on that specific wall, if they need some changes, if they're too heavy. It's a collaborative process, selecting the work, overseeing the production, co-ordinating the installation and, in many instances, installing the work themselves. LCA frequently comes to the studio during production to work with us first-hand on problems that arise between the artist and the criteria for ship safety."

"Mostly we work with architect Njål Eide's projects," says McMartin. "He handles the biggest areas onboard and perhaps the most complicated. He pushes the limits all the time, because he wants every ship to be better than the last one. Some of the changes he makes are what distinguishes an RCI ship from a ship from another company." ■

Paramount Parks

Paramount Parks has produced the beautiful stage curtains for the theaters onboard nine RCI cruise ships.

Paramount Parks, headquartered in Charlotte, NC, is the parent company of Paramount Show Services International LLC, a division of Viacom International, one of the world's largest entertainment and publishing companies and a leading force in nearly every segment of the international media marketplace.

Paramount Parks owns and operates five amusement parks around the US and North America for which it provides all of the costumes, scenery, and amusement park rides. One Paramount division is called Global Entertainment Services. About 80 percent of the work done in this division is for the cruise industry.

The Maritime Operations Department has provided consulting, costumes, rigging, curtain packages, and general maintenance services for the cruise ship industry for over a decade.

The Paramount Parks production facilities are situated in Charlotte, North Carolina, an area of the South with a strong tradition of women who quilt, weave and spin. Stan Morrell, who directs Global Entertainment Services, explains that a lot of women in the Charlotte area are highly skilled in fine, detailed handwork.

"We are able to manufacture soft goods, hard goods, welding, woodworking, art decorations and scenery," explains Morrell. "We have developed professionals, meaning we can produce varied and complex works. We provide services, including developing turn-key live entertainment programs, designing and maintaining theatrical rigging equipment, creating custom art pieces for art suppliers such as London Contemporary Art, and designing and fabricating theatrical scenery, stage curtains, and costumes.

Gwen Turner, Sharon Ratchford (Production Supervisor), Meta Thompson, Pratibha Suthar working on the stage curtain for Rhapsody of the Seas.

"We were heavily involved with the *Voyager of the Seas*," continues Morrell, "providing goods and services for the Ice Show, the Game Show, the Royal Promenade, Cleopatra's Needle, and La Scala Theater. We maintained a significant crew at the yard in Finland to execute the installation of all of the Paramount-provided equipment and artwork."

Morrell explains that the process of developing the elaborate stage curtains starts with the architect, who develops the look of the theater onboard. The style of the architecture sets the tone and approach for all of the decoration and art in the theater, including the main curtain, he says.

"The artists produce elaborate models and sketches. We send a sample section of the curtain to the client with all the appliqué and jewelling that will be present in the final piece so the Steering Committee of RCI can see what it will be like. At this stage, comments and suggestions will come back from LCA, the architect and the RCI representatives," explains Morrell, adding: "We have developed a strong relationship with London Contemporary Art. They direct us in the design brief for the

> *"We have a staff of artists and a battalion of craftswomen – we can do anything you want."*
>
> *– Stan Morrell*
> *Director, Paramount Parks*

artist to follow, the interpretation of the artist's work and translating the artist's vision into the Austrian curtain, while maintaining the integrity of the piece."

Chief designer Steve Rundle first has the artwork prepared; then it goes to the costume shop where the supervisors discuss the approach to translating it into fabric and paint. "We take different textile elements and try to get as close to the interpretation as we can," Rundle points out. "We use different fabrics, some printed, some solids. We have to over-dye them sometimes to come up with the correct color. We use a variety of techniques, weaving fabrics together, adding all different types of embellishments, some of which might appear silly when viewed up close, yet are the perfect touch viewed at the distance from which the audience views the finished drape. These guys are tremendous at interpreting into fabric the intentions of the artist and the designer."

"Then fabrics can be ordered and production can begin on the full-size curtain. The artwork is digitized and full-scale patterns are produced for the stitchers and painters to work from. While we use computer technology to assist us with cleaning and enlarging the original artwork, the process of keeping the life and essence of the original is still very much a hands-on thing. A flat picture with the design printed on the fabric comes back to us from the printer. But then we go back in, with paint and appliquéd fabric, with jewels and other stuff. This is what makes everything come alive," remarks Rundle.

Depending on the artwork and approach, the artwork is then recreated on a large scale, frequently using a combination of techniques that can include paint, appliquéd fabric, trim embroidery, sequining, beading and jewels. "Near the end of our 12-week production period, we may have 10 to 15 of our quilting ladies working on the floor at once, all hand stitching appliqué and jewels," says Rundle. "By the end of the production people are actually lying all over the floor sewing and stitching things on. Sometimes we put a machine on a platform equipped with wheels. We have to move it along to get to the different areas."

In the last stage before the work is finished, the rigging rings must be stitched on so the curtain can be raised and lowered by lift lines once it reaches the theater. "To sew on these rings, one person actually has to stand behind while another is in front, feeding the needle back and forth to one another through the curtain," explains Rundle. "It's really a trick to get the rigging attached right. The attachment should not be visible, without puckers to create shadows. The curtain should move up and down easily and drape nicely without disturbing the visual impact of the art," he adds.

"The curtain making process is long and intense," says Rundle: "Working on one of these curtains is like a marathon. When we finish we are all so tired and very excited; the ladies bring their cameras to get a shot of their craftsmanship, and everybody from the interior design and architecture departments comes over to see it. Even those of us who didn't take part in the work directly take pride in the finished product. It is a major event when one of these curtains is completed. We put a label on it, proudly listing the names of all who contributed to its fabrication under the Paramount Parks Banner. After all the fanfare, it is taken down and transported to a yard in France, Finland or Germany, to be installed." ■

Key staff Paramount Parks, from left: Stan Morrell, Executive Director of Global Entertainment. Sharon Ratchford, Costume Shop Supervisor. Lisa Brantmeyer, Supervisor. Steve Rundle, Scenic Design Supervisor. Melanie Fearnow, Manager Costume and Character Shop. David Reitterer, Director, Entertainment Operations. Michael Salzman (with glasses), Scenic Softgoods Supervisor.
The curtain on the table is for the Explorer of the Seas, *Studio B theater.*

Kyrre Andersen and Liv Anne Lundberg

Kyrre Andersen and Liv Anne Lundberg have worked together on every art/decorative commission since 1987. They divide the work between them. Lundberg has an illustration studio; Andersen is more the craftsman. Lundberg is usually the one who sketches out the first ideas on paper as a basis for discussion. Andersen often begins with a model, or even several three-dimensional models.

"We work together for a while and then go our separate ways to do what needs to be done. Then we talk things over again and work towards a design to show the architects and London Contemporary Art. In the production phase, however, we work together the whole time although it varies a little based on who has the most to contribute during this phase," says Lundberg as Andersen nods in agreement.

When it comes to works of steel like that done on the *Voyager*, Andersen's background in metal is the most relevant, while Lundberg applies her talents mostly to flat compositions, colors and painting.

"We have created several hanging sculptures, but nothing as elaborate as the one onboard the *Voyager*. We've made many pieces of public art in our time, but we work differently on a ship than we would on land. On board there are a lot of people who have strong opinions about how things should be, including both the architects and LCA. You really have to give it all you've got to satisfy them. On land, you can allow yourself a little latitude when it comes to such matters. Demands are still made there, but one is often a little freer in how one meets specifications," adds Andersen.

"Ship's interiors are more expressive than in public buildings, where they can be completely empty premises with little to consider except for the dimensions. The opposite is true on a cruise ship. There aren't very many large areas of empty wall space. It's essential to be able to communicate well with the architect when working on such a large, complex project. We have to understand what was intended with the architecture and we need to follow along the line of what they want," interjects Lundberg.

"We thought that 'our wall' was well suited for using colored lighting, and we also tried to add transparent elements. We associated the white wall with a sail.

"We also decided to have the sail sort of billowing in the wind. We wanted to imply speed, lightness, something that was not overt but sort of dissolved in the form – not so concrete, a little abstract," comments Andersen.

"We made a plastic model, and we also thought plastic would work well with the steel, lights and colors. It turned out to be too much of a fire hazard, though, so we ended up using perforated steel plates. We did a lot of experimenting before we found a way to make steel plates seem transparent. In addition, we polished the surface using a special technique that makes it reflect light especially well.

"The work, which was to be finished in May, was probably hung too early, which resulted in problems with dust. The timing for mounting demands a fine balance between the shipyards' desire to have everything in place as early

Kyrre Andersen and Liv Anne Lundberg during installation work on Voyager.

"In large part we must do our work on site. After all, we are painting with light."

Liv Anne Lundberg and Kyrre Andersen

as possible and the artists' fear that the work might be damaged during construction of the ship," continues Andersen.

"We wanted to achieve our idea of the sail billowing in the wind, which could be illuminated in different colors to create various atmospheres: the sky, dusk, sunrise. We ran into certain technical problems, though, and we continually had to come up with new solutions for carrying out our vision. We think we managed to achieve it pretty well," says Lundberg.

Kyrre Andersen and Liv Anne Lundberg: "Spin". Stainless steel illuminated by coloured light. The artists' interpretation of the curved wall as a sail has inspired them to fill this sail with wind and light. They want this artwork to express speed, lightness, movement and alternation.

Kyrre Andersen did all of the steel work on the *Voyager* sculpture himself, with the help of an assistant. "Our little workshop was piled with steel from floor to ceiling and we crawled around in a kind of nest of steel parts and pieces," recalls Andersen. "We had made a model which was very close to the end result, down to every last detail; we took measurements of each and every part, calculated the full-size dimensions, and began to form each piece. When we finished one piece we went on to shape the next one in proportion to the others. Without such an exact model we never would have managed it.

"We were really in suspense when the sculpture was mounted. There was this huge scaffold in front of it, and we didn't get to see the whole work until the scaffolding was taken down. Well, we thought it worked very well in relation to what we'd done in the model," says Andersen.

"We do a type of work that is extremely dependent on good cooperation among differing groups onboard. Our installation on the *Voyager* can't be compared to painting a picture at home and then hanging it on a wall onboard the ship. It had to be produced in Norway, mounted in Turku, Finland and the final adjustments were made when the ship arrived in Miami, especially the setting of the lights. It's difficult to plan in advance how and where the lights should point to attain precisely the colors we wanted. When we use several different spotlights with different colors, they combine to create a new color when they hit the wall. Spotlight placement is critical. The fine adjustments must be done on site. We have to work by trial and error as a painter does in his studio. We are, in fact, painters who must do their painting on site. After all, we are painting with light," reports Lundberg. ■

Kyrre Andersen and Liv Anne Lundberg working on a model for Enchantment of the Seas.

This interview with Kyrre Andersen and Liv Anne Lundberg took place in Miami as they were completing the huge installation of colored light on steel for the Voyager of the Seas.

CV

Liv Anne Lundberg:
National College of Art and Design, Oslo
Institute of Clothing and Costumes 1979-83.
Kyrre Andersen:
National College of Art and Design, Oslo
Institute for Metal 1978-83.

Exhibitions:
Installation, RAM Galleri, Oslo 1993.
"Oktett" Solbergelva /
Ål Community Center 1994.
"Panorama" RAM Galleri, Oslo 1992.
Spatial installation "Kuben", Tromsø 1990.

A number of public decoration commissions, including:
The local government administration building, Svalbard 1999.
The Quad, University of Bergen, 1999.
Høgtun Upper Secondary School, Troms 1998.
Finnsnes Community Center, Troms 1995.
Telenor Headquarters, Oslo 1995.
"Light sculpture", Håkons Hall, Lillehammer 1994.

Commissions for 11 cruise ships, 5 in the Royal Caribbean fleet.

John Ashworth

John Ashworth began in engineering, but had always wanted to be a sculptor: "My parents said I should take an education as an engineer; as an artist I would be poor. Engineering would be suitable as I was very good at

"I think I have achieved a wonderful little marriage between art and engineering."

– John Ashworth

making things. I quit my job with Rolls-Royce in the 1960's and after that I designed textile machines. Then I thought I'd do what I always wanted to do. I left engineering and spent seven years in art schools, first in Manchester and then at the Royal College of Art in London.

"My connection with RCI began with the great Sand Clock for the Library on the *Sovereign of the Seas.* That happened well before London Contemporary Art entered the stage. When they did, they saw the clock, and commissions for the *Vision Class* came along.

"If you look at my art, you'll see that I'm taking engineering for a walk. I do like movement, tension and that sort of thing. As an engineer it's very straight stuff, but as an artist I push my machines far beyond what they're supposed to do. I think I have achieved a wonderful little marriage between art and engineering. And after all, there are not a vast number of sculptors who can use engineering in this particuliar way.

"There is a strange relationship between commissioned art and other art projects. I found when I was teaching that there was almost a golden rule: If you were teaching for one day a week, you could get back to your own work within a couple of hours. If you taught two days a week, you could be pretty certain that the work you did the day after would be absolute rubbish. If you did three days' teaching you would be in deep trouble; it would be very difficult getting back your own work. When I'm doing the RCI pieces

***The great Sand Clock for* Sovereign of the Seas**
"It was a wonderful clock to build," says Ashworth. "It has 16 glass bells, the sand is taken to the top by a bucket chain, pipes and different buckets. Then the sand is poured over the glass bells, making a very ghostly sound. This is reproduced outside the glass case through loudspeakers with exactly the right volume. It plays like an orchestra. It is driven by compressed air and controlled by two computers. And it's all suspended against movements and vibrations. Part of the clock was built onboard. "At any time, there were about 60 people watching me. It was sometimes a little tiresome. On the last trip one guy asked the obligatory question: 'How is it driven – is it perpetual motion?' 'No. It's driven by compressed air'. 'Where do you get that from?' I couldn't resist the little devil inside me who said: 'We get it from Miami. If you look outside you can see the hose as a red line in the sea. We follow exactly the same course back and pull it up again.' And off they went to see this mysterious thing. I performed a miracle. It took a very long time, but the clock is still working."

I just go totally into it, and I'm very singleminded. It's one of my problems, but also one of my gifts."

John Ashworth's background as an engineer reveals itself clearly in the large Pool Deck sculpture on *Grandeur of the Seas*: "I was asked if I could do a sculpture about propellers. It was a great chance to do a nice big sculpture. I like working big. A ship's propeller is actually an exquisite object. There are various different kinds of ships' propellers, but aesthetically they are all wonderful things, which is why you find them in harbors at the end of piers. Part of your mind says: 'If you want a sculpture about a propeller, just get a propeller, they are so wonderful.' What you really have to do here is something like shopping. If I want some dishwashing liquid and some potatoes, I go to a supermarket and pick up the stuff and go home. But many people would look around and pick up all sorts of things – when presented with a problem like 'do something with a propeller', I go to every source I can think of that has anything to do with propellers.

"You go around with an open mind. What I did discover is that they do these wonderful tests to find out how propellers behave. You see, there's a problem with propellers; on one side there is a vacuum, and on the other side there is high pressure. On the side of the vacuum the water is almost boiling, and that causes an enormous amount of pitching and erosion. When they design propellers, they do tests to really minimize that. And you are left with all these wonderful spiral forms that get compressed and then open out. That is what that sculpture stems from; looking at all those tests. I got photographs of them in the National Maritime Museum.

"The Triglobal for the *Vision* library came about because I've always been fascinated by things moving very close to each other. When I was a child I had to go on trains quite a lot. It was such a thrill when a train came the other way and you realized that the trains were just inches apart. Initially when I first set up, I had a little bronze foundry. I can actually cast bronze and other stuff. I did a small version; in this little bronze piece I tried to push myself on a particular feature. Not only does that piece have these sections which move very slowly in opposite directions, but also at different speeds. One of the things I tried to find out was how thin I could cast the bronze. It was originally a little trial piece and I worked it up to the final piece that is on the ship."

For *Voyager of the Seas*, John Ashworth has made the sculptures Pi, Golden Rectangle, Pyramid and Sirius. "The peculiarity of working with ships is having to work with themes. To me that's quite unusual. *Voyager of the Seas* had themes like the Greek and Roman Empires and Ancient Egyptians. I thought that "Empires" were an odd sort of choice for an artistic endeavor.

"It can sometimes be difficult to work to a specific theme. It's easier if they ask you to make a sculpture for a specific site than if they ask you to make one about the British people. You have to think in a particular sort of way, but it's good for the mind – good exercise," concludes John Ashworth. ■

CV

John Ashworth, b. 1942, British.
After Manchester College of Art and Design and Royal College of Art (1971-74), Ashworth taught at the Central School of Art, London; the Royal Academy of Art, London; the Bristol College of Art; the Portsmouth College of Art; and the Hornesy College of Art.
He was elected Associate of the Royal Society of British Sculptors in 1997.
Awards: Arts Council of Great Britain, Award (1974), Major Award (1978).

Shows:
Since 1970, he has had more than 20 solo shows and group exhibitions in distinguished galleries in London and the UK.

Public Collections:
Arts Council of Great Britain,
City of Nottingham Arts Department,
Leicestershire Education Authority,
Manchester Metropolitan University.

Private Collections:
Dr. Carl Nelson, Massachusetts, USA.
Hans and Dot Bøhler, Gjettum, Norway.
Mr. and Mrs. R. Noble, London, UK.
Kenneth Draper, Minorca, Spain.
William Bailey, Manchester, UK.
Unilever, London, UK.
5 cruise ships in the fleet of Royal Caribbean Cruise Line, Miami, USA.

Since 1970, John Ashworth has executed 16 commissions for churches and cruise ships.

This interview with John Ashworth took place in the artist's studio in Old St. Patrick's School in London.

Marc Berlet

"I have always been a sculptor," begins Marc Berlet. "During the war my father was in a German prison and we were living on a farm where I spent most of my time herding cows from pasture to pasture. The only thing I had to do all day long was to carve with a knife. That's how it started. Then I went to the Ecole des Beaux-Arts in Paris. Since then I have been a sculptor for 45 years. It's in me. Making money has never been a consideration.

"When I was young in Paris, I met famous people: Miró, Giacometti, Samuel Beckett; Riopelle and Joan Mitchell who became my friends. Jean Paul Riopelle was the one that taught me all about the great cars, the Duesenberg, the Bugatti. He's still alive and lives on an island off the coast of Canada. He was a brilliant painter. My friendship with Riopelle put me in touch with some incredible people, writers and painters mostly. It was an amazing time and I was just a kid, but everybody loved my work.

"It was not overwhelming. I felt I was part of the group. They accepted me as their peer. We had fun. Life is not only about fame and talent, it's about relationships and how you deal with each other. At my age, being cocky and very young, I took their friendship and acceptance for granted. They made me feel as good as they were and I loved them. People like that don't only influence your work, they influence your life. Just by their presence.

"You realized that they had seen something that you had not seen yet. It was enough to be close to them. Giacometti took the time to listen to and encourage a 19-year-old, to give advice. These things don't happen today. There's no time. Too much Internet with communication between one TV screen and another, e-mail and all that bullshit. There's no intimacy so that people can really

"The painted metal and wood sculptures by Marc Berlet display not only unusual technical competence, but also what is far rarer and more admirable: a forceful capacity for creating aesthetic pleasure ... Berlet is also at ease and fluently conversant with the artistic language of the 20th century ... I salute his style, his resolve, his humor, his versatility, his skill and his achievement – in a word, his art."

– James Lord (Art historian)

Marc Berlet in his Miami Studio. (Photo: Rod Dickinson)

love each other or spit in each other's faces.

"I happened to be part of that deep human contact when I was very young. It transformed my life. It also transformed my way of thinking. The way I look at things, the way I look at money, at fame. There was no glamour, it was all about works of art. Glamour is for movie actors. Today's painters and sculptors don't understand that. I'm not dissatisfied, I just feel that I missed the boat being so young, in many ways. The world was wide open for me, but I was more interested in life and sex. Mind you, that is not a bad thing at 19. It gave me a lot more pleasure than a fat bank account.

"In 1969, I came to the US with James Baldwin. We spent the whole summer in Provincetown. I started to work as a studio helper for a great American painter, Mark Rothko, stretching canvases and all that. I managed to get a studio that summer and sculpted, and Walter Chrysler, the son of the automobile family, bought seven of my pieces. He had just opened a museum and offered me a show. He combined my sculpture with Auguste Rodin's. The show was called 'Rodin and Marc Berlet'. It was a tremendous success, an unbelievable time in my life.

"As you see, this is my world and it's a great place to work. I'm at ease here. I work when I feel like it. I can work 20 hours a day for six months. Then I will take a break. I'm not a workaholic. I have been working now for the past three months, but not because I have to. I can clean the tools, build a roof, do some odd jobs around the house, then suddenly one morning I wake up, go to work and don't stop. I don't work every single day, however. That would be too much like a job. I like having the freedom to decide when I want to work. I look at it, I prepare it, I build up. I arrange things so that they will suit my aesthetical sense. Right now I just look at it – like a tease.

"There are lots of works in my studio. I have 450 pieces of sculpture in here and about 500 drawings. They are in crates all over the place. I've got works everywhere in the world: Europe, South America, different parts of the United States. Sometimes I feel I can't keep track of them. So now I'm not sending anything to anybody. I'm just keeping the whole lot here: If you want it, you have to come get it. I'm going to leave a legacy of a lot of work because I intend to live another 120 years. I have a lot of energy and I work very hard.

"For the *Rhapsody of the Seas*, I made two pieces, musical instruments in painted metal, and some small sculptures by the elevators. For *Grandeur*, I made two sculptures for the Main Theater entrance. They were commissioned by Gro Nesjar of London Contemporary Art. I believe I did something that was not overly pretentious. I kept my own personality and was given great freedom in my work for this ship. The theme for *Rhapsody* was musical, so I stuck to my instruments. I made a harp and a cello. I blew the original harp, destroying it by using too much heat on it four days before it had to be delivered. So I went to the workshop, where I worked like a maniac with a helper, and we made a new one in 24 hours.

"I no longer work with pieces like the huge instruments on my own. I don't want to do it. It's too much hard work for one person alone. Now I'm casting in aerospace aluminum. This is my new avenue. I've been involved with bulls and animals for too long.

"I did the best I could for the ships. It was good work, not conventional. Just honest hard work. I believe I did a good job. Let's face it, the art is a great complement to these ships. People come on board because they want to have fun, eat good meals, play at the casino, or swim in the pool. The art enhances their environment." ■

This interview with Marc Berlet took place in the artist's home in Miami, Florida.

CV

Marc Berlet was born in France in 1938. Educated at Ecole des Beaux Arts in Paris, Lehigh University, Bethlehem PA USA. Solo exhibitions in important galleries in USA, Argentina, France, Belgium, Italy. Participated in distinguished group exhibitions in the USA and Europe. Marc Berlet is represented in permanent collections:
Musee d'Art Moderne, Paris, France.
Musee des Beaux Arts, Rennes, France.
Chrysler Museum, Norfolk, VA, USA.
Collection of President Perez-Balladares, Panama.
Monumental works/commissions: Skylake Professional Building, Miami, FL, USA.
Village Market, Boca Raton, FL, USA.
Rhapsody of the Seas and *Vision of the Seas*, RCI, Miami, FL, USA.

Jacques Berten

A French textile engineer migrated to the USA. Worked as a waiter. Got fired. Now travels the USA, buying the finest maritime antiques and artifacts through his own personal channels. Some of his finest pieces can be seen onboard the RCI ships.

Jacques Berten's cooperation with RCI started when Gro Nesjar from London Contemporary Art came into his shop "Ettamogah Shipwreck" in Fort Lauderdale and wanted some model ships. The shop is named after a memorable Australian pub.

"I don't like partnerships," says Jacques Berten. "I don't want to share. It took me so long to build what I have. I was a textile engineer, but now I'm in antiques and other business. And I love it. When I met my wife I said I'm going to do what I want. 'OK, I will go for that,' she said.

"When I met Gro Nesjar for the first time, she approached me in perfect French. I didn't want to share my secrets with her but I thought 'Why not?' It took me one second.

"I read books to find places that were under maritime influence in the past. I just go with some introductions, a head full of knowledge and my good walking shoes. And little by little, very methodically, I 'clean out' the places I go to. I talk to a lot of people, and they refer me to somebody else who refers me further on. After all, it's just a question of patience and dollars. Last year I drove 85,000 miles and flew 45,000 miles; that's 130,000 miles or 208,000 kilometers – Eh, oui, that's a lot, but it was fun and very interesting."

Berten buys pieces that have historical value and that could easily fit into a maritime museum. "I buy nothing for decoration of restaurants, and I never buy replicas. I am a maritime dealer, not a nautical dealer. That's why it's so difficult, and that's why you need a head full of knowledge. One small mistake can cost a lot of money, and you have to pay for that experience. There's no substitute for learning from your mistakes.

"The maritime business is a circle, a sort of club where everybody knows everybody and everything.

> *"When it's too good to be true – pass. Something is wrong somewhere."*
>
> *Jacques Berten*

So you just have to break the circle and go where nobody else goes. Success depends on luck, helpful people, a good alarm clock to wake you up at 3:30 a.m. to be at the market at 5 a.m., the nose of a hunting dog, and split second timing to say YES, because if you say 'let me think', it's gone. Normally I don't know who I'm buying for and what price I can take, and that can be a problem.

"When I'm digging through a store, I look thoroughly. Everywhere. I take my time. I look around and I often find strange things. Like the coconuts carved by the British sailors 300 years ago. When they didn't have ivory, which they didn't have on the routes to the South Sea and the Caribbean, they carved coconuts. It's unbelievable what they could do. Nobody knew about them. Now they are fetching high prices."

For *Radiance of the Seas*, Berten dug up an impressive old black cannon: "A Californian friend who is a diver and a collector,

Jacques is finding the finest maritime antiques for the RCI fleet. (Photo: Rod Dickinson)

discovered the wreck of a Spanish galleon in the Bahamas. She went down in 1520, loaded with silver, gold bullion, precious stones – and the cannon. I always told him: 'If you want to sell it, I want to buy.' It's an exceptional piece. One day he rang: 'Do you still want to buy the cannon?' I did."

When *Rhapsody* was built, a very old model ship was crushed by an unfortunate cleaner who dropped a heavy piece of glass on top of it. It was worth USD 25,000 and was bought from Berten. “They called me from London and said they needed a first-class model ship for *Rhapsody*. I had five days to deliver,” Jacques Berten relates.

After a few phone calls, he found a man in Newport, RI who had been treasuring this model ship in his dining room for 25 years, but now he was short of money. Berten flew from Miami to Boston the same day, while a friend was preparing the wooden cradle. He rented a truck, drove to Newport, bought the model and loaded it on the truck. Then he went to Boston’s Logan Airport, and slept in the truck in front of North West Freight to be ready at 5 a.m. to put the model on the first plane so it could be delivered on time. “That shows the power of being in the business. You don’t have the time to think, you just have to act. That day I was tired, but very happy,” recounts Berten.

The broken model was later restored in London and now sails the Sevens Seas onboard *Rhapsody* as was originally intended.

Berten doesn’t keep a shop full of antiques anymore. “It’s just trouble and expensive storage. I have my own customers who know me. If one of them calls for something, I start to look around. Last June I had three customers collecting coconuts, so I went out to look for some. I found one very beautiful one. The problem is that I just had to keep it. I now have seven myself.

“About 80 percent of the things you find in the market are fake. What you see on the London market of sextants, octants – a pocket sextant Stanley, they sell for 100 pounds. When you look at the discs they are pale yellow, pearl green and pearl pink. The problem is that you can’t look at the sun in pearl yellow or pearl pink. You need something that is dark. If you buy a fake – it’s a fake. It may be a good one, but it’s still a fake. But they are selling fakes for real. I said to this guy: ‘You are selling fakes.’ He looked at me and said ‘No problem, you don’t have to buy. If you can’t see the difference between a fake and the real thing that means you are stupid.’

“That’s why you need to know exactly what you are looking for, where it goes, etc. I have a golden rule: When it’s too good to be true – pass. Something is wrong somewhere.

“Last year I stopped by Vermont. You have to go places where not everybody goes. If you’re looking for something from the sea, go to the mountains. Vermont is not far from the sea, but it has no shore. In six days I drove 1,800 miles. I scanned places, knocked at doors. And in six days I had eleven items. Enough to organize a lot of decorations on some ships – and even some pieces for other customers.

“When you find a genuine old model ship, you can’t say you need to think about it. Otherwise, when you come back, it’s sold. Every time I find a model, I go for it! People are fighting for the good models and prices are high. But first you have to find them, and that’s not so easy. One day they called me and said they needed four model ships for the *Voyager*. Same day delivery. I had just one that I owned myself – ‘The Dundee’. Took the truck and drove down to Miami. Now it’s cruising the Caribbean. To find these models you have to be at the right place at the right time. Sometimes a museum needs money. This is America, not Europe – European museums don’t sell.

“If you know the right people at the right time you can get into the private auctions that are held for a very limited circle of people. They buy it for you, they get a commission and you get your model.”

The model of the submarine Nautilus on board the *Vision of the Seas* is actually the model used by Disney for the movie about Captain Nemo. Says Berten: “Luck was on my side. I had one chance in a million to find the *Nautilus*. But LCA wanted one. I was looking wherever I went. Sometimes you find things where you don’t expect them. Suddenly, right out of the blue, this guy pulled a model of the *Nautilus* out of his car! I asked if it was real. He said ‘Yes’. It had come from Atlanta. He was working with Disney. I said ‘I want it. How much?’ ‘Any price?’ ‘No limit’. We negotiated. I didn’t even ask for the best price he could give me. I always say ‘there is a God for the drunks and the antique dealers.’ For that one, I was in the right place at the right time. It was my lucky day. Period.” ■

This interview was conducted in Jacques Berten’s home in Fort Lauderdale, Florida.

Helaine Blumenfeld

At work with a "Mayan figure" for Vision of the Seas.

Helaine Blumenfeld is an artist who is continually reinventing herself in the search for a vocabulary of form, writes Nicola Upson in "Mythologies: The Sculpture of Helaine Blumenfeld". Sculpture for her is never concerned simply with observation or narrative, but with experience, with a knowledge which is far from obvious but which advances us in our understanding of who we are and how we fit into the world around us. Blumenfeld's work communicates on a number of different levels, visual and imaginative, tactile and emotional, but underlying everything is an insistence on growth and development. For both the artist and the viewer, this sculpture represents a journey of revelation and discovery.

"Pietrasanta is really the home of sculpture as a profession," Helaine Blumenfeld says.

> *"The eye you are working with when you are really creating – it is not an eye that really sees – it's intuitive."*
>
> *Helaine Blumenfeld*

"It combines an ethos of passion, enormous vitality, a shared sense of pride in workmanship and an acknowledgement among sculptors working here that sculpture is their number one commitment. Pietrasanta is the center for almost all the resources that support my work; marble, skilled artisans, specialized tools for working and superb, as well as competitively priced bronze foundries.

"But there is another very interesting thing: being an artist you end up being an egomaniac, whether you mean it or not – you have to. In normal life you have to repress that, because people can't take it. But here, everybody is like that. So you don't have to make any excuses - and that's very helpful. You feel liberated from the pressures of general society. When I'm working, no one expects to see me for lunch. I don't have to cook for anybody. I don't have to be nice, and people understand that."

"I have been working here for more than 25 years. It is only in the last five, however, that I have really found the two sides of my commitment to sculpture coming together. For many years I have had the opportunity, through numerous commissions – to create large works in both stone and bronze. I have always distinguished between my "public work" which seemed to refer back to earlier simpler forms, and my "experimental work" which continuously ext-ended boundaries and encouraged me to take risks.

"Since I have been working with RCI, this distinction is no longer necessary because all of the sculptures they have commissioned have come from my "experimental" models. These have been sculptures that are on the edge of where I am, creatively speaking. To be able to take these pieces further, to enlarge them and to try to "perfect" them, has been a dream realized. Seeing these works on the enormous ships, where so many people can admire and enjoy them, has been not only rewarding but also inspiring.

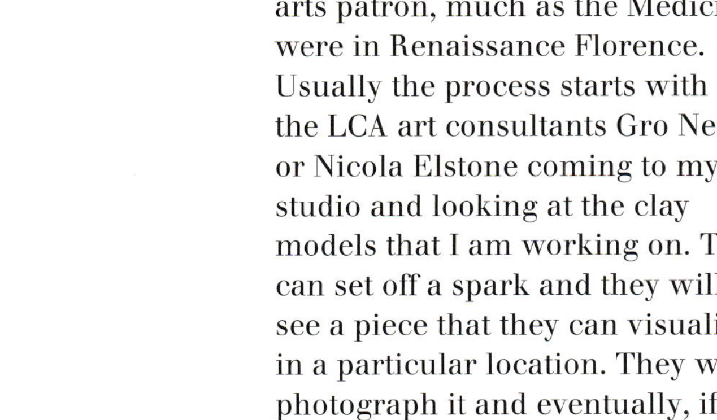

"RCI has become a modern arts patron, much as the Medicis were in Renaissance Florence. Usually the process starts with the LCA art consultants Gro Nesjar or Nicola Elstone coming to my studio and looking at the clay models that I am working on. This can set off a spark and they will see a piece that they can visualize in a particular location. They will photograph it and eventually, if it gains approval from RCI, I will be asked to create the work on a particular scale for a specific space. On other occasions, I will be asked to submit an idea for a project and specifically, to create new works. This is tremendously exciting. For example, the first sculptures I did for *Grandeur of the Seas* resulted from being asked to think about doing standing "Moorish" inspired figures. Later, for *Enchantment of the Seas*, I created wall reliefs on Indian themes, and for *Vision of the Seas* I did a series of "Mayan" sculptures as well as some amazing marble wall reliefs for the central stair case.

"In creating sculptures for these incredible floatng cities, many people are involved: RCI, LCA, the architects, designers, the craftsmen at Studio Sem, and the Fonderia Mariani where my bronze works are cast.

"The sculpture I did for the Champagne Bar on *Voyager of the Seas* is another example (See page 238) of creating works that stretch my creative boundaries.

"This is one of the most advanced and complex pieces I have ever created. Most of the major companies that have commissioned my work in the past would never have chosen such a daring, dramatic work. Its complexity and power would have worried them. LCA people saw the model of it in my studio and immediately recognized that it would fit in the Champagne Bar. They then

Helaine Blumenfeld builds full-scale models of niches to get proportions right.

"Moorish figures" for Grandeur of the Seas.

"Angel" for Voyager of the Seas *being made at Studio Sem.*

showed it to the architect, Njål Eide, who liked it, saw its potential and LCA presented it to the Steering Committee at RCI, where it was approved. So this process speaks for the enlightenment of the consultants, the architects, and – above all, the client," says Blumenfeld, adding that this is "a rare and wonderful position for the artist. At every level there must be a high degree of cooperation; the important thing is for me to be very clear about where I'm going. I put a lot of energy and effort into the initial model. I often try to see the space – visit the ship – so that I can plan the scale of work intelligently. That's very helpful. When this has not been possible, I have counted on LCA to act as my eyes – filling me in on the surroundings for the given sculpture – and of course studying the plans as well. Working to a specific site imposes another level of responsibility. The sculpture must not only succeed in "absolute" terms, it must also really work well in its designated location."

Blumenfeld says that in the five years she has been creating sculpture for RCI, she has done some of the most important pieces of her career. "And that is not only because my best works have been selected by them, but working to a deadline has in itself been instrumental. I disovered that I could work in a new way – more rapidly and with more certainty. I have always worked quickly in clay, but I discovered that I could achieve some of the same spontaneity when working marble. Deadline also seemed to encourage my inspiration to come faster and my nagging doubts to disappear. It is important enough to complete a major work in time, but it is also vital to keep up the momentum of creativity."

The hanging sculptures for *Explorer of the Seas* are the result of a new development. Blumenfeld says: – LCA's Gro Nesjar saw a sculpture in my studio and suggested it would be very good for the curved wall in the Centrum of the *Explorer*. When Njål Eide saw it, he felt it should be a free hanging sculpture in that area rather than a relief. I was reluctant about this, telling him that I had never actually done free-hanging.

"The piece in question would not be appropriate as I had designed it as a wall relief. Njål advised me to try developing a few new models that could be suspended. He was extremely positive and convinced me to put aside my resistance and experiment. And because of his encouragement, that's what I did. I began to really get excited about the challenge, about developing a new aesthetic. I loved working in a totally new way. I began to discover that I could still do work that was clearly "Blumenfeld" but was not fixed to a base; that was modelled in paper or sheet metal instead of clay and stone. The result was two atrium sculptures, each ten metres high!

"But if I don't like it – I can't take it away. When I have signed the contract, I'm committed – this is going to happen. I have never taken any job about which I was so excited and so worried. I was quite worried about the Indian wall reliefs and I was worried about getting the Mayan figures just right, but nothing like these sculptures. They were like three-story buildings.

"I went into completely unknown territory with these hanging sculptures. I had never done anything like them. The risk was about continuity versus change: in order to move on you need the continuity, but you also have to be willing to take the risks of change if you are to grow. All too many artists, when they succeed, stop experimenting, stop growing and simply continue on the path that brought them that initial applause.

"A finished piece may work for everyone else, but first of all, it has to work for me. People think I am a calm and confident person. I am confident, but I don't think any artist can be calm. It was fascinating for me that the further I went into the process of fabricating the atrium sculptures with an engineering firm, the more assured I became and the less apprehensive.

I believe you have to have two eyes: The eye you are working with when you are really creating – it is not an eye that really sees – it's intuitive. And then you have your critical eye. But if you open that critical eye too soon, you'll destroy the work which isn't fully born; you take away its power; it becomes contrived and loses its magic. You have to get to a certain stage, and then look at what you have done – establish a certain distance, a new perspective. If that distance comes to soon it's dangerous. We then interfere with the development of our own language if we try to control it before the right moment. We're in a kind of twilight zone between rational and emotional, between control and freedom, and it's in that area that the artist's greatest work can be realized.

I think art is an effort to go into the subconscious. It is the artist who finds the language which is extraordinary enough to express the magic of the subliminal, whether through sculpture, music or poetry. And I think that when an artist succeeds, the response is amazing. That's what I have been trying to achieve." ■

This interview took place in Helaine Blumenfeld's studio in Pietrasanta, Italy.

CV:

Helaine Blumenfeld's life is divided between Italy, where she works, England where she now lives, and the United States where she was born.

In 1964 she received her PhD in philosophy from Columbia University, New York.
In 1965 she studied sculpture with Ossip Zadkine in Paris and had her first solo show of polished bronzes in Palais Palfy, Vienna.

From her first major show in 1966, Helaine Blumenfeld captured the attention and respect of international critics and collectors alike. Her sculpture has been exhibited both solo and with renowned sculptors like Henry Moore and Brancusi. She has exhibited her works in USA, UK, Italy, France and Norway, and her works are incorporated in important Public and Private Collections throughout the US and Europe.
She was elected as Member of Royal Society of Sculptors in 1993.

Luchio Brieva

"My cooperation with RCI started like a well-timed coincidence, like many things in my life – from an artisan's point of view. I consider myself an artisan. I enjoy that label better than any other," remarks Luchio Brieva, an intense native Colombian. "I was an architect at one point, but I recovered from that, and I became interested in philosophy and religion. I spent a few years with that; it became a sort of marriage that suited me perfectly. I started making my particular pieces in a beautiful little garage in London. It used to be a stable in Victorian times.

"After that I had my studio in a chocolate factory, but I still kept the lovely feeling of horses. I had the park next to me. I had a good business. I used to sell a lot without any advertising. People used to come by and buy my little pieces. They were all based on symbolism, geometry and that kind of thing. Then I was on my own, but I had this friend, a former fellow student of architecture, Jason Moul. He wanted to do things together. He was working for Mike Newby, the glass artist. And on one of his trips to a ship to install works for Mike Newby, he showed some of my work to Nicola of London Contemporary Art.

"A few weeks later she called and said 'look, give us a proposal'. A few days before the presentation someone had broken into my studio and taken everything. All my tools, everything. Three days in a row they broke in. Anyway, LCA liked what we had made and

Voyager of the Seas was built at Kværner Masa Yard, Turku, Finland. From left Joan Blackman, LCA, Artist Luchio Brieva, Anne Cecilie Thidemansen, LCA and Art Installation Supervisor, Chris Gottelier.

"Art is about basic communication. It's about my life. I peel off all the things I don't need."

– Luchio Brieva

it eventually became copper, shell and glass on *Grandeur of the Seas* in the Windjammer Café. Jason and I did a few works for RCI cruise ships together. Now I am on my own again, and I do some pieces that I sell, but I also work for LCA and RCI. I loved working with the ships right from the beginning. Also from an engineering point of view. Coming to the yards, seeing these huge man-made vessels, it was wonderful. We worked very hard all day, and at night there was this sense of friendship.

"These ships are a world apart. Especially when they are built. It's hard to describe it, how they put the huge pieces of metal together, the beautiful shapes. It's a piece of art in itself. The first time I saw these little guys welding this big ship, and realized that was how it was put together, through teamwork, I loved it.

"I like to work with commissioned art. Forget about the differences. Forget the label 'artist'. I love working with artisans. In my other pieces, I mean those I get commissioned to do for private individuals, I am completely closed to this modern concept of art. I don't like that sort of position where everything is divided and the artist is seen as a modern-day Christ. Some people use fashion a lot, artists use art, but they sometimes live in a little world that I don't understand. One of the joys of my work is meeting people who actually know more than I do about putting things together, who know about materials and tools. That's my reward. They are people with big hearts.

"The commissioned art completes my work. One day I go to

the studio and I get inspiration to start working on a piece I know is going to be sold. It's very serious. I believe that you always have to play the whole field. On the one hand, I have this quest for understanding and wisdom and my relationship with God.

"On the other hand is the work level, where all this fits in. To me, the commissioned pieces are always fun, they always put a smile on my face. I need to make both gallery art and commissions. They interrelate, and you learn from it. New insights hit you when you don't expect them. Ultimately, I have a very romantic relationship with all these works for ships. And I love it.

"I did a couple of things for the architect Njål Eide, but I mostly talk to the LCA people about the frames, the shape of the rooms, the colors. They talk to RCI and the architects.

"I know the mechanics of putting up a piece, so I know that you have to leave enough room in every department to play with. And that's fine. We have to respect that. From my position, this is like working for friends. I deal with them all the time. Even if I don't have any work for them, we always keep in touch. With LCA I became part of a family, and I love them. If I didn't, I wouldn't work with them.

"My last commission was for *Voyager of the Seas*. It was not difficult, and I had a bit of room to play with. But I was tired after a lot of partying in Barcelona. However, the yard was fantastic. The fascinating part is the efficiency. You have a problem. They solve it. Day or night. It's a whole adventure. And the LCA people treat you fairly. If they didn't, it wouldn't work. The whole thing would come tumbling down.

"I'm in a special position. If I did not want to work, I really would not have to. Something I did in the past paid off well so I am comfortable. The key is that I work because I love these people.

"My main concern is that I like what I'm doing. There is a very dangerous phase before we even get to the ship. It's when we're making a piece in the studio. My guys, myself, all of us; we all get so involved with the piece. For me, this is the main part. After me, the next group is the people I'm dealing with – Gro, Joan and Anne of the LCA family, and that includes the engineer and the architect.

"What members of the public think is not all that important. Naturally, you think about people, and how they perceive it, but not first and foremost.

"My work is always about relationships. If someone says 'we need this' for a theme, I just humbly do it. I don't question it. Whatever money they pay me, I will not remember in five or ten years. But the nights during the installation are unforgettable. That is my true reward - just being with all these people. It's a way of life. In the beginning, I said to my friend Jason that I would not make too much of this work, but then I realized how much fun it was going to be. Going to one of these ships, meeting everyone, going through all the different departments – it's fascinating, like a childhood dream come true. My favorite pieces, and the ones that have been most challenging, are probably the figures high up on the wall above the Sports Bar in the Royal Promenade on *Voyager of the Seas*. I've never done anything like them before, so I worked like hell. They were all done by hand, every single piece was cut and molded; no machines involved." ■

"Baseball Player". Royal Promenade, Voyager of the Seas.

This interview was taped in London.

Laurence Broderick

"I put notices up in my exhibitions: 'Please touch the sculptures'. I want people to experience the shapes and forms that I have enjoyed myself in making that sculpture."

– Laurence Broderick

Predominantly a stone carver, Laurence Broderick has devoted his art to capturing the vitality of wildlife and the grace of the human form. He aims to combine abstraction and realism using subtle forms and curves to create a sense of movement, simplicity and timeless beauty.

"LCA approached me for a mermaid for one of the ships. I was busy organizing my annual Skye exhibition and wasn't quick enough. So after a week with me getting a place to do it and getting materials organized, they said: 'Forget it – we found somebody in New York.' So we lost that one and didn't hear anything for some time. Until suddenly a Swedish architect, Lars Iwdal of Arkitektbyrån, liked my 'Goddess Athena'. He had seen it in one of my catalogs and wanted it for the *Grandeur of the Seas.*

"I certainly enjoyed working with the three ships in the *Vision Class*: *Enchantment, Grandeur* and *Vision of the Seas.* RCI have succeeded with their concept. When I first worked with RCI, I thought that "my" architect Lars Iwdal was responsible for the whole ship. Then I learned that he was doing about half a deck! And how many architects do you need to design a ship? Wherever you went, there was this richness about everything. Our architect was responsible for the Solarium deck. He put 'steam' into his deck. So it seems to me that the 'competition' between different architects is a good idea. And the art makes the character of the ship.

"My stone carvings are different from my bronzes; a solid thing with its own form. The turtle comes from the West coast of Scotland. As soon as the commission came through for the Solarium on the *Vision of the Seas*, my wife Ingrid and I looked around to see if we had any turtle of that particular size. LCA didn't actually say what color stone they wanted.

"I carved one yellow, and they said 'Oh no, we wanted it red'. And we wanted two tortoises, but as you have carved the turtle already...' I carved a red one. Then we realized we hadn't enough stone to carve two tortoises. We drove 600 miles to a beach in the North. You can't go to a particular quarry; you don't go to a shop and buy this kind of stone. We went to the beach on a Sunday morning when everybody was at church and collected about a ton. We went for the biggest pieces first, when we were fresh and energetic. As we got tired, the stones got smaller.

"The sight of Ingrid and me going up to Scotland in a red van to get a piece of stone from the beach just to go onboard a ship is ridiculous to think about. But we enjoyed it and made a holiday out of it. And it brought more stone to our collection in the studio, so I can carve more turtles.

"I have turtles in the Mayan Solarium – a big turtle and a big tortoise and two figures on the bar. They are females actually. The make-up of the stone is so strong that you can't see the design. It disguises it, and it's not until you run your hand over the piece that you realize you are stroking her breasts.

"This point also applies to the elephant for the *Enchantment of the Seas*: I want people to touch my sculptures. I put notices up in my exhibitions: 'Please touch the sculptures'. I want people to experience the shapes and forms that I have enjoyed myself in making the sculptures. It is not like a painting on a wall. Whereas a picture takes you into a scene or into a color and a combination of ideas, a sculpture you have to live with. It becomes a part of your life; it's an object like a chair or a table. What I'm trying to do is to reeducate people into seeing these objects and enjoying them. Sculpture really is a combination of hard forms, soft forms, light, shade and color.

"I was asked: 'Stone or bronze for the Solarium? Definitely stone'. If you use bronze on the solarium deck, you could fry an egg on it. They used to slide back the big roof in the Caribbean, and the heat is so intense, you wouldn't be able to touch something cast in bronze.

"The Solarium where it was to be installed had an Indian theme, so it was to be an Indian elephant calf, not higher than 100 cm, small enough for children to climb on. I know that Henry Moore actually liked children to play with his sculptures. So why shouldn't I? If the forms are smooth enough it works very well.

Elephant for Enchantment's Solarium.

CV

Laurence Broderick, b. 1935, British.
He studied painting, illustration and sculpture at the Regent Street Polytechnic and Hammersmith School of Art. He began his artistic career as an historical and educational illustrator and painter. After a period of teaching, he became a full time sculptor in 1981. His studio and Art Gallery is in Cambridgeshire.
Broderick has shown his work in successful one-man shows throughout the UK and abroad as well as group shows with the Royal Academy, Royal Scottish Academy, Royal Society of British Artists, Contemporary Portrait Society, Society of Wildlife Artists and the Royal West of English Academy. Broderick is a regular contributor to Christie's Wildlife Art Auction and was awarded associate membership of the Royal Society of British Sculptors in 1991.

Laurence Broderick's work can be found in private and public collections worldwide. Commissions have included a portrait to celebrate the 80th birthday of conductor June Gordon, Marchioness of Aberdeen and Temair, CBE. The bronze head, also including Lady Aberdeen's hands and baton, was presented by His Royal Highness Prince Edward.

"The design was modelled in clay, 10 cm high – a compact shape. It had a kneeling leg for easy foothold for young climbers and the trunk as a handhold to climb easily onto the calf's back. As it had to be high-density and strong to avoid easy scratching, I decided on Indian green marble, 'verde kay'. The next stage was to enlarge the small maquette into a working model, half size, i.e. 50 cm, in plaster and the work of carving could begin.

"The stone proved to be extremely hard, almost like granite. Chisels broke in quick succession. Diamond saws and diamond grinding proved more successful. Diamond polishing discs and a final waxing brought out a wonderful rich green color. However, the completed elephant proved to be too heavy for the ninth deck of the vessel, and so the painful decision of coring it out had to be taken, which reduced the weight by a quarter of a ton to one and a quarter tons.

"I'm most happy with the elephant for *Enchantment* because I was allowed to do what I wanted. 'The Goddess Athena' I had designed already some time ago. The architect said 'I want it enlarged, white and in stone'. So I did it like that. The elephant came from nothing." ■

"Self Portrait". Clay.

This interview with Laurence Broderick took place in his studio in Cambridgeshire, UK.

Fredrik Brodersen Lyngør Seilmakerverksted, Norway

The maritime rigging works in the Schooner Bar of the RCI ships were made by sailmaker Fredrik Brodersen in the beautiful town of Lyngør, which is built on four islets facing the open sea some 250 kilometers (155 miles) southwest of Oslo, Norway. The old sail loft is teeming with activity, and the youngest apprentice, Marius, is more than happy to serve three years of apprenticeship.

The sail loft towers over the little white houses of Lyngør. So beautiful and well preserved is the small harbor town that it has been included on UNESCO's World Heritage List. This harbor has seen sailing ships and shipping since time immemorial. It is an environment deserving of historical preservation, but that doesn't mean that it's dead, despite the disappearance of the sailing industry with the advent of steamships. In Lyngør, the sailmaking tradition has seen a renaissance.

The 150 permanent residents of Lyngør are delighted to see light in the attic windows of the old herring house during the dark winter months. And they are happy that the business is not only based on the older citizens who soon will disappear, taking with them their knowledge and expertise forever. Lyngør Seilmakerverksted (Sailmaking Workshop) is about the only one in Scandinavia that still makes sails in the traditional way.

The picturesque sail loft was started by Brodersen in 1976 and strategically placed among the most powerful of Norwegian summer icons: little white wooden houses built practically in the surf, surrounded by white picket fences, islets and reefs. Brodersen trained in textiles and sewing and served his apprenticeship in another sail loft before he struck out on his own. The decision to set up shop in Lyngør was not difficult; there was a conveniently located and intact, one-hundred-year old building, previously used for herring processing, available.

The sail loft looks as it has been there since the beginning

of time, but it is in fact a foreign element in Lyngør. At the turn of the century, enterprising souls from western Norway wanted to start salting herring in Lyngør, but there were no buildings suitable for the job. Since building materials were expensive and labor practically free, they simply

brought a herring saltery from the west coast.

The building has now been modernized and equipped for the sailmaking business, but it also offers showers and laundry facilities for the pleasure boaters who come to Lyngør by the thousands each summer. These days it is mostly the sloping floor, designed to let water from the barrels of herring run off and out into the sea, which reveals the building's past.

Fredrik Brodersen splices rope for the RCI rigging and sews sails for museum ships himself. This is the real thing – no shortcuts, no cheating. Such an approach

"It's incredible what you can do with canvas."

– Fredrik Brodersen

is time-consuming and demands strong motivation.

"The collaboration with RCI began when I met the head architect for the RCI ships, Njål Eide, at a boat show. He was interested in the canvas and the smell of tar and what we were doing in the Sail Loft," says Brodersen.

"He asked if I could make a decoration for the Schooner Bar in the form of some sails, ropes, a rigging or some such thing. The very first piece was a very simple installation on one of the pillars in a Schooner Bar.

"Over the years, we have made many pieces. We have made works for all of the ships – plus some refurbishments. We were in Miami participating in the re-outfitting of the Song of America. That was when the curtains were further developed with many small spars and sails between the window openings. Since the mid-1980's, we have completed a new project for a new cruise ship every year," says Brodersen.

"We have made some frames stretched with canvas for the *Voyager of the Seas* – a combination of sails and a hull with a keel and the whole bit. It's a fabulous thing which is mounted like a sail over the bar.

"For another ship we made many small gaff sails which function as 'curtains' between the windows, in mahogany and brass and canvas. It's very effective – it's incredible what you can do with canvas.

"We haven't gotten to the point where there are plaques on the pieces of art telling what they are and who made them. So feedback is rare. But people who know us notice. We often put a label with 'Lyngør Seilmakerverksted' on the sails. And sometimes I get a postcard from people who have been on a cruise. I also get good feedback from the owners. They are satisfied and that makes us happy out here on the edge of the wide open sea," concludes sailmaker Fredrik Brodersen. ■

(Photos this page: Jon Lie)

David Buckland

London Contemporary Art first commissioned Buckland to produce three large art works for *Enchantment of the Seas*, each work based on a festival in Mysore, India, (see page 148).

His latest works are onboard the magnificent *Radiance of the Seas*, and *Brilliance of the Seas*.

"Usually during an exhibition of my work I get proposals for

"A stretched slice of time – that's photography to me."

– David Buckland

commissions, but I am asked to produce a piece of work similar to the work shown in the exhibition," says David Buckland. "But when LCA has commissioned the works for the ships I have made art for them – unique concepts – they went right to the edge of what I can possibly do. They are unique in their approach and inventiveness.

"The technology I am using now is right at the cutting edge, that is, right at the forefront of what is being discovered and developed, and still LCA wants to see what's possible beyond that. They never want to take a safe option.

"I was first introduced to LCA and RCI by the sculptor Helaine Blumenfeld. I have known and admired Helaine's work for many years, in fact, so much so, that I have done two books on her work. Initially, I showed Nicola Elstone of LCA a portfolio of my work and she asked me to work on a presentation based on the theme of festivals in India. My point of contact is always through the art consultants at LCA. It is they who sell and promote an idea. I think there was an initial resistance to the use of photography; is it really fine art? I still believe the possibilities for the "photographic image" are endless, constantly expanding and with the capability of unique expression.

"Oddly, during the past three decades, I believe the perception of what is possible with photography has actually gotten narrower. If you go back to the Victorian era, photography was a very physical media. The artists working then had to make their own plates, devise new ways of producing emulsions, develop new chemistry. They reinvented photography every day! And they ended up with something so physical that just by looking at it, you could envisage its process of creation. If anything, it was more akin to an oil painting. Viewing this early work, you are seduced by the depths and nature and quality of it. All the way through my career in fine art, it has been this potential physical quality of the photographic image that has excited me. I think LCA really picked up on that in my work when they commissioned the Indian project.

"The works for Radiance of the Seas *were demanding in terms of both visuals and technology, and were always at the cutting edge of development. Each level of the vessel has a theme based on a major design movement of the 20th century. For the forward stairs, I created huge 400 cm glass works, each of which is inspired by one of these major art/design movements. All the works are made on glass sheets floating away from the wall, and each of these sheets contains a photographically-generated image, sometimes carrying real information and sometimes just a color or a graphic design. Some of the glass works are set against painted canvases while others are backlit with the latest LED lighting."*

"I often combine the use of painting with the photographic image. A lot of this work has developed during my work as a theater designer, which has also enabled me to work on a huge scale. Huge photographs usually end up looking like posters or billboards. By combining a fragment of a photographic image with the pure physical quality of the painted color of red or yellow, you have a chance to step out into new visual territory and also be able to produce work on a large scale. New ideas are always difficult to get into the marketplace. Again, it is the courage of LCA's commissioning that helped me develop this work.

"For the artists, these commissions by RCI and LCA are wonderful opportunities for them to show their commissioned art works to a sizable audience. Probably more than 500,000 people will view these works aboard the five ships every year.

"As an artist you can make whatever you like, but unless people see it, in many ways it doesn't exist. It's like really good theater, you can put on the finest production of a first-rate play, but if only twenty people turn up to see it, you've failed. The nature of art doesn't change or diminish, it just means that the work is out among the audience to stimulate, entertain and be discussed.

"My darkroom is now all computers, and computers really make the most brilliant darkroom. I can change a little bit of color here, add a little energy there. I can remove or add whatever I wish, simplify the image or complicate it. It is much like a painter working with a canvas. You keep making it more energetic until it works. But the strangest thing about the computer is that you work with all this high-tech electronic information, but the print you end up with is so very physical. I have an Iris 3047 printer in my basement connected straight up to the computer. All this electronic information is converted into minute squirts of colored dye. You can literally print on anything: art paper, canvas, high gloss or even glass. It is very physical, almost full circle back to the early days of photography and the wonder and possibility of the photographic image."

For *Vision of the Seas*, David Buckland made two triptychs based on the Mayan culture in Mexico.

"Again, using the computer and the Iris 3047 printer, I had been experimenting with putting images onto glass. In a way, they were almost like stained glass free-standing sculptures. I showed the work to LCA and they asked if I could develop the idea, working it as a wall hanging. Although the work was eventually to be based on the Mayan Culture, it was necessary to try to establish how the glass could best be structured

Two "Mayan" triptycks from Vision of the Seas.

and lit. I worked with Mike Newby at Glassworks, a very inventive small company in London. The works were wall images on art paper bonded to aluminum, which would have three 10 mm glass sheets floated 4 cm in front of the images. The glass sheets would have a photographic image etched on the reverse and a deep etched line image on the front surface. Most important though, was to edge-light the glass with fiber optics that could be varied in intensity.

"To produce the imagery, I spent 10 days travelling the Yucatan Peninsula, photographing many of the Mayan ruins and collecting copies of drawings and photographs. These were digitized and the three layers of each triptych evolved. For example, on one panel the front deep-etched image is a line drawing of a pyramid, showing its secret interior whilst on the rear of the glass you have a photographically etched image of a female goddess, and the real image on the back is of a pyramid with golden Mayan bird sculptures flying around it. The fiber optic lighting changes constantly, so the whole triptych is moving and

changing in front of your eyes. Incredibly so.

"It was a complicated work to evolve, and there were many failures and discarded ideas along the way. LCA was wonderful. They were constantly seeing possibilities and pushing, pushing, pushing." ■

This interview was recorded in David Buckland's studio in London.

CV

David Buckland is a British-born artist whose scope encompasses the photographic arts, portraiture, installation designs, most notably for RCI, and set and costume design for theater and film direction. His career in the photographic arts spans almost 30 years. Having graduated from the London College of Printing in 1970, he was awarded the first two-year fellowship in photography in Newcastle and subsequently a two-year Kodak fellowship. His first one-man exhibition was at the Northern Arts Gallery in Newcastle in 1972. Since then, he has had solo exhibitions in many international venues: The Sander Gallery, Washington, DC; the Musée National d'Art Moderne (Pompidou Center), Paris; the Minneapolis Museum of Art, Minneapolis, Minnesota and the Museum of Contemporary Photography, Chicago, Illinois. He has also had touring exhibitions in France, Italy, Australia and the USA. The artist's principal one-man exhibitions include the Photographers Gallery in London 1977 and 1987; the Air Gallery in London 1978; the Espace Photographique de la Ville de Paris 1988; and the National Portrait Gallery in London 1999.

Buckland has designed sets and costumes for more than twenty theatrical works. In 1999, he designed the set and costumes for "A Stranger's Taste", performed by the Royal Ballet at the inaugural evening of the new Covent Garden Opera House in London. Buckland's books include two monographs on his own works and two books with the sculptor, Anthony Caro. His work is exhibited and held in major collections worldwide, including the National Portrait Gallery in London and Metropolitan Museum in New York.

Jonathan Clowes

"A fine piece of sculpture communicates the artist's love of spirit and form."

– Jonathan Clowes

Jonathan Clowes with model of "Diadem", Rhapsody of the Seas.

Jonathan and Evelyn Clowes create some strange and wonderful wooden sculptures that seem to float in the air. For RCI, they have made two Centrum sculptures, "Diadem" for *Rhapsody of the Seas* and "Canticle of a Blue Planet" for the *Explorer of the Seas*. Big sculptures for big cruise ships, built in the middle of the quiet New England countryside. These pieces of art are built by a highly skilled team of craftspeople, giving Jon and his wife Evelyn the chance to do the vital, creative part. To produce this kind of art, you need peace and serenity. Their setting is correspondingly quiet.

We travelled to the village of Walpole, New Hampshire, to meet the people behind these remarkable sculptures. Tucked into a hollow beside a rushing stream is the studio/shop of Jonathan and Evelyn Clowes, who create immense wonderful bent wood sculptures that are at the same time delicate and playful. We met a husband and wife team who are as filled with energy and humor as they are talented.

"A fine piece of sculpture communicates the artist's love of spirit and form," says Jonathan Clowes. As the work evolves in the mind and in the studio, aesthetic concerns interact with the requirements of the materials to create a uniquely balanced whole. The success of a piece depends on the artist's skill and attention to both demands. A good piece elicits an appreciative knowing or wondering from others. Practically, the work must also reflect a consistent and visible level of intention and care in its crafting. Beyond that, I believe each piece must engage the viewer's spirit, encouraging it to move beyond the bounds of daily existence. As an artist, I seek to attain such integrity.

"Random relationships alone are not good enough in art. You have to control the relationships between forms in a meaningful way. I enjoy making forms for particular spaces. It's like building a marriage or any kind of relationship. I enjoy the process immensely."

Jonathan Clowes has been making hanging sculptures since he was a child. He discovered early on that he was handy and he loved to build things. "I have been building things my whole life, beginning with small carved objects, boats and mobiles. In this wonderful country of ours, we don't have to have a lot of formal training to determine whether or not we are qualified to do whatever we want to do. My training took place in boatyards and cabinet shops and in short stints at art schools.

"I studied briefly at MIT. My background really is a whole hodgepodge of different things I've done. Fortunately, I learned something important from each of these experiences which ultimately can be applied to creating sculptures. Now I have been a 'serious' sculptor for more than25 years."

Jon's father was an avid yachtsman and Jon grew up on the ocean. "Being a sailor, I've hung things up in the air all my life. I've always been involved with the wind and the sea. Quite literally, I grew up on sailboats on Cape Cod, Massachusetts. I sailed with my father on trans-Atlantic voyages, in Europe and along the northeastern coast. My father was not a warm water sailor, so we sailed the waters of Maine, Nova Scotia and Newfoundland. As North Atlantic sailors, we dealt with many challenges and saw some beautiful country. Watching a sail unfurl into the wind has always been a big moment for me. Installing Diadem in *Rhapsody* was even better.

"Evelyn and I love the design process. We need a sense of the space involved and then our ideas flow freely. We believe that people interact with the spaces they are in. The role of our sculptures is to enhance that interaction, and hopefully to infuse it with wonder, beauty and peace. Evelyn really helps me keep my attention on these aspects. During the building phase of a project I get very involved in its engineering and fabrication.

These aspects of a project excite me greatly, but in the end we must achieve a synthesis of fine design and careful crafting to produce an awesome work of art. Evelyn helps us hold the focus on that goal during the building of a piece. These large pieces we made for Royal Caribbean have moved us into

The whole Clowes family helped assembling "Diadem" for Rhapsody of the Seas.

tighter collaboration, opening up a whole new facet of our partnership that we both truly enjoy. My hope is that the sculptures we make will enhance people's lives as they have ours.

"When LCA first approached us about putting one of our hanging sculptures in the atrium of a cruise ship, my first response was, 'You can't swing a gigantic pendulum in a moving ship!' But the consultants were persistent, and architect Njål Eide in particular was adamant that there were solutions to the problems of motion. So with the help of a team of engineers and a very involved modeling process, we found a way to stabilize our kinetic sculptures, making them seaworthy."

Jonathan and Evelyn Clowes: "Canticle to a Blue Planet". Painted metal and wood sculpture. Centrum, Explorer of the Seas. *(Photo: Edward Hill)*

Jonathan's artistic sensibilities grew more out of the crafts tradition than is the case with most artists: – "That gives me a fair amount of intuitive insight into engineering. I talk the language enough to understand what engineers are up to. I don't have the formal training to do the mathematical calculations myself. But just as doctors should never try to heal themselves, sculptors should never engineer their own sculptures! They should have somebody test theories and challenge their assumptions. It takes a creative engineer to help us with the big projects for RCI. I approach these projects with a strong sense of what's possible. As a craftsman and an artist I can recognize what can be built and what can't. We've got to be sure the ship's housekeeping crew can keep the sculpture clean, that no part of it will fall on anyone's head or that the whole piece won't start to vibrate on some strange harmonic note that could ruin everyone's vacation. Thank God we have a team of engineers who say, 'Design what you want and we'll find a way to build it.' And they leave what we all jokingly refer to as 'the art part' to Evelyn and me."

Evelyn then spoke about another indispensable player in the process of building these enormous floating sculptures, Njål Eide, the architect for the huge *Vision Class* and *Voyager Class* ships. "Njål Eide has been an important source of inspiration for us along the way. Njål has a very good eye for possibilities and at an early discussion phase of the Diadem project, he said, 'We've seen your work. We like what you do. Do whatever you think is right for this space, and I'm sure it will come out right.' When we came back to Oslo with our conceptual model, his critique was absolutely in line with where we thought the piece ought to go. We extended our stay a day and worked through the night, modifying our model to come to agreement with Mr. Eide on the final form for the piece."

Mr. Eide was also involved in the piece they were currently making for the Centrum on *Explorer of the Seas*. "He came over to our studio to give a final artistic review before we began the actual piece. He stood on the viewing scaffolding we made for him and suggested one adjustment: a slight lifting and rotating of the 'sail'. That change, once made, completed the approvals process!"

The experiences from *Rhapsody* were very useful as they constructed the new Centrum sculpture for *Explorer of the Seas*.

"Yes, our experiences with *Rhapsody* did influence the building of this new piece, but they are not as directly translatable as you might think! This piece is constructed in an entirely new way. It is actually made of aluminum. We designed it for composites, because we had learned how to use composites, and because it was one of the most logical materials to use. But to meet the stricter fire codes for the *Voyager Class*, we decided we had to use fireproof materials. So we started to do some research and some soul-searching.

"We wanted the opportunity to build this design. We reached back into the past, not my past, but to old metal crafting traditions, including the hand-crafting techniques used to make armor and coaches in the middle ages and, more recently, to make airplanes and automobiles. We combined this old technology with the latest materials of the aerospace industry. Our long, rotating, spiraling shapes look like bent wood and are very light and strong. We've had to retool our shop and train our people in these old arts and new materials, a real learning experience for all of us.

"But all this is behind–the–scenes stuff and when the piece is done no one will see the carefully constructed internal structure of the piece. What I hope they see is an elegant collection of shapes and colors. A sculpture that makes them stop, look and look again. This piece has everything to do with the sea as the nurturing cradle of life. It is about the interface between sea and air, the place that spawns life. We are trying to capture the underlying harmonies that nourish not only our survival but also our spiritual life. We hope it sings an essential song to all who view it." ■

The interview with Jonathan and his wife Evelyn Clowes took place in the their studio/shop in Walpole, New Hampshire, USA.

CV

Jonathan Clowes, American.
Born in Toronto, Canada.
Independent sculptor and designer since 1974.
He now works in close cooperation with his wife Evelyn Clowes, an ordained minister, textile artist and designer.

Education:
Phillips Exeter Academy, Exeter, NH.
Massachusetts Institute of Technology, Cambridge, MA.
The Museum School, Museum of Fine Arts, Boston, MA.
The Portland School of Art, Portland, ME.

Related professional background:
Concordia Boatyard, So. Dartmouth, MA.
Damariscotta Boatbuilders, Rockland, ME.
Paul Luke, East Boothbay, ME.
Dan. W. Clark, Inc., Woods Hole, MA.

His works are exhibited in distinguished galleries and art shows in the United States.
Jonathan Clowes has won several important awards for his sculptures.
His works have been bought by important private and public collectors in the USA.
Among his commissions are Centrum Sculptures for the RCI cruise ships *Rhapsody of the Seas* and *Explorer of the Seas*.

Jonathan Clowes has also designed and built important residential and liturgical furniture.

George Cutts

George Cutts makes complicated and sophisticated, large and subtle sculptures that are generally in continuous, majestic motion. His studio looks like a mix between a well-stocked second-hand store and a mechanical workshop. There's no plaster or clay in sight. In addition to form, Cutts' work involves pumps, nozzles, clutches and electrical motors. Small mistakes can have huge consequences. A couple millimeter's miscalculation on a pipe at the bottom of a water-based mechanical system can cause the top of a nine-meter high sculpture to rotate too fast, resulting in water raining down on innocent customers in a shopping center.

Cutts' pool sculpture for the *Enchantment of the Seas* is made of shining stainless steel pipes that are to be in perpetual motion.

George Cutts at work on a full-scale model outside his studio in East Sussex, UK. (Photo: Jon Lie)

"I've got to do some work now. I'm a maker, not a chatter."

– George Cutts

The elements must each follow their own paths, one clockwise, the other counter-clockwise. The work is full of optical illusions, and sometimes it looks as if the 'screws' are going in the same direction. "Timing is critical with movement; if it is too fast, it's disturbing, if it's too slow it has another effect," explains Cutts. "So I spend a lot of time timing it. But when the work is finished, it has a stable speed that cannot be changed.

"LCA said they needed a pool sculpture and asked: 'Can you do something?' They have never told me what to do. There are only the natural constraints of working on a ship that control you; weights and movement and things like that.

"The sculpture I'm working on right now is completely new. Nothing like it has been done before, and I have a commission to make it. I don't have to be struggling on my own. I'm being paid to make what I want to make. These commissions for the cruise ships have taken the place of the renaissance patrons, really. And the system works without somebody taking a huge cut so that I can afford to make what I really want to make. And the commissions for RCI get me somewhere else: they allow me to be seen by people outside the normal art scene.

"I always make everything myself, including all the engineering. After exhausting jobs I have decided to start delegating parts of the work to other people. But when they say 'This cannot be done, it has never been done before', I just have to do it myself. I seem to have a mechanical mind. When I was young, my hobby was repairing clocks and watches.

"I always had to struggle for money. With such complicated works one can never get rich as an artist. It's almost impossible to calculate these pieces. The result is that there is little or nothing left in the end. Even for the big prestigious pieces.

"And it's a pity that I have not passed what I've learned of my mechanical skills on to anybody else. My sons were not interested. In the old days your sons would take what you've learned; that's how they built the Gothic cathedrals. My knowledge cannot be reinvented. I am inventing all the time. There is never the same sculpture.

"The next job poses different problems. But if I get another like the Pool sculpture for *Grandeur*, I will know how to do it. The problem is that people who shop for nine-meter tall sculptures tend to want an original rather than a copy.

"Making all my own sculptures gives me an understanding of scale. The large installments are physically demanding. You walk in fit on Saturday morning and, when you come out, it's Monday and you are finished in every sense of the word. After that I don't want to go in the studio for a week, but I will be back in two days.

"As a boy I was an apprentice in a shipyard up in Yorkshire. I thought there was something more to life than shipbuilding. My mother was a dressmaker, and I decided I wanted to do fashion design. Then I got a scholarship to art school. It was fantastic! So I got to the place and I worked my arse off, because it was lovely. They used to lock the doors after class, and I climbed in through the windows to work at night as well. I was so badly educated; I didn't know who Michelangelo or Leonardo were.

"There was a block of stone there, and one day I found out about sculpture. I picked up a chisel – the figure is in fact still in my garden – and I carved into this block of stone and thought:"This is my life – this is what my life is about."

"It was only in the early 1960's I started putting steel into it; the first mixed-media stainless steel and stone came out then. I could cut them out, like my mother would make a dressmaking cut. It was the same process, the same form. My mother could look at some fashion in a shop window, and she could go home and cut out a pattern exactly the same – just by looking at it. She could fit a pattern on somebody virtually without measuring them. So I put stainless steel sculptures together in the same way. I would cut a pattern, then I cut the forms out and welded them together. It works the same way.

"There has been a lot of struggling. I wouldn't sign up with a gallery. A major London gallery offered me a 20-year contract when I left college because I had won a competition. They would take 85 percent of what I sold and I would pay for my own materials. I said: 'You must be joking.' They replied: 'But we will make you a star.'

"I refused to go through a gallery system and I suppose that's why we had to struggle. I've done everything to make a living. I was a male model and I did stunt driving for films in order to carry on doing sculpture as I wanted to. Not as the galleries wanted. This gallery said they wanted 40 pieces of the sculpture I won the competition with for an exhibition of my works. All the same, but slightly different. I said 'That isn't art'. But that's how they build names and how you make it big."

Cutts' studio is overflowing with strange treasures. He says: "I have a friend who is a painter and is desperate to come in here and do a painting of it. But no way! I would have him here for a whole year. And he drinks as well; I wouldn't be able to get rid of him.

"When I have a terrible job on, I work and work until I can't move in here. Then my wife Grenie will come in and send me off to the pub. She will clean it up. If I were to try to do that job, it would take me months, because I would pick things up and stare at them, wondering how I can use them. I can't do it.

"But I've got to do some work now. I'm a maker, not a chatter." ■

This interview with George Cutts took place in his studio in East Sussex, UK.

CV

George Cutts, b. 1938, British, Rugby, Warwickshire UK
Lives and works in Cousley Wood, East Sussex.

Cutts left school at 14 to begin a sheet metal work apprenticeship in Goole Shipyards, Yorkshire. 1955: Doncaster School of Art, Yorkshire. Won scholarship. 1957: Royal College of Art, London. Won a rare scholarship. Youngest ever student, at that time, to attend.

Selected One-Man Exhibitions:
1970: Sculpture in Crystal, Mineral Gallery, Albermarle St, London
1972: Title Unknown. Ben DuBose Gallery, Houston, Texas, USA
1976: Contemporary Steel. Folio Gallery, Burlington St, London
1978: Cutting Edge. Gallery 24, London;
1990: Steel Reflections (Two-Man Exhibition). Art in Industry, Breda, The Netherlands.

George Cutt's sculptures are represented in important private and public collections, among them: Lord Rotschild, Waddeson Manor, Buckenhamshire; Dr. Hans Rausing, Wadhurst Park, East Sussex; Senator John Glenn, USA; King Fahd, Saudi Arabia; Mazda Head Office, Tinbridge Wells, Kent; Sheik of Qatar, Qatar; Storm King Art Center, New York, USA; Dordrecht Museum, Dordrecht Park, The Netherlands; The Ulla and Heiner Pietzsch Collection, Berlin.

George Cutts is an elected Fellow of the Royal Society of British Sculptors since 1996.

Nini Anker Dessen and Magne Austad

Nini Anker Dessen has created a number of large tapestries for RCI ships. Her textile works are filled with imaginative inventiveness, visual lushness and a strong sense of color. She also paints, including watercolors.

"Njål Eide (the architect) allows me to work freely with ideas for decoration," says Dessen. "He shows me drawings of the ship and points to which areas he wants me to decorate. Together we determine the materials, colors and sizes of works of art which will best harmonize with the ship's interior. Eide has confidence in my ability to understand the interplay between artworks and their surroundings. The freedom he grants me is very inspiring.

"Sometimes the framework is already decided, as in the *Legend of the Seas*, for which I made the large 'Romeo and Juliet' piece for the Dining Room, which stretches two stories high. I had to rent Edvard Munch's studio in Ekely, Oslo so that I would have enough space to work with the large sketches. The largest tapestry was 5.5 x 5 meters.

Dessen says it would never have been possible to complete the largest projects for RCI without professional assistance. The tapestries were therefore woven at a workshop in the French town of Aubusson. "The weaving workshop has a 500-year tradition," she says. "Mostly it's men who sit at the looms – men who have learned their trade from their fathers. These are people who are adept in their handicraft and are able to deliver amazing results in the course of three to four months. They have mastered all the techniques from the 'Gobelin' techniques to modern weaving methods.

"For the *Voyager of the Seas*, I used a multi-dimensional weaving technique in which I brought forth the feeling of a woven layer on top of another in a sort of relief. There were some rougher parts, with coarse yarn, together with areas of finer yarn. It was a very demanding job!

"I'm not so interested in the actual weaving process as in the technical expression. My strength lies in my many ideas, which I want to see realized. In Aubusson they have worked with artists through the generations, but they decide themselves who they will weave for, so the artist should be knowledgeable and experienced. This works very well for me," says Dessen.

Nini Anker Dessen and Magne Austad.

"The weaving workshop at Aubusson has an enormous selection of yarn, especially wool," continues Dessen. "But I have to make my own palette for each tapestry. By mixing several thin threads together I usually get the exact color nuance I want. Each color mixture gets its own number. If one of the colors isn't exactly

"These large commissions for cruise ships have given continuity and the opportunity for development. They have provided challenges one otherwise wouldn't encounter as a pictorial artist."

– Nini Anker Dessen

Tapestry "Romeo and Juliet" for Dining Room in Legend of the Seas.

right, I can always dye the yarn to my specifications.

"While the work is underway, I mark every last area in the sketch with the correct color number. It takes time to make such a detailed work layout for the artisans, but by doing so, I retain 100 percent control over the end result. Even after 14 years of cooperation, I travel to Aubusson to maintain a full overview. This also allows me to make small changes spontaneously – for example adding a bold thread if I feel the desire. If the result is to be my artistic expression, I have to control its production. Some people think you can just send a sketch to the workshop and let them do the job. Then it doesn't take much for the result to come out totally wrong."

Dessen feels that her tapestry 'Romeo and Juliet' on *Legend of the Seas* was a successful creation. "The composition's perspective makes the room seem to extend into the picture so that those sitting close to it don't experience it as a

"Curved Art", Legend of the Seas.

wall that blocks their vision, but as something beckoning them to venture into," she says.

For the *Voyager of the Seas*, it was decided to use non-figurative tapestries. Njål Eide wanted a kind of 'relief' effect in the large tapestries to be hung in the main staircase on the starboard side. "Two of my finished tapestries were bought from the Haaken Gallery in Oslo for this project," says Dessen. "I built on these by lengthening them with the addition of two new tapestries, 'Vision Rouge' and 'Silence Bleu'. I also used the relief technique in the third tapestry, the 'Vision Maritime'. In a fourth tapestry, the 'Eclair Bleu', I made a kind of frame which was woven in a rougher structure above and below the picture's mid section.

Nini Anker Dessen: Tapestry. Main Stairs, Voyager of the Seas.

"I think it's interesting that the tapestries are different on each deck. Åse Frøyshov created the beautiful tapestries for the other staircase. Thus all the decks on the *Voyager of the Seas* are decorated with tapestries by two Norwegian pictorial weavers. They are very different and express some of the breadth of Norwegian pictorial weaving."

With textile commissions of this size, the final touches must always be done on site, according to Dessen, and it can be critical that the artist herself is there at the time. "Fortunately, both Åse Frøyshov and I were allowed to travel to Finland to hang our tapestries. It's a tough phase. Tapestries are easily damaged. There's always someone polishing marble or laying carpet underfoot just when you need to climb the ladder to hang the piece. On the Voyager, the ceiling in the stairway had been made 50 centimeters lower than what we had been told. A ventilation pipe had been forgotten. Several tapestries had to be adjusted. It was good there were two of us on site."

Dessen had never done ceramic work when Njål Eide proposed a project for the Windjammer Café and Indoor & Outdoor Café on the *Legend of the Seas*. "In Norway it's not usual for ceramists to cooperate with other artists in their workshops," explains Dessen, "although the Danes have a number of workshops that help and guide artists from the 'outside' with ceramic-painting work."

"At that time I had suffered a whiplash injury that made certain work tasks difficult for me. I contacted my good friend Magne Austad for help. Magne Austad's works are light and open, with clear color nuances that are difficult to recreate on clay. He prefers to use tempera, oil and acrylics and often blends different techniques together. He likes to 'bake' the pictures, to paint thick, layer upon layer, until the desired effect is achieved. He has always worked hard on his techniques. He has taught in the profession and knows that one doesn't get far without mastering the technical aspects.

"We found a workshop that made samples which were accepted by Njål Eide. We had to create our own color palette for the ceramics, and got to know the colors thoroughly so that we could use them without fear. When you paint on clay, you have to know what the finished pieces will look like after they are fired in the kiln. During the firing process, the colors change, and take on a whole new appearance. It took us quite a while to figure out this mystery.

"For the *Legend* we made a collage, 'Curved Art', for the Windjammer Café. The result was a blending of Magne Austad's painting, in the upper part of the picture, and my collage with paper applications and textiles in the lower part. We managed to integrate this into a collective form of expression. In the rest of the café, we made large ceramic reliefs with Windjammer motifs around the walls, covering 45 square meters of surfaces altogether.

"We were also given the task of proposing coloration for the table tiles. Each table was decorated with a hand-painted tile in the middle, each of which was unique. One of the special things about hand-made ceramics is that the result has an exclusive quality, that is, the colors are livelier than mass-produced work. Working with clay represented a new and exciting challenge."

Dessen and Austad's painted ceramic panels also liven up the ship's rest rooms, together with lavish marble floors.

The challenge with these works was to create an impression of continuity while at the same time preserving the uniqueness of the individual panels. Dessen and Austad created these kinds of works for four ships, producing more than 50 ceramic panels for each vessel.

"Shipowners Gjert and Arne Wilhelmsen have always taken the initiative and made sure that Norwegian artists have had the opportunity to compete for commissions onboard RCI ships.

"The large commissions for cruise ships have provided continuity and the opportunity to develop. They've offered challenges a pictorial artist would otherwise not be able to experience. Large dimensions are demanding; it's much more difficult to compose in large format than in small format. You can't just make a model in small format and expect that this can be blown up to the desired size. The task requires an entirely new perspective in size, scale and surfaces. The lines of a ship also demand a different kind of approach. But you learn a lot, especially new techniques and the ability to cooperate.

"I get a kick out of working for these vessels. You won't find such close cooperation other places in the art world. It's an educational process and we meet many capable people: outfitters, craftspeople, and not least, the architects and art consultants.

"But one prerequisite for being involved in several projects is that you must be able to renew yourself. In addition, you must be technically precise and predictable. You must be reliable and deliver on time," concludes Dessen. ■

CV

Nini Anker Dessen, b. 1957, Norwegian.
Education: studies in architecture and textiles at the National College of Art and Design, Oslo, Norway. Art Academy in Bonn, Germany. Central School of Art and Design, London, UK.
Solo exhibitions, Norway: Gallery F15, Moss; Munch Museum; Gallery of Modern Art; Haaken Gallery.
Solo exhibitions, International: Galerie Robert Four, France.
Collections: National Foundation for Publicly Commissioned Art, University of Oslo; the Oslo Muncipal Art Collection, The Bank of Norway; Østfold and Vestfold Counties; Borre Muncipality; The Cathedral School, Oslo; Commissions for tapestries, applications, paintings and ceramics for RCI, Princess Cruise and Radisson Cruise Lines. Corporate collections: Norsk Hydro; Furuholmen Invest; Molde Stadion; Bergesen and others.

Magne Austad, b. 1946, Norwegian.
Education: National College of Art and Design; student teacher. National Academy of Fine Arts, Oslo; The Royal Art Academy, Stockholm, Sweden.
Solo exhibitions, Norway: Kunstnerforbundet; Haaken Gallery; Haugesund Society of Arts; Karmøy Society of Arts.
Collections: The National Gallery Norway; The National Touring Exhibitions; the Norwegian Council for Cultural Affairs; and a number of works in public institutions, companies and RCI cruise ships.

This interview with Nini Anker Dessen took place in her studio in Oslo.

Michele Oka Doner

Nature is Michele Oka Doner's starting point, and she uses this inexhaustible source of inspiration to confer new life on familiar forms. Doner's imaginative designs of chairs, fireplace tools, trays, lighting fixtures and other practical everyday pieces have earned her a place among America's most innovative artists. She has made major works of public art in New York, on sidewalks and in subway stations, on airport floors in Miami and Washington, and striking floors onboard the RCI cruise ship, *Voyager of the Seas*.

"Fame is a word I don't know the meaning of," says Doner. "Ideas mean something. Dialogue means something. Thinking about how to make materials apply to something new; this is what it's about. The rest is silly. Fame is there to replace the death of many things that were important, the death of religion. In a last gasp, they put artists in there.

"Rarely do people survive that kind of exposure. It robs them of privacy and the ability to go back to the well. The public is thirsty. We live in a homogenous society. We are losing what's unique and special, as people collect by brand name. I am not a brand name. I see no need to accelerate," comments Doner.

"I believe there is a great life source, and that everybody's birthright is to connect. Everybody has within themselves the power to transform their own life. To take life as energy. To take their energy and to put down another layer in this long human endeavor – however grand or modest; that's what life is," says Doner.

"The old structures are finished. Something new is being born. I would like to be engaged in the exploration of both the past and the future. I have sons. I would also like grandchildren. It's a wonderful thing to be part of something greater than yourself. I don't lament what is gone. On the contrary. Every generation is supposed to separate the wheat from the chaff, to harvest what's good, to replant seeds for the future. Living is natural. There's more nature in New York than most other places. Imagine all the people who live there. People can live out among the trees and the grasses and have the stars every night, but they can be unconscious. Nature is not just the absence of man-made things. I love nature – I am nature.

"The old structures are finished. Something new is being born. I would like to be engaged in the exploration of both the past and the future."

– Michele Oka Doner

"Everybody asks me why I live in New York. I don't separate myself from anything. I am woman. I am partner to man. I have a very primal sense of order in my world. New York is filled with nature. First of all, it's man's creation.

"I've always threatened to do a work of art called Urban Botany. Every day I find the most beautiful images just down the street. I find somebody has eaten grapes and thrown the stem in the street where a truck drove over it and flattened it – something that looks like algae, with its primitive form. Then I find scallions someone has stepped on lying on the sidewalk in front of the Korean grocer, and they remind me of octopuses and squid. Then I find somebody has peeled an orange and it was heart-shaped when it got pulled out. So there is an orange heart on the sidewalk.

"I go into Chinatown, I see seahorses in a jar, I see these beautiful fruits they bring forth. I see melons. I see: this is nature. All of this I take home and I lay it out. I find so many things that speak to me every day. I walk up to the flower district. I see everything from a hundred miles around New York brought in. Then I see what they fly in. I eat it every day – I'm eating nature."

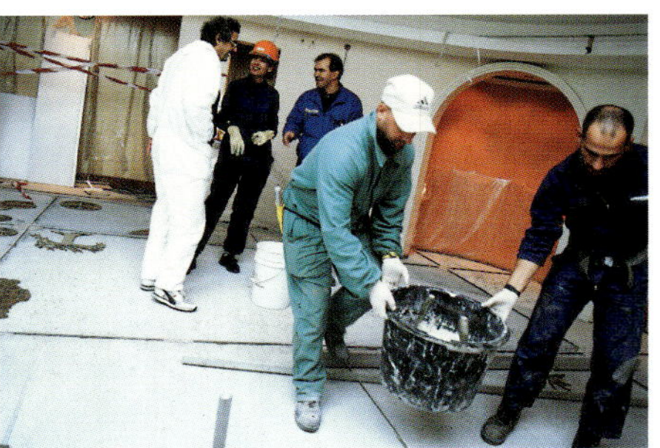

Doner says that commissioned work allows her to develop ideas on a much grander scale than she would normally have the ability to do. She says her work has developed over the years, when she was her own client: "I needed certain things, so I created them. It always starts like that. But commissioned work takes it a step further. Even if I did my own floors of maybe 5,000 square feet," she explains, "it's a far different scale than the

Miami Airport where there were more than 30,000 square feet.

"I have worked all over the United States and Europe and I have been commissioned by cities, counties, states, local governments as well as private people to make giant parts, fireplaces of stones from the river for a community center. I made a wall 165-feet long in Herald Square subway station in New York, composed of 11,000 handmade gold luster tiles from the last remaining Pewabic pottery of the American Arts and Crafts Movement in Detroit, Michigan. It's fascinating to be involved in so many different projects. Then you interface on a commission with an architect who has his own visions and dreams. I find it very stimulating.

"So commissioned work pulls me out of my own universe, into something that is quite astounding. And I get a lot of feedback from people who see my art.

My works for the Miami International Airport are site-specific. Every image there was something I picked up or saw in a book. For this project, I spent time on the beach in South Florida – it's like no other coastline in the world. It's wonderful to walk on the beach, just looking. Sometimes the images are things that one could only see with a microscope, so I provided this for an audience. There are enough pieces there that are recognizable so that people key into it. They begin to look at them. And then there are things that come from a French book on microscopic photography. I took foam from the beach and examined it under a microscope. In the rotunda there is a little essay on the structure of life, the origin of life, how it began in water; algae and early life forms. Had I not become an artist, I thought I was going to become a biologist."

Michele Oka Doner works with her Terrazzo/Bronze Feature Floors on Voyager of the Seas.

Doner comes from a long line of artists. Her grandfather was a painter trained in the Imperial Academy in Odessa, Russia. "My parents were both trained in music but I also grew up with painting because of my grandfather. He moved from Odessa to the USA. Genes are powerful. He came from a long line of scribes; the written word, the eye-hand coordination are, I feel, in the genetic code. I've always loved painting, writing and dancing. He was the rebel who didn't want to become a scribe. The world was changing and people were becoming literate, so he became a painter.

"I had lived near Cranbrook School, Michigan. It was designed by the Finnish architect Gottlieb Eliel Saarinen. I went to the University of Michigan in Ann Arbor. My teachers were Finnish. They had come with Saarinen to build Cranbrook School, and then they went to the University of Michigan and were teaching design courses. I was 17 years old.

I met these masters and it was wonderful. I somehow absorbed the idea of art being part of buildings and buildings being artistic, and integration as opposed to separation.

"When I moved to New York in 1981 I took my sons to the Planetarium. Then we came out and there was broken asphalt, a deteriorating situation. So I called an architect I knew in New York and he measured the outside of this area. He made a scale model and I created a concept of embedding what I had seen in the planetarium dome. It was at your feet, in cement, when you walked out. As luck would have it, I had done a piece of art for a medical company called Becton & Dickenson. And the CEO came to my studio with his wife. She noticed my maquette and asked what it was. I explained and she asked if I knew anybody at the Museum. I said 'No, I've just moved here.' She knew a Board of Trustee member who was brought back to the studio. The idea went to the museum and funding was found. I did the model in 1984, it was exhibited and in 1987 the project was installed with 300 bronzes embedded in cement.

"Once I did that I realized it was very difficult to keep it maintained outside. I then had an idea to try it inside in terrazzo, and I won a competition for the Sacramento Central Library in California. That was my opportunity to test this. I always sign a contract saying: 'Yes, I can do it, but I have no idea if it will work.' And fortunately I found these old craftsmen and they taught me a lot. I moved out to Sacramento and worked with the craftsmen and I learned a lot about terrazzo and about materials in terms of expansion and contraction.

"I think expression is very much a question of technique. Man's conquest of material; from early man finding clay by the riverbank, understanding that the soft clay can be used to hold something together. It fell in the fire overnight and became hard. These moments of melting iron, handling it, forging it, seeing that fire transforms clay, iron and bronze – extraordinary!

"This is still something that I get excited about. That I'm part of that really links me back to our ancestors. We are still a part of that story. I am a continuation of an old story, and I love the fact that ideas can live on in materials." ■

Blue Terrazzo and bronze floor, Voyager of the Seas.

This interview with Michele Oka Doner took place in Turku, Finland, when Doner's artwork was being installed in the floor of the Viking Crown Jazz Club onboard the Voyager of the Seas.

CV

Michele Oka Doner is a native of Miami Beach, Florida. She lives in New York. She received her Bachelor of Science and Design and Master of Fine Arts from the University of Michigan.

Michele Oka Donor is an internationally acclaimed artist. Her work is in major public collections, including the Metropolitan Museum of Art in New York; the Art Institute of Chicago; Virginia Museum of Fine Arts; and the National Design Museum-Smithsonian Institution, New York. She is also well known for her monumental works in public places, including "Radiant Site", a 150 foot long wall composed of 11,000 gold luster tiles at the Herald Square Subway complex in New York; "Codex Sacramento" at the Sacramento Central Library; and "A Walk on the Beach", the celebrated 22,000 square foot floor of Concourse A, Miami International Airport.

Peter Esdaile

Peter Esdaile started out as a graphic artist and painter. The sculptor in him only blossomed in the past 10 years. The pendulum of his artistic expression has swung between figurative and abstract; from intuitive expression to strict and concise geometry, not all at the same time, but, rather, in periods.

"I've been involved in decorative art since 1973," says Esdaile, "but my first cruise ship work was in 1992. Ship projects involve a somewhat more challenging work process than making something for a stationary building," he explains. "You rarely have the opportunity to make an 'on-site inspection' to see and feel the physical space. And you can't wait for motifs or formal solutions to come to you. You develop a kind of first-hand instinct for how the result should be. You quite simply can't allow yourself the luxury of cultivating doubts. Instinct, adrenaline and some sleepless, creative nights have usually kick-started the whole thing into action pretty effectively for me.

"My versatility has at times made things confusing for me. On the other hand, it's given me a broad basis of experience. I'm a restless, curious and searching type," says Esdaile. "The swinging of the pendulum is an important part of my nature. I have also been influenced by the fundamental extremes of the many schools of thought of the 20th century, and the tension between them."

Esdaile's collaboration with architect Njål Eide began in 1995 with the *Splendour of the Seas*. He created artworks in wood and Plexiglas for the Viking Crown. "I enjoy working in a dialog with other creative people," reports Esdaile, "and have found the architects' and art consultants' vigorous involvement in my work to be refreshing."

In 1995, Esdaile made his first attempt to use Plexiglas as a material in his sculptures. "I had a lot of broken glass around and wondered how I could recycle this completely usable material in a creative way," he recalls. "I realized that it had a lot of potential, as it could be laminated, planed, and formed. Plexiglas is formable, with a resistance somewhere between hardwood and marble. In addition, its optical qualities and light transmission create a strange and unpredictable aesthetic.

"Another advantage is that you can easily associate it with the other materials used on the ship," says Esdaile. "Matisse talked about *'Calme, luxe, et volupté'* – calm, luxury and abundance. I have tried to imbue my pieces with calm, as well as to communicate a sense of luxury through the choice of materials. This works well with the ship's interiors, which are dominated by mirrors, brass, marble and crystal. There is so much that is competing for attention onboard. At best, I hope to have provided something contemplative, sensual and elegant, whether the material is wood, steel or Plexiglas," says Esdaile.

"I imagine women checking their makeup in the steel surfaces of my sculptures. A cruise ship

Peter Esdaile in his workshop.

"My versatility has at times made things confusing for me. On the other hand, it's given me a broad basis of experience."

– Peter Esdaile

can't be a forum for Arte Povera, Trash Art or provocative art. The art on a cruise ship is meant to please."

On the *Legend of the Seas*, Esdaile was in charge of portions of the decorations in the Viking Crown. "I used a lot of copper and wood," he says. "Large, sandblasted, tar-burned wooden panels, with objects and jewelry from Viking times, together with a miniature Viking ship. I took the work with the Viking motifs very seriously. I spent a lot of time at the Viking Ship Museum and let myself be seduced by the ornamentation and artistic style of the Viking Age.

"On *Splendour* I also did pieces for the Viking Crown," continues Esdaile. In the stairways with the spades and the tapestries, the masculine and the feminine are intertwined, resulting in a freer and more personal style. This liberated approach can also be seen in the four high reliefs. They lead to associations with the sea, birds, fish, waves, and a stylization of water as an element in a waterfall – an abstract approximation of what the Vikings saw on their voyages. I've been on the ship many times and feel that these pieces work," says Esdaile.

In the aft lounge, Some Enchanted Evening, on the *Vision of the Seas*, Esdaile created a series of sculptures in Plexiglas, wood, steel and copper, which he calls 'Illusory Nature'. "In this series of sculptures, I was initially fascinated with the nature of the South Pacific Islands," says Esdaile. "Water, waterfalls and vegetation are a constant theme that I play with. Water is depicted with a tranquil, rhythmic movement: waves, ripples and waterfalls. In this, I chose a combination of natural and synthetic materials that allow for abstraction, as well as create organic variations that occur in the creative process. Plexiglas in particular has been a useful material in portraying the interplay of water and light that results in varying colors and hues that mirror and filter their surroundings.

"I have chosen to portray vegetation with a focus on mathematical symbolism wherein flowers and trees are portrayed as regularized, configured symbols – symbols that mirror their own complex molecular composition, as well as the complex and delicate interplay between nature and man. Man's creations also appear subtly here and there in this Pacific idyll, as metaphors in man's search for belonging."

Esdaile says he is proud of what he did with the Guest Relations Desk on the *Voyager*: "I call the work 'Kaleidoscope'. It expresses the underwater life in the Caribbean in blue, green, turquoise, yellow, and red – almost the entire color spectrum orchestrated over nine meters and 10 different 'segments'. If you abstract everything you see under the ocean, you could maybe say I have captured the essence of it.

"I felt that the initial parameters were given. It was to be a completely simple, rigid architectural design: 10 squares that curve behind the Guest Relations Desk. I didn't know much about the other details of the interior, but I chose to make something that gave the impression of moving as one walked by. This was to be in a rotunda in the middle of the ship.

Pigmented Plexiglas Wall Relief, "Kaleidoscope".
In creating this piece, the artist became fascinated by the sharp contrast of the vibrant colors of the fish, shellfish, aquatic vegetation and sand found in the Caribbean. These colors are reflected and refracted by sunlight passing through the depths of the sea, as well as by the constant motion of the sea itself. The result is, of course, a limitless constellation of colors and shapes. The sculpture "Kaleidoscope" is intended to be a playful mirroring of this interplay of colors and the beautiful randomness of nature.
Voyager of the Seas, *Guest Relations Desk, Deck 5.*

"I had this work on my studio floor for a half a year while I worked on it. It looked like a city built of glass blocks – a colorful, spacey, futuristic affair. Then I was struck by my other interpretation: Human voices. Music like a choir, or perhaps rather a cheerful cacophony like many different voices in many different languages. The colored bands in the glass blocks can literally be associated with vocal chords and therefore tones or resonance.

"I was at the yard in Turku to install these works myself. I was the only one who could do it. Nobody else would have figured it out. I had exact measurements for each picture that had to be mounted on the back side of the glass. I think it would have been hard for anyone else to figure out which side was up and which side down. The pictures were made up of 380 pieces that had to be placed exactly as I had them on my studio floor. I am of course happy with the installation. This is the first impression people get when they come onboard. Everyone has to pass by the Guest Relations or Purser's Desk. You could call it an important strategic artwork location.

"The wall is nothing more than a partition between a room behind, i.e. the Purser's Office, and where the pursers are out front serving the guests. The pictures were to have a partitioning function. The challenge was that the artwork was not to block the window because the people behind it were to be visible through it. At the same time, it was to be something that hovered there, giving an almost stereophonic experience.

"I couldn't have made a work like this four years ago. My collaboration with RCI has been a learning process. Today I can attack material with a greater sense of respect and know that I can handle the technical complexities that will occur. After a while, you get to know what you are made of when it comes to courage and self-confidence so that you can take on larger and more complex jobs.

"Without these commissions, artistically speaking, I would be in a completely different place today.

I've found that I can do things, not merely think what might be possible, but actually do it. In fact, I've already done it. I am therefore enormously grateful to have been allowed to do these things. We've had generous budgets and have felt the lift that comes from that." ■

This interview with Peter Esdaile took place in his studio outside of Oslo, Norway.

CV

Peter Esdaile, b. 1947 in Montreal, Canada, Norwegian.
Education: National College of Art and Design 1966–68. National Academy of Fine Arts 1968–73.
Solo exhibitions: More than 20 solo exhibitions since his debut at Young Artists Society, Oslo in 1971.
Group exhibitions: More than 20 exhibitions in Norway, Denmark, Iceland, Germany, England and Austria.
Peter Esdaile's works have been purchased by a number of museums and collections.
Norway: The National Gallery;
The National Touring Exhibitions; the Norwegian Council for Cultural Affairs; the Oslo Municipal Art Collections; Rogaland Art Museum.
International: Eskilstuna Society of Art , Sweden; Brandts Klædefabrik, Denmark.
He has executed major commissions for a number of public buildings in Norway and for many cruise ships, including seven of RCI's large vessels.

Åse Frøyshov

"Commissions like decorating cruise ships are very challenging. The parameters are given and the work makes quite different demands on you than gallery art. You have to make something that fits into a context. That alone is quite a challenge.

"It all started with an exhibition I had in New York in 1996. Somebody who knew Gro Nesjar, who managed the LCA office in Miami at that time, showed her the exhibition catalogue and recommend-

ed me to her. Three months later, I was contacted by LCA. They initially asked me to make tapestries for alternate decks on the main stairs of the *Rhapsody of the Seas*. In the end, I was asked to make sketches for all eleven decks.

"I accepted, although I knew it would be a huge challenge. All my sketches are made in paper collage. I made a sketch that was one-and-a-half meters tall; I cut and pasted and designed something that would be appropriate for every deck, and sent it to Miami. It was given the name "Rhapsody in Blue." It consisted of 17 tapestries, and was easily approved by the Steering Committee. The only change they wanted was to include an element that would differentiate each of the decks. I thought of including a symbol in every tapestry; these became butterflies, fish, palms and stars. And I have to say that I found it useful myself to have these symbols when I came aboard to install the tapestries.

"I had a tight deadline for the Rhapsody project, and weaving yard upon yard of tapestry demands a certain amount of time. The project was approved in September and was to be delivered in April. Finishing all those tapestries on time was probably the greatest challenge I have ever faced. First of all, I had to measure and make a mock-up of all the decks myself. I had to dye all the yarn for all the tapestries, and when I began the project, I was completely on my own. I set out somewhat haphazardly because I had no time to waste. I wasn't quite in tune with what color palette I needed. All I had to work on were the sketches and measurements, plus a color

"Work is like a walk in nature. The surroundings are always changing, and I am always moving forward."

Åse Frøyshow in her studio outside Oslo. (Photo: Tomaszewicz)

sample from the carpet and the walls. I worked my way into the project from September until November, when I hired an assistant. Another assistant joined at Christmas time. We managed, and the tapestries were delivered in April.

"The completed vessel was to leave the shipyard at St. Nazaire in France. There I was, with one assistant and an enormous amount of tapestry to hang. We mounted the works on huge boards. I had never had to hang anything on a boat before and wasn't sure exactly how to do it. However, since the ship moved with the waves, I quickly realized that the tapestries would need to be very firmly attached.

"When I was originally given the commission to decorate a staircase, I thought of it as a second-rate placement. That's what I was used to from commissions for buildings on land. "Oh, well – a staircase," I thought to myself. But on the ship, only the Centrum is larger and grander. The main stairs featured one major artwork medium – clearly the best location on the ship for my textiles.

"The confidence shown me during the Rhapsody project was incredible. I have worked on smaller projects with committees that have poured directives on me. RCI, the architects and LCA trusted me and left a lot to my judgement.

"Fantasy Garden" is one of Åse Frøyshovs huge tapestries for Main Stairs, Voyager of the Seas.

"Making the five tapestries for the *Voyager of the Seas* was actually a simpler project. I had learned a great deal from the work on the first ship. I was more confident, and knew more of what a ship demands. For example, it is very important to consider the patterns of the carpeting.

"I didn't think I would be able to make tapestries for *Voyager* as beautiful as those I had made for *Rhapsody*. I thought that the work would be a little poorer the second time around. The tapestries for the first ship were a success, and it would be a difficult act to follow. But fortunately, I had a whole year between the two projects. This gave me time to calm down, to readjust, to move on. I had time to leave behind what had been. It's okay for artists to copy each other, but preferably, they should not copy themselves. Now I feel that the two ships have turned out completely different from one another. And that's a good thing.

"The way I work is that I enlarge my models and place them in full size on the floor. Even though the full-size model is a completely accurate enlargement of the maquette, I still have to do a lot of weaving along the way. The enlargement creates its own strange set of problems. Then I cover the pattern with yarn that I have dyed myself. This phase takes a very long time. I 'paint' the tapestry on the floor with colored yarn. I had a problem with the *Voyager* project: I made two sets of sketches, and the first was the best. But the colors were too bright, and I had to 'shift' the colors of the tapestries between the two sketches.

"I discovered this when I showed the sketches to architect Njål Eide (architect of the stairs) and Gro Nesjar. The carpeting samples had arrived, but they were different from what I had first seen. I was told that the colors of the first sketches were too bright. That was true, and I knew it as soon as I saw the samples on the blue floor.

"Changing the colors was quite a demanding job. I had to create a whole new color scheme in my head. I had never done anything like that before, and it took some time. We're talking about thousands of yards of yarn.

"I actually dyed the yarn for all of the five *Voyager* tapestries at the

Working on "Rhapsody in Blue" for Rhapsody of the seas. (Photo: Tomaszewicz.)

same time. Then I labelled the yarn, rolled the patterns away, and wove the tapestries one by one. The finished tapestries were put down on top of the pattern, on the floor.

"I dye up to 14 bundles of 100 grams each at a time, and I can do 28 bundles, in two big pans. They need to reach 100 degrees Celsius, and the yarn must soak for half an hour at that temperature for the dye to set. If you've put in too much, you have to start all over again. You must constantly be mixing the colors, and it can be difficult to get the right balance. This is my way of cooking – I'm not so interested in food, but I know how to dye.

"The tapestries for *Voyager* have the collective title 'Fantasy Garden'. I was told that a 'Millennium Ship' was under construction, and that the theme was to be about different eras. The decks were to be Egyptian, Greek/Roman, and of every other era, right up to the Space Age on the upper deck. This was a little difficult for me; my works were to hang between the decks. I knew that I had to figure out something that would tie the epochs together, and realized that nature has always been there.

"For me, work is like a walk in nature. The surroundings are always changing. New elements keep coming into view, and I am always moving forward. I can never stand still. And I think it is very difficult to go back to something I have left behind.

"Work of this magnitude forces you to delve into new areas of yourself and bring forth things you might not have thought you had inside. You have to break through inner barriers, and it's risky. I've been 'climbing stairs', not taking great leaps, but moving upwards slowly. So I feel reasonably confident that I can handle these challenges," concludes Åse Frøyshov. ■

This interview with Åse Frøyshov took place in her studio at Gjettum Farm outside Oslo, Norway.

CV

Åse Frøyshov, b. 1943, Norwegian.
Lives and works in Oslo, Norway.
1967–69, Royal Danish School for Educational Studies.
1969–73, The National College of Arts and Crafts, Oslo.

Åse Frøyshov has had 27 Solo Exhibitions since 1974, most of them in the USA and Norway. She has participated in numerous Group exhibitions in Norway, the USA, the UK, Sweden, France, Russia and Romania. Her works are represented in several Private and Public Collections, among others in Norwegian Council for Cultural Affairs; North Norwegian Museum of Applied Arts; The municipality of Trondheim; The Gallery of Trøndelag; and The Norwegian Parliament – Stortinget. Among Åse Frøyshov's numerous public works are tapestries for SINTEF, Trondheim; The Bank of Kreditkassen, Trondheim and Oslo; Statoil Stjørdal and Trondheim; Trondheim Courthouse, Olavshallen, Trondheim; Norsk Tipping, Hamar; North Norwegian Conservatory; and RCI cruise ships *Rhapsody of the Seas* and *Voyager of the Seas*, Miami, FL, USA.

Philip Jackson

"When you do a public sculpture like those on a ship, you have to identify your audience." Philip Jackson firmly believes that it has to appeal to the people: "It would be rather arrogant to create a sculpture that you know will not be understood by the majority of the people who see it. I enjoy watching the public's reaction to my work, which is why I try to spend some time at each of my own exhibitions, listening to what people say and watching how they react. A sculpture is a form of communication. If it doesn't communicate, if it only means something to me, then it has failed.

"Parts of the art world scare people away because their works don't communicate. It's egotistical and inward looking. In the past ten years or so, there has been a tendency for artists in this country, and in other countries, to shock their audience. The shock is often accomplished by simple tricks like using crudeness or vulgarity, or by employing some taboo in the artwork. People are supposed to have a violent reaction to it. I feel that shocking people is something that is rather easy to do, and it's a transitory thing anyway. What shocks today doesn't shock anyone tomorrow, and there has to be more to art than that."

Jackson endeavors to make his sculpture somewhat mysterious, elegant and slightly reminiscent of something glimpsed from the past, but he does so in a contemporary way. "I want the work to stir emotions by evoking memories. I have had wonderful letters from people, telling me what my sculptures have done for them and while some admittedly say they find them quite sinister, the majority are very kind and observant, often picking up on very subtle things that I have put into the sculpture. People who collect my work tell me how strongly they are affected by my imagery.

"Where a sculpture is located can be the make or break of it, so when possible I will advise a collector about where it should be placed. A great location can make a good sculpture sensational. It really is very important."

When works are installed on a ship, the problem is often that there are too many other distractions.

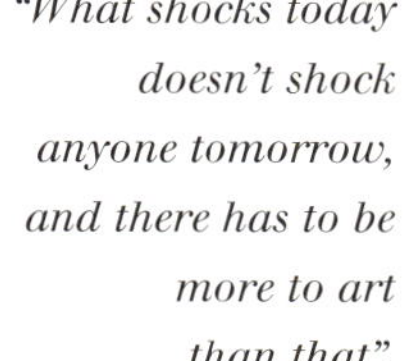

"I try to get some feeling of beauty, grace, mystery and human emotions into my sculptures. In art you can only do what you feel strongly about - I can't follow a trend, I just have to do what I feel is right."

– Philip Jackson

When people are in a gallery, they know exactly what they are there for. On a ship, art is one of many "entertainment opportunities". Jackson thinks the image has to be less subtle, more easily read than it need be in a gallery. Of course, doing work for a ship's interior entails other problems for the sculptor. The detailing and color scheme of a ship's interior is beyond the sculptor's control, and one cannot generally isolate a sculpture in its own neutral space as one can in a conventional gallery or when placing a work in a landscape. Lighting can also present problems as the ambient lighting on a ship is designed for passenger safety and not necessarily for illuminating art works to their best advantage.

"Of course one sees drawings of where the work is to go, but because of the complexity of fitting out these enormous vessels, it is basically impossible to alter the location allocated for the work to any significant degree. However, once the work is installed onboard, you know that it will be seen by a very large audience, some of whom would probably not venture into a conventional gallery."

For *Legend of the Seas*, Philip Jackson created two Shakespearean works.

"'Romeo and Juliet' is a play that I know very well so it was a most enjoyable commission. I had a fairly restricted amount of space for each figure on the ship as they had to fit into specific alcoves.

"I modeled the sculptures in clay in a reasonably impressionistic way, working the head and the hands, the expressive parts in some detail, but leaving the robes fairly rough and textural so they looked as if they were made of wood or rock. Consequently, they had a more abstract feel."

Jackson has used masks a lot in his work. "In fact I have done a whole series of works that I refer to as the 'Masks Series'. These started many years ago following a visit to Venice where I was installing a sculpture on a ship being built in the dockyard.

"Venice made a tremendous impression on me. And because I was there for some time, I was able to visit museums, galleries, walk the streets and generally get to know the city and its history quite well. In the paintings of Guardi, Canaletto, Bellotto and Longhi, I was fascinated to see the use of the mask by the 17th and 18th century Venetians.

"During this period Venice was the great hedonistic capital of the world. The rich patrician families who had built their palaces on the Grand Canal occupied their time with carnivals, balls, opera, the theater, processions, festivals and

Background: Shakesparian figures from Romeo and Juliet for the Dining Room on Legend of the Seas.

The "Don Giovanni" is from Grandeur of the Seas.

other lavish types of entertainment. Everyone knew everyone in this small, vibrant and exciting city. Constraining the excesses of the period, however, were the strict and complicated social conventions of Venetian society. To circumnavigate these, the Venetians took to the mask, behind which they could go about the city unrecognized, have illicit affairs, conduct secret assignations, vendettas and so on. They could live a double life."

Says Jackson: "The great painters of the day, of course, painted scenes of every day Venetian life inhabited by these masked figures and I was intrigued by the fact that you could tell whether the figures were male or female, angry or passive, sad or happy and so on, in spite of their hidden or masked features - all by virtue of body language. It then came to me that it would be very exciting to make a series of figurative sculptures in which the body was hidden but where the viewer read the sculpture by body language. This was the birth of the 'Mask Series'.

"The mask proved to be very successful as an idea, and a few years ago I had a major exhibition in Venice where these sculptures were seen by a large international audience. I was slightly worried about it because I thought it was a bit like taking coals to Newcastle, but the exhibition turned out to be a great success. The 'Mask Series' struck a real chord with the public and the response was most heartening.

"I think that even nowadays, at the beginning of the 21st century, we sometimes still go round in a kind of mask, except that now we call them cars. We have ways of hiding our identity; if you get into a Ferrari, you can't help behaving like someone who drives a Ferrari. If you get into a Morris Minor, you become someone quite different. This idea of people having different personalities which they change from time to time is quite intriguing.

"I also endeavor to give my work a feeling of theatricality, which is why I think that location and lighting is so important. At the Venice exhibition, the sculpture was lit at night, giving a truly exciting and dramatic change of gear to the exhibition after dark. It was almost like having two exhibitions. I always encourage those who buy my works to consider installing lighting for this very reason.

"Other things that inspire me are music and the theater. Many of my sculptures are derived from the music I love or the drama of the opera. When I am creating a new piece, I play music in the studio and this actually affects the way the sculpture develops. It is interesting that I have gotten letters from musicians who have been kind enough to say that my works have been very inspirational to them. One particular person who became a good friend and who is a cellist of great renown was inspired to compose a piece of music about a particular piece of my sculpture. In a way, that completes the circle." ■

The interview took place in Philip Jackson's studio/gallery in Midhurst, West Sussex, UK.

CV

Philip Jackson, British sculptor, was born in Scotland and now lives in West Sussex, UK.

1987–89: Winner of National Peace Sculpture Competition, Manchester City Council 1987. Elected Fellow Royal Society of British Sculptors.
1990–92: Awarded Otto Beit Medal for Sculpture. Awarded Silver Medal by Royal Society of British Sculptors. Winner of Mozart Bicentenary Sculpture Competition – Belgravia London 1991. Solo exhibition, Solothurn, Switzerland. Falklands War Memorial Sculpture unveiled at Portsmouth by Baroness Thatcher.
1993–95: Winner of Liberation Sculpture Competition, Jersey, Channel Islands – the sculpture was later unveiled by HRH The Prince of Wales. Solo exhibitions: Stansted Park Foundation, Chichester Festivities, Chelmsford Cathedral, Jersey Museum, Jersey UK and Casanova Gardens, Venice, Italy.
1996–99: Solo exhibitions: Pashley Manor, East Sussex; Parkview Gallery, Bristol, UK; and in Naples Florida, USA.
The Wallenberg Monument unveiled in London by HM The Queen. The Ghurka Memorial unveiled in London by HM The Queen. Constantine the Great unveiled at York Minster by Lord Coggan. Christ in Judgement unveiled at Chicester Cathedral by Lord St. John of Fawsley. Empress Elisabeth of Austria (Sissi) unveiled in Geneva, Switzerland. Sculpture for the Royal Hospital Chelsea. Sculpture of St. Richard for Chicester Cathedral. Portrait of King George VI for Darthmouth Naval College.
Philip Jackson has works of art onboard the RCI cruise ships *Legend of the Seas*, *Grandeur of the Seas*, and the third *Voyager Class* ship – *Adventure of the Seas*.

Larry Kirkland

(Photo: Jon Lie)

"My work is really about the place that it's in."

– Larry Kirkland

Larry Kirkland has created over 150 large-scale art commissions throughout the world. These site specific environmental installations are more than something that hang in the air or sit on the ground. "My work is really about the place that it's in. I try to define a space more than just make an object in that space," says Kirkland.

Writes Jean Lawlor Cohen about some of his large installations: "Larry Kirkland creates art in the high and wide interiors designed by many of today's architects... They add color, form and movement to the architectural spaces."

Kirkland utilizes the expertise and teamwork more often associated with architects and builders than with fine artists. He works closely with engineers, fabricators, tradesmen and, of course, the client, with the same efficient friendliness. The scale of the work demands that many other people contribute their abilities to realize the monumental artworks. He takes pleasure in the logistical and political complexities and relishes the problem-solving.

Among his works are two large installations for the huge atriums onboard the RCI ships *Splendour of the Seas* and *Voyager of the Seas.* In 1995 RCI gave him the opportunity to present some ideas for their new ship, *Splendour of the Seas.* His work had been presented by an American art consultant and caught the eye of *Splendour* architect, Njål Eide. A visit to Oslo by the artist resulted in a mutual appreciation between the artist and architect.

"The two large installations for *Splendour* and *Voyager* involved large engineering issues, as does anything on a ship. Weight is important. The higher the artwork is placed onboard, the less it should weigh, says Kirkland. There is enormous concern that if the ship is top-heavy, it will change the center of gravity. Movement is another. On land, movement can be an interesting aspect of a work of art, and sometimes quite wonderful, like the mobiles of Calder. But on a ship, movement can be disturbing to some passengers – it can cause motion sickness. If a ship encounters rough seas, a hanging sculpture or chandelier could swing erratically in the space and make the visitors feel uncomfortable. I don't want to contribute to anyone feeling ill so we have tried to create an illusion of motion and airiness. What we want to remain stable should remain still.

"There are many issues that must be considered: elegance, beauty, memorable aesthetics,

"The Dancer and the Tutu" Centrum sculpture, Voyager of the Seas.

technical difficulties and installation complications. The engineer's mind and my own must be together from the beginning of the conceptualization."

Kirkland's fabrication team works carefully with the shipyard to time the installation. Kirkland's large works come in multiple pieces, or modules. "We actually assemble them within the ship on the site of the installation. I have watched other artists have difficulties bringing on very large pieces that can't fit through the doors to the ship. We not only ship over the artwork from the States to the Yard, but every tool and bolt necessary

for installation. Our efficiency makes a good impression with the workers at the shipyards. That's important when you are an American working in France, Germany or Finland!"

Splendour of the Seas

"On *Splendour*, the piece titled Terra Soleil Ciel is really in three parts: the earth, the suspended solar ray and the wall relief of the constellations. This sky-map was inspired by an original zodiac map drawn by Albrecht Dürer hundreds of years ago. I wish this piece was illuminated more effectively. It seems to disappear. With a wash of light it would glow above the sun-ring and the earth below. The earth globe is an important part of the tensioning device of the sun-ring. All the cables go into the globe and are held in place by a special device that keeps the stainless steel cables in constant tension. We use similar hardware on sailboats; marine fittings, in concert with some specially designed items of our own. Each cable has it's own tiny spring which allows the piece to have some give and take with the motion of the ship. Think of it a little like breathing.

Model for Centrum sculpture, Splendour of the Seas.

the *Voyager*. The Dancer is an airy sculpture that ascends from Deck three to ten. Hundreds of cables, threaded with gilded rods, spheres and acrylic discs makes an effervescent cone of reflected light. At night the special lighting washes the elements in softly swirling color, like an enormous glass of bubbly champagne.

"I tried to make the entire artwork slowly rotate, but there was resistance to the idea of a complicated mechanical device. We tried to accomplish the illusion of movement with the lighting. The piece was created to be very transparent to allow the passengers to see through it from the Royal Promenade up into the atrium." says Kirkland.

The *Voyager* installation was also created with the collaboration of Oslo architect, Njål Eide. "Together we understand the entire experience of the space and conceive of sculptural additions to enhance the viewers experience. With such a large ship, the artwork must work together as both a collection of artworks, as well as memorable way-finding devices for the passengers."

The other artworks by Kirkland on *Voyager* are found in the center of the Royal Promenade ceiling on Deck 5. The dome-like Oculus and Beauty Ring help define the small amount of natural light coming in from the skylight at the pool on Deck 10. This opening upon Deck 10 is capped by the Jewel Pyramid, an eight sided cone of dichroic glass.

The piece is made to react to the slightest movement and adjust back to the original position. We learned from looking at a sculpture on a previous ship that this ability to "breathe" was important.

"In the first test crossing the ocean, the cables snapped because they were overly tight. You can't have cables be overly stressed because of the dynamic movement of a ship. Ships float on moving seas and respond to this motion. Everything attached to the ship affected by this force must be able to 'breathe' with the ship."

Voyager of the Seas

There are several Kirkland sculptures in the Royal Promenade of

"The Jewel Pyramid" also called "The Beacon". Glass pyramid. Voyager of the Seas.

Complex state of the art lighting within the three pieces creates an ephemeral cone of moving light and color. The Beauty Ring is a three dimensional Compass Rose with eight points of the compass in a constant evolution of color. Above it the glass layers of The Oculus are defined by lines of light and color in constant motion that lead the viewer's eye all the way up, through the vessel, to the Deck 10 Pyramid – quite spectacular. The Jewel Pyramid acts both as the central focus of the skylight but also as a sculptural form on the pool deck. "I was inspired by an Italian baroque cathedral in Turin I remembered from my art history classes. The building up of geometric forms and ending with a small opening for natural light to stream through to illuminate the lacy forms of the dome was translated into glass and moving light."

Kirkland presents his ideas directly to the RCI Steering Committee and CEO Richard D. Fain. The scale and complexity of Kirkland's work demands a direct communication with this group. "It all begins with listening. It is so important that I hear from Richard D. Fain, the Steering Committee and ship designers what they are trying to achieve for the ship. We have an opportunity to review some of my past work, discuss the ideas for the current sculptures, consider new suggestions and refine the form, color and scale of the work in progress. I also bring along the engineering team to discuss the pragmatic and structural issues of each project."

"With work on the ships, trust is important. The older I become, I find that trust by people in any situation is the key to success. So far, RCI has exhibited a lot of trust in me and our work together has been a reflection of that. I am offered many project opportunities and find that the most satisfying ones are those in challenging places with unique parameters directed by people who are looking for innovative and exciting results. RCI has certainly provided me with these!

"I think that architecture, even at its most inspiring, is made to provide a shelter for us. Art is the something that brings us alive – or attempts to. We identify not so much with the spaces as the touchstones within them that create a memory. Hopefully, the art in our environment becomes one of those memorable touchstones. Art is about being moved in some way and that should be the soul of our dwelling spaces."

"Artists are looking for an ideal. Their creative struggle is to find perfection; and perfection may have little to do with truth. Most of the time I don't like the word 'artist' because it has been so abused. My desire is not to be so much of an 'Artist' as to live a creative life. I strive to bring creativity to the places I work in. I bring a strong understanding of design and art to an environment and always remember that it will be inhabited by people. They are at the center of the experience." ■

The interview took place in Washington, DC, USA.

CV

Larry Kirkland, b. 1950, American. Graduate of Oregon State University (B.S. 1972 with Honors) and The University of Kansas (M.F.A. 1974 with Honors). After returning to O.S.U. to teach in the Department of Art, he moved to Portland, Oregon and established a studio in 1976. Since that time he has concentrated on the creation of artworks in public spaces. Kirkland has installations in diverse places and environments including: Putra World Trade Center, Kuala Lumpur, Malaysia; Kansai International Airport, Osaka, Japan; John Hopkins University, Baltimore, Maryland, USA; Oregon Health Sciences University, Portland, Oregon, USA. Major work for RCI Cruiseliners: *Splendour of the Seas* (Centrum Sculpture) and *Voyager of the Seas* (Centrum Sculpture and Glass Pyramid) and *Adventure of the Seas* (Centrum Sculpture).

Globe, Centrum, Splendour of the Seas.

Peter Layton

> *"Our aim is to exploit the reflection of light and color."*
>
> *Peter Layton*

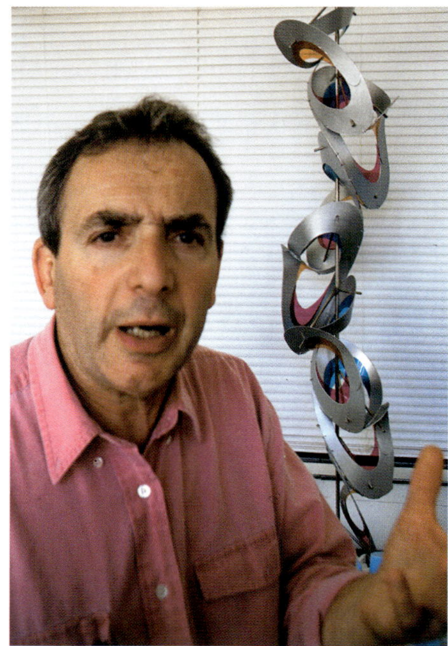

Peter Layton in his London Studio. (Photo: Jon Lie)

In collaboration with Simon Moss, Peter Layton has produced two large Centrum sculptures for RCI ships, "Janus" on *Legend* and "Ariel" on *Vision of the Seas.*

"Working for RCI has been a very interesting and worthwhile experience," comments Peter Layton. "It's enjoyable being in an environment like shipbuilding. It is a world apart seeing those structures at the yard in France. Working with the French has been pleasant. Most of what we have done onboard the ships has been in France. Dealing with the language – you need to be part psychologist, part engineer, part artist, part businessman: It's been a very fascinating experience – one I wouldn't have missed for the world, really. And we don't feel restrained by the brief. In fact, we like the brief in a way; the challenge of that space."

Layton and Simon Moss work very much as a team. They collaborate very closely on everything they use for the ship. There are some pieces where Layton has initiated the idea and there are others where Moss has been the originator: "It's very much a back and forth, to and fro, give and take relationship," Layton remarks.

"We consult one another on virtually every stage. Simon Moss has a design background and handles the technical aspects to a large extent, although we both tend to meet with engineers. Most of what we have done for the ships has been a combination of metal and glass. We have worked exclusively with one metal worker – John Crisfield – he is in effect the third member of our team.

"On the initial project, for the Centrum onboard the *Legend of the Seas,* we worked very closely with the head architect, the Norwegian Njål Eide. He had a lot of input. At our first meeting, he said 'I want something like this,' and he made a drawing. We translated that in two or three different ways. Our first glamorous proposal was rejected. We were one of two or three teams that submitted. But we got a second chance. And it took a long time before we came up with this piece that we called 'Janus'. He is a two-headed god, looking both forwards and backwards. He is also the god of entrances and exits. We regarded the Centrum very much as a meeting place, and the gap between the elevator shafts as an entrance.

"It was very interesting when we were actually putting the piece up. We were in France at the shipyard in St. Nazaire. It was freezing cold, blasts of icy air blowing through the ship. We were desperately putting this sculpture together. It had never been completely assembled, and there's always that gamble: Is it going to work? We were working against very tight deadlines. It was a hair-raising experience. The French workers were standing around, looking at it, wondering what the hell it was going to be. They could see a school of dolphins diving, and it was really interesting to hear the kind of interpretations they were giving the piece.

"It really was a tough job, and we sweated blood. We could not have given more during the installation. We worked for two weeks, morning, noon and night. Breaks were on the job. They wanted to get the scaffolding down, because it was holding things up in the Centrum. We had to extend the deadlines because we were not ready. Because we were a bit inexperienced, we were terrified that the Chantiers yard would use us as an excuse for delays. We didn't intend to be that delay, so we were determined to get it finished. They wanted the scaffolding down by the end of the week. I think it was on a Saturday the ship finally departed. By Wednesday they were agitated, and we still needed another couple of days. There were two pieces and a fountain below. We were working flat out and they said to us that everything is supposed to be finished at 12 o'clock Saturday and that there's going to be a little reception with drinks etc. Therefore the scaffolding had to come down at 5 a.m. Saturday morning. Absolutely. No argument.

We worked through that night, installing the fiber optic lighting. What they did not tell us was that at midnight they were going to switch all the lights off for an alarm test, and that they would be off for several hours. We were up there on the scaffolding – very high up – when the lights went out. I rushed to the security people to borrow a flashlight. We would have bought flashlights if we had known. One of them lent me a flashlight that was useless after five minutes. The only thing we could get was a small pencil light. We finished the job, eight stories up, with me holding the pencil flashlight in my mouth, so that the three of us up there could have our hands free to finish working on the fiber optic lighting. We worked until five – I didn't sleep one minute that night as there were other small pieces to be finished. At about 11:30 a.m., I could see that the waiters were already there, and at 12 the guests arrived. We finished just in time. Perfect. And it was sheer magic when the scaffolding came down. We had never seen the piece assembled before but it was worth all the problems and pain of installation. It was one of those peak moments – on top of the mountain – there are few of those in one's life. It had worked – and it looked fantastic!

Legend of the Seas*: Big sculpture – hard work.*

"One of our reasons for using polished metal is that we had this magnificent lighted environment. Our aim was to exploit the reflection of light and color. In the end you can't see the steel, you see color, areas of color, areas of light – and the glass and the metal are almost interchangeable. Peoples' movements help create a kinetic quality derived from the light and color.

"The first crossing of the Atlantic, from St. Nazaire to New York, was in very stormy weather, and we were quite worried. We had no idea how these pieces were going to survive. I remember asking someone from LCA. He said: 'The piece was wonderful, it moved majestically.' It was certainly never meant to be kinetic in that sense!

"The piece on *Vision of the Seas*, 'Ariel' is altogether different, but it is also related to the 'Janus' – a further development. We went through many stages. Obviously, the

Steering Committee is the final arbiter, but Njål Eide was very involved and very much the inspiration for this whole group of works.

"We often start out with little cardboard models, then we expand them and eventually do large metal ones. With this *Vision* piece, we progressed through many versions before we arrived at 'Ariel'. Njål suggested some changes. He is a visionary guy, and I have a lot of respect for him.

"There's a certain spin-off from one project to another. You don't make two pieces look the same, but if you have a space like the atrium or the Centrum in an RCI ship, you want to make the most of it, and there are certain problems you have already solved when you do the next one.

"We've been very lucky, particularly with *Vision*. The architect more or less said: "Here's the space. Do something". Njål was confident, knowing what we had done before. We also did the niche pieces for the stairways, we did not want just to produce some little object of art in a niche. We wanted the niche to work as a whole.

"Nevertheless, Njål Eide likes to have input, and also likes to have a degree of control. But he wants us to initiate the work. He is happiest when we come up with something and he can say, 'yes, but …' He knows he needs something, but he doesn't quite know what, and is big enough to allow us to make our proposal. The Centrum sculpture on the *Vision of the Seas* was entirely our idea, but he made a suggestion that improved it. That's the sign of a good working relationship." ■

The interview took place in Peter Layton's workshop and studio in London.

"One of our reasons for using polished metal is that we had this magnificent lighted environment, says Peter Layton. Our aim is to exploit the reflection of light and color. In the end you can't see the steel, you see color, areas of color, areas of light – and the glass and the metal are almost interchangeable. Peoples' movements help create a kinetic quality derived from the light and color." Peter Layton (left) and Simon Moss with model for Vision of the Seas.

CV

Peter Layton, b. 1937 in Prague, Czech Republic, British.
Educated at Bradford College of Art 1960–62 and the Central School of Art and Design 1962–65. Lecturer at various colleges of art in the USA and Britain 1972–80. In 1976, he opened the London Glassblowing Workshop which he is still running.
Exhibitions include shows in major galleries, glass museums, and craft fairs in Britain, Germany, Luxembourg, France, USA, Slovakia and the Czech Republic.
Public collections include: Liverpool Museum; Castle Museum, Nottingham; Victoria and Albert Museum, London; Broadfield House Glass Museum, West Midlands; Royal Scottish Museum, Edinburgh; Glasgow Museum; Norwich Museum & Art Gallery, in the UK; National Museum, Prague, Czech Republic; Gus Khrvstalny Glass Museum, Russia; International Glass Museum, Ebeltoft, Denmark.

Simon Moss, b. 1967, British.
Education: Somerset College of Arts and Technology 1985–86, Ravensbourne College of Design and Communication, BA Hons Degree Product Design 1986–89. His role in the collaboration/teamwork with Peter Layton has become progressively stronger since he joined the London Glassblowing Workshop in 1990. Initially working with Layton on small sculptural designs for exhibitions and commissions, he now takes major responsibility for all commissioned works.
Simon Moss has cooperated with Peter Layton on all the sculptural commissions for the cruise ships. He has contributed to 16 major exhibitions since 1991.

Victor Lind

"The first art piece I made for a cruise ship was six meters high. It towered a meter over my studio roof. On the outside. It was cold painting out there during the winter," recalls Victor Lind. "You need to be organized and practical, and that agrees with me. You can't make a six-meter painting on a whim. You have to have a good rough draft."

Lind explains the process of art commissions from beginning to end: "It usually starts out with my answering machine. 'Call Njål Eide,' says a voice. It turns out they have a ship in Finland, and they'd fancy having something to cover a certain wall.

"Things are pretty unclear in the beginning phase. We discuss it a little bit. It takes some 8 to 10 months from the conception of the idea to the finished work. Overall, it is an advantage to have clear agreements, a set timeframe and delivery date, but not necessarily time pressure. An amount is an amount, and a date is a date.

"RCI doesn't want the same thing every time, quite the contrary. We have to constantly figure out new things, pose new questions," says Lind. "These commissions also mean freedom, not least to say 'no' to jobs I don't really want to do, jobs that involve unprofessional committees and difficult people.

"The draft models are important. I make new proposals for the large pieces while I work. 'Is this what I had in mind?' I ask myself. I can then return to the big piece when I've figured out what I want. It's always different to actually see a work than to think or talk about it.

"In the old days, they called it 'studies'. An artist made 'studies' as he worked. Once I started out painting a motif based on Mount Spåtind in Norway, where I had a cottage. I ended up with a painting of Mount Arrarat where Noah ran aground with the Ark after the water receded. It is a privilege to be able to let my imagination run free. I don't need any concrete references from the real world. But that is the starting point," says Lind.

At first Lind did all his paintings on canvas, including works for the ships. But this was a complicated process. "When the painting was finished, you had to take the canvas off the frame and screw a 3-millimeter aluminum plate onto the frame," he explains. "After that, the canvas was stretched over the plate. This made it strong and fireproof. But then we figured out that we could just as well paint directly onto the aluminum plate. This also

Victor Lind in his Oslo Studio.

"Art doesn't come into being through a majority decision. I am the one who decides – but there are many others who contribute."

– Victor Lind

had the advantage of making it much easier to redo something if you weren't satisfied with what you had done."

However, it turned out that the aluminum posed its own set of problems. "When you paint on metal, you can't assume that the paint will just stick," clarifies Lind. "In order to make it work, first the metal plate has to be roughly sanded and acid-washed to remove any oils. After that, it's rinsed with Lynol and alcohol. A lot is based on experience from working with graphics. I've been involved in a lot of unusual techniques. I've also been a teacher at the Academy of Art. When you teach you are forced to figure out how things are supposed to work. I often run into technical problems when I am working. A solution can generally be found, but it has to be a good one.

"In order to test out the technique, you can paint with different kinds of colors on different kinds of plates that are prepared in different ways," Lind continues. "You can let them dry for a week and then put them all in a bucket of water overnight. Then you can see which ones can tolerate moisture and therefore can be used."

One of Lind's works is a 12 meter-high painting on the *Voyager of the Seas*, which spreads over four decks, equivalent to five floors in a large building. It is located next to the elevators at one end of the Royal Promenade. The shipyard managed to mount this work without any problem, but the installation instructions were a chapter in themselves. They had to be totally accurate, without any possibility for misinterpretation or misunderstanding.

"We have to know exactly where the crossbeams behind the wall are and how much weight they can handle. Large works have to be divided up into smaller elements and the workers must have an installation plan and instructions to follow," says Lind. "But sometimes it happens that the wall has been made smaller than in the original design.

"and you get someone to assist you. You go to work in high boots, a hard hat and a boiler suit. It's a far cry from the image of a painter out in nature with a beret and easel. And the guys at the workshop got a kick out of this 'art' stuff. They saw someone who works rough and dirty just like them."

"Midgard". Painting on aluminium plate. Main Stairs, Enchantment of the Seas.

"The placement and dimensioning are almost as important as the actual painting," Lind continues. "A work has to be seen as a whole with many elements. The pieces on the *Voyager* are a series of 2x4-meter aluminum plates that are etched with hydrochloric acid. Because of the size and weight of these plates, you need at least two men to carry them. You feel that in your back."

Lind explains that his work couldn't be done in a normal studio. He made his artworks at Hamy Sveis outside of Oslo. "There they have industrial equipment, lifts, cranes and a 1,500-square meter floor," he says,

Now the plates are installed on the *Voyager of the Seas* and Lind is pleased with the results. "They work extremely well," he smiles. "They are true originals – full of traces from a calculated process. This work is about seeing possibilities, directions, solutions. It's not just drawing a sketch and then enlarging it."

Lind enjoys the work he does for RCI and feels it is a great opportunity for an artist to develop. "This is interesting work," he concedes, "but it's not the kind of thing you start on just to try it out. You need to have a commission and a professional reason. Then you can experiment with techniques that you never would have been able to try otherwise. The economics are in place, you set aside the time you need and you get a hold of at least one assistant."

Lind says there is a mutual trust in his collaboration with architect Njål Eide and the art consultants from LCA. "If I went to another architect and another employer with my proposals, I would have to make many more drafts, but Njål Eide understands what I'm doing. He says that it sounds fine – 'Try it'. So we give it a try and it usually turns out well.

"Trust is a key concept for Eide," Lind continues. "We throw the ball back and forth about what can be done and how. He has ideas himself, he senses the direction, but he's not sure exactly. I often have the answer. This back-and-forth dialog is important. We are both professionals. And during this process, with its tight deadlines, feedback comes quickly. When I have a proposal ready, I call Eide, who is a very busy man. He comes and sits in the loft of my studio and drinks coffee and looks at art. That way he gets a little break too. After a while, the art consultants at LCA enter the picture. But the same goes for them. You are talking with people who are qualified to take part in this discussion; they usually have comments, but they are too busy to waste time with small talk. They don't flatter – they say what they think. This is something entirely different than figuring out things on your own," says Lind, adding: "Art doesn't come into being through a majority decision. I am the one who decides – but there are many others who contribute. And this is really how one should work in this day and age."

Lind says the final phase is the most exhausting. "There's often a rush period during which you work extremely hard to finish the work. When everything is delivered, all the boxes have been sent to the shipyard, all the instructions for mounting have been understood, you can be pretty exhausted." ■

This interview with Victor Lind took place in his studio in Oslo.

"Full of traces from a calculated process". Etched aluminium. Voyager of the Seas. *Niche sculpture by Pearl Levy.*

CV

Victor Lind, b. 1940, Norwegian.
Lives in Oslo.
Educated: National College of Art and Design, Oslo, 1966–67. National Academy of Fine Arts, Oslo, 1966–69.
Teaching: Associate Professor, National Academy of Fine Arts, Oslo, 1972–87.

Represented in museums and collections in Norway: The National Gallery; The National Touring Exhibitions; the Norwegian Council for Cultural Affairs; Kunst på Arbeidsplassen, Oslo; Municipal Art Collections; The City Art Collection, Bergen; Rogaland Art Museum; The Gallery of Trøndelag; Haugesund Art Gallery; Rogaland Kunstmuseum; Lillehammer Art Museum; the National Museum of Contemporary Art.
International: Musée d'Art Moderne, Liege, Belgium; Museum of Contemporary Art, Skopje, Yugoslavia; Museo de Arte Moderne de Campina, Sao Paolo, Brazil; Biblioteque National, Paris, France.

Victor Lind has made numerous monumental works since 1965 in schools, banks, factories and several cruise ships.

He has participated in a great number of international exhibitions and biennales all over Europe and in America. More than 30 solo exhibitions since 1962.

Carl Nesjar

Carl Nesjar, known for his ice fountains and many years of sculptural collaboration with Pablo Picasso, has many irons in the fire. If he's not on an airplane on his way to give an art lecture somewhere in the world, he's hatching a new project in ice and steel. As usual, he has large commissions ahead: on top of the list is a park project in Kristinehamn in Sweden, where he will erect huge propeller shafts and other industrial forms.

Nesjar has a matter-of-fact way of expressing himself. Celebrity is not his style. He's never been a prophet in his own land; he has a more prominent name out in the world. In addition to the ice fountains he has made in many different countries, Nesjar has left his mark in the form of monumental, sandblasted Picasso sculptures.

"Think how much easier it would have been to stand in the studio and paint watercolors," reminisces Nesjar, thinking back on all the architects, engineers, casters, carpenters, construction workers, plumbers, and electricians he has worked with throughout the years. The meeting between technology and art can sometimes be frictional, but it mostly affords great pleasure," explains Nesjar.

In the interface between natural sciences and art, Nesjar is probably the only Norwegian painter who has made stop-overs at the Institute for Refrigeration Techniques at the Norwegian University of Science and Technology and at Massachusetts Institute of Technology (MIT). That's how things can develop when one has more than paintbrushes at hand – sandblasting equipment, for example.

The road leading to the creation of the first water and ice fountain in

Ås, outside Oslo, began with a concrete Picasso frieze in Barcelona. After that came the USA. An extended stay at MIT gave Nesjar a glimpse of what could be the art of the future: large holograms that can be projected over more than a kilometer. "Imagine the Egyptian Pyramids projected three-dimensionally upon the night sky," says Nesjar. "Energy is a function of interest; one masters what one is interested in."

Nesjar's Centrum sculpture for the *Enchantment of the Seas*, called "Northern Light", is made out of huge acrylic prisms that hover and shine in space. The prism form is again repeated in a sculpture sitting in a small circular pool at the Champagne Bar on Deck 4.

"Energy is a function of interest; one masters what one is interested in."
– Carl Nesjar

It is like a bouquet in a circle under the large installation on a convex steel platform, and is sprinkled with water to liven it up.

"We started with a large Atrium with a glass ceiling," Nesjar continues. "The ship was to sail in the south, where the sun is high in the sky, and we decided to make use of that as much as possible. We discussed the possibility that the light scattered by the prisms might have a blinding effect at certain times, but fortunately this was not the case.

"The installation was built partly at Hamy Sveis outside of Oslo, and partly onboard the ship. First we made a working model in 1:10 scale in a steel frame. Here we defined the space perpendicularly and with circles. We worked for weeks on it with string and paper prisms. Njål Eide came out to see it and didn't want it to hang as low as I originally proposed.

"Each section of the sculpture was made at the workshop. The boys at Hamy did a great job with the sections that hold the parts of the sculpture and the relationship between them. It was difficult to make these large forms 'float' in the air in the Atrium while at the same time remain relatively stable at sea. But when we came on-board, we found that it was even more of a challenge than any of us had expected. We toiled with the installation for 14 days, but we eventually got it up. The final touches were made the night before the ship was to leave the yard in Helsinki. Now it is sailing around the Caribbean."

Nesjar is accustomed to trying new techniques. "If you do something that hasn't been done before, technical problems will inevitably occur," he says. "The main point is that the work functions as it was intended." In the case of the Enchantment installation, the high sun was an important factor that Nesjar used to his advantage.

Carl Nesjar is now older than Picasso was when they first met. Yet he doesn't appear ready to rest on his laurels. As a fountain sculptor who uses ice as his medium, he has a different perspective on time than most people. Once he drank glacier water from a 'hanging glacier' in Alaska, he recalls, and afterwards an engineer calculated that the water had fallen as snow at the time of the Trojan War. "Imagine that," says Nesjar. "A peaceful snowfall up in Alaska while Achilles and the boys were fighting."

"We made a working model in 1:10 scale in a steel frame".

There can also be other perspectives and dimensions to a sculpture, as Nesjar relates. A four-story high, naked Picasso woman that he had constructed in 1975 stood in Chicago until a wealthy Japanese bought it as part of a package deal that included a park, laboratory and the art. The woman, weighing in at 100 tons of concrete, was put into a steel box and sent as special freight via New Orleans and Le Havre to the Japanese buyer's enormous golf complex in Normandy – complete with swimming pool, two Henry Moore sculptures and a large farm fixed up to nearly plastic perfection. Everything was fine until the Japanese encountered money problems and a new owner entered the scene. The gigantic Picasso sculpture was prepared for yet another journey, this time to an unidentified new owner.

"Nobody should complain about the lack of movement in the art world," says Nesjar laconically. ■

This interview with Carl Nesjar took place in his studio in Oslo, Norway.

CV

Carl Nesjar, b. 1920, Norwegian.
Education: Pratt Institute, N.Y.C.; National School of Art and Design, Oslo; Royal Academy of Art, Oslo; Columbia University, N.Y.C.

Carl Nesjar participated in decoration of the government building in Oslo the last half of the 1950's. In 1957 he came in touch with Pablo Picasso, who made the drawings for this project. His works were ended in 1971. Together with Picasso, Nesjar has also made several monumental sculptures, in Europe, Israel and USA.

Nesjar has produced many works in Europe and USA where water, ice and light are part of the sculpture. His last project was a seven-meter-high year-round fountain with water in the summer and ice in the winter for Statoils Forskningssenter in Trondheim. In addition to his activities as painter, graphic artist and sculptor, Carl Nesjar has also worked with photography. As a painter he is influenced by French and American painting and his abstract works often derive inspiration from nature.

Centrum-sculpputure "Northern Light" for Enchantment of the Seas *was made of huge acrylic prisms that hower and shine in space.*

Michael Newby

"The word 'no' is not in my vocabulary."
– Michael Newby

Michael Newby and his Glassworks Studio have made several large glass sculptures and panels for the RCI fleet. Their relationship began in an unusual way, back in 1990, as Newby recounts: "A design company in central London kept asking us for samples of etched sandblasted glass. When it took 10–15 minutes to make and send the samples, it was fine. But these things got bigger and bigger, yet we didn't get any work from it, even though we were spending more and more time. I got tired of this and was about to start charging for any amount of time more than 30 minutes. Then – out of the blue – they rang and asked if we wanted to make a glass sculpture of Marilyn Monroe. I said, 'fine'. We had never done anything like that before. Nobody had.

"They wanted to know the costs," continues Newby. "How do you calculate something that has never been done? I came up with a figure that didn't mean anything to me. I phoned them up and said 'OK, but it's going to cost you this'. I thought, 'thank God, that's gone away.'

"After four weeks we got a purchase order in the mail. That's how the artwork projects started for my studio.

"However, it turned out that Marilyn Monroe was copyrighted, and the rights were very expensive. So instead, it was agreed that Newby would do a rendition of Fats Waller playing the piano. "I found a still photo taken from a 1943 film," says Newby, "where you could just see Fats Waller playing the piano at the back of the band. I blew it up, and said 'we'll do something like that'. 'Go ahead', they said. So we did Fats Waller for the *Sovereign of the Seas*. It was quite a big piece."

Initially, Newby was not very happy with the result, he confides. "You can start off with an idea in your head – this is what it's going to look like. Then you look at the finished work and are dissatisfied. If you didn't know how it was meant to look, it might look fine, but the artist knows that this is not what he started out to make.

"We finished Fats Waller late on a Wednesday night. I looked at it and thought 'it's awful, just terrible'. We went to the pub and got drunk. I remember thinking that it might look better in the morning. But then it still looked like rubbish. I saw it six months later when I had forgotten what my perceptions were, and actually it was not bad at all. It wasn't brilliant, but it wasn't bad. This was before we got in touch with London Contemporary Art.

"We never saw it go onboard. And we heard nothing from RCI. After a while, times were bad and we employed an advertising agency to help build new business. It turned out to be pretty useless. Except for one thing, they wanted to put together a brochure on us, and for that they needed a good quality photograph, so they asked RCI if they had one of the Fats Waller sculpture. RCI responded by saying that they had been looking for us for several years. RCI's CEO, Richard D. Fain, had seen the Fats Waller sculpture and liked it. So we started to get regular commissions from RCI and their art consultants after that."

Ben Jenkins (top) and Michael Newby building "Aurora Borealis/Ice Ship" for Vision of the Seas.

Newby was asked to make three stained-glass windows for the *Enchantment of the Seas*. The theme was 'Carnival', featuring three main carnivals: Pasadena Festival of the Roses; Trinidad and Tobago Carnival; and Mardi Gras in New Orleans.

"I went to Norway to see the head architect, Njål Eide," says Newby. "There was a big meeting where I presented the panels. They liked them, but not quite. They thought I was trying to do too much, that I should make it simpler. They were right," Newby readily admits.

Another project Newby completed for RCI was a glass ship for the aft lounge on the *Legend of the Seas*. "That has many stories attached to it," smiles Newby. "We made a lot of proposals and sketches. They went back and forth across the Atlantic until we had five months before delivery date.

"Fats Waller". Glass Sculpture for Sovereign of the Seas. *The team was so busy making the sculpture of the man that they almost forgot to make the piano.*

We started working, but there was tremendous weight involved. I had no idea what would happen if you put that much glass on top of a base. It might crumble.

"On a Saturday night at nine o'clock, with the glass ship in a large scaffolding crane, we all stood around it; nobody spoke. We put it down on the base and expected all hell to break loose. But it didn't. We ended up being satisfied with the job," recalls Newby.

"We had mayhem getting it out of the workshop though. It was so big. They closed off the road for a day just to get this thing out. I went to the St. Nazaire Yard in France to have a look at the ship. Ben Jenkins, who was working with me, was on the other side of the gate. He'd been there for some time to supervise the fitting. He rushed towards me and said: 'Before anyone else tells you – they dropped it!' The problem was that the glass ship was supposed to go on deck seven, but they couldn't get something so big onto that deck. They tried for two days with big cranes.

"Somehow, I still don't know how, they had finally got it up there. But in the process they had taken the ship with the waves away from the base. The base was too large, so they tried to cut it, and that's when they dropped it. And the piece of glass that covered all the lighting was the only piece of glass you couldn't get to. That was the piece that cracked of course. So we agreed to cover the front and the back with stainless steel."

Newby says that his cooperation with RCI and the art consultants of LCA has been vital to his studio's development. "I started glasswork 20 years ago with a stained glass studio. And I like to think that we have done some good stained glass work," he says. "But if it were not for RCI and LCA, we would still be a stained glass company. They've had the vision and the money to allow us to develop ideas that we would not possibly have thought of. The word 'no' is not in my vocabulary. So when they ask for a glass ship, I say 'yes'. It's only afterwards it strikes me that 'no' might have been the right answer."

Newby adds: "Every piece we have made for RCI is a prototype. We are exploring the possibilities of glass and how it interacts with light and fiber optics. Natural light can give some amazing effects. Fiber optics and color are like punching light. You see how far it will go through glass. What happens when the glass stops the light? Do you need a broken edge to keep the light in the glass? These are the kinds of questions we ask." ■

This interview with Michael Newby took place in his studio in London, UK.

CV

Michael Newby, British, born 1943.
After graduating from the University of London with an honors degree in Economics, Mike Newby had a successful career in industry, both in the UK and the United States.

In 1980 he decided to change careers completely and follow his creative leaning. He began *Glassworks* as a stained glass studio in London but since then he has expanded its technical and creative repertoire to include most forms of glass decoration. He has undertaken major commissions for private and corporate clients worldwide using glass in a two and three dimensional context.
Mike Newby has important works on several of the RCI cruise ships, including *Legend, Splendour, Grandeur, Rhapsody, Enchantment, Vision and Voyager of the Seas.*

Fin Serck-Hanssen

Fin Serck-Hanssen took nearly all of the photographs in this book. He is an art photographer who has exhibited works in several countries. A large number of his works can be seen in the forward stairs onboard the *Voyager of the Seas*.

The motifs in Serck-Hanssen's *Voyager* photographs are taken from the Jostedal Glacier, the largest glacier in western Norway.

"If I have a need for it,
I find a technique.
Everything else,
I don't bother with."
– Fin Serck-Hanssen

Fin Serck-Hanssen likes his pets.

He wanted to avoid references to size in the images so that they could be seen as microscopic sections or as vast landscapes; they have both qualities. They seem abstract, almost anatomical, and can bring to mind Lennart Nilsson's close-ups of the body's internal organs, with the same sort of shifting of hues. Serck-Hanssen works in a blue spectrum, however, as opposed to Nilsson's warm red tones.

The glacier project came about as a commission for the Winter Olympics in Lillehammer in 1994, as a part of an artistic presentation on the theme "Winterland". These works provided the starting point for the series that now hangs on the *Voyager of the Seas*.

Serck-Hanssen says that taking these photographs was demanding work. "We went out to find the ice, weighted down with heavy equipment for the large-format camera. I had an assistant and we made quite a few trips between Oslo and the Jostedal Glacier in the course of the half-year the photography took. It was a long hike from the car to where we found the crevasses and caves we were after. We passed danger signs with warnings that the glacier could calve, but after a three-kilometer march we were not in the mood to turn back. We just stepped over the fence and went on."

Serck-Hanssen was interested in the melting process: "I wanted to show what came out as the glacier melted; that the ice was not pure, and that dust particles appear, giving the pictures a certain tangibility. Glaciers are not clean – they contain pollution from many hundreds of years. The layers are pressed together and concentrated from the weight of the glacier," he explains.

"We had no experience with glaciers. There was a lot of noise from the glacier. You felt very much 'there', with water gurgling and the ice creaking. The glacier gave a powerful feeling of being inside a living organism. Things don't go very quickly with a large-format camera. You need to use a tripod and lots of delicate equipment, so we had some long and tiring days. The job was quite dangerous. I wouldn't want to do it again."

"The whole series was taken on the Jostedal Glacier, with the largest number taken on an arm on the west side, the Bødal Glacier in the Western part of Norway. That was the part that offered the most interesting motifs and which was most accessible during the late summer and fall when it wasn't too cold."

At one point when they went back to the same place they had been the day before, Serck-Hanssen recalls, everything had changed: "Pieces of the ice walls had fallen down and melted and the space had changed character."

When the commission for the Olympics first came up, Serck-Hanssen was a little hesitant to focus on the glacier: "It was almost too 'set up' or predictable, given that the theme was winter and Norway," he says. "But on the other hand, I wanted to do it. I had worked a lot with water before. It was enticing to develop that theme further.

"Water envelops the objects that are in it. The light dies out quickly. The light is 'compact', and you see it in a different way. You don't get the same feeling of light outside of the water. You don't see that it dies out. Under water you can see the light getting weaker as the distance from the surface increases.

"In addition, the light is scattered by the water's surface, almost as with glass. Exciting changes take place. Also, water is a powerfully charged concept. Water was one of the four Greek elements, together with air, earth and fire. Our body is almost totally water. We come from the sea," expounds Serck-Hanssen.

The glacier pictures are full of tonal values with very small nuances that change within a limited color spectrum, but with rich abundance within this spectrum. This is the very reason that Serck-Hanssen used a large-format camera to capture these images. He says that these pictures depend on the small tonal nuances, which would have been lost if he had used a regular 135-mm camera.

"I was forced to learn how to use a large-format camera," says Serck-Hanssen. "I saw the possibilities and was curious about the technique. If I have a need for it, I will find a technique. Everything else, I won't bother with."

In fact, Serck-Hanssen had not originally intended to become a photographer. He didn't even get his first camera until he was 18 years old. He had planned to raise fish and was certified to be a fish farmer. He appeared destined to end up in the water. But he became interested in photography through his interest in music. He liked punk and new wave, and one day a journalist friend of his asked if he would take some pictures at a concert. In return he got a free ticket.

One photo job led to another, and after a while, Serck-Hanssen became interested in using the camera to express the culture associated with the music. "I thought that this was something I wanted to delve into," he recalls. "I went to England, both for the music and to learn more about photography. Since then, it has been my living. In Norway, photography wasn't thought of as art, but the photography scene in England was exciting, and training opportunities were abundant."

"Glacier". Photos for Voyager of the Seas.

Serck-Hanssen says he had always considered technology unimportant. "But after a while, I discovered that there were things I wanted to do – and then technique became important as a tool. I learned whatever techniques I had to in order to accomplish what I wanted. The point has always

been the object, not the technique. But to the extent that it will help me towards my goals, I will learn the technique. Computerized photography is nothing more than a digital darkroom," he says.

Serck-Hanssen says that he no longer even needs to view a subject through the camera, as he can visualize the final result without seeing it. "When you've been doing this for a while,

you see differently," he discloses. "When I worked in black-and-white, I visualized the result in black-and-white. Now I'm working intensely with colors and I see differently."

Although Serck-Hanssen has had many exhibitions, he is not overly concerned about what the public thinks of his work. "What's important to me is to make pictures," he says. "The exhibitions tend to come so long after the photographs are made that I have a distant relationship to them. Exhibition openings are mostly a social event: You stand there with a glass in your hand and say 'Thank you very much'. But occasionally someone comes up to me and says that one of my pictures has moved them. That makes me feel happy." ■

This interview with Fin Serck-Hanssen took place in his studio in Oslo, Norway.

CV

Fin Serck-Hanssen, b. 1958 in Oslo, Norwegian.
Education: 1981–84 BA HONS Photographic studies, Derby, England.
Since his first solo show in 1983, Fin Serck-Hanssen has exhibited widely in Norway and in Europe. Among them at Henie Onstad Art Centre, Høvikodden, Norway; Sølvberget Gallery, Stavanger, Norway; Riis Gallery, Oslo, Norway; Bergen Society of Arts, Norway; The Artists' House, Oslo, Norway.

Fin Serck-Hanssens photos have been shown in more than 20 Collective Exhibitions in Norway, Denmark, Sweden, Finland, Italy, UK, USA, Germany, The Netherlands, Canada, France, and Poland. He has executed art projects in cooperation with Yoko Ono, Per Barclay and other artists. Fin Serck-Hanssen is represented in numerous Public and Private Collections, among them: Victoria & Albert Museum, London, UK; National Museum of Photography, Film and Televsion, Bradford, UK; Henie Onstad Art Centre, Høvikodden, Norway; National Photography Museum – Preus Photomuseum, Horten, Norway; Rasmus Meyer Collection, Bergen, Norway; the Oslo Municipal Art Collections, The National Museum of Contemporary Art, Norway. His series from a Norwegian Glacier is on board the RCI ship *Voyager of the Seas*.

"Glacier", detail.

Inger Sitter

Inger Sitter and Terje Lundaas in Lundaas' Miami studio working on glass and marble reliefs for Radiance of the Seas. *(Photo: Rod Dickinson).*

The Norwegian painter Inger Sitter has done some of her best work in marble. Most of these large, characteristic reliefs can be found in the stairways on the *Vision*, *Rhapsody*, *Voyager* and *Radiance of the Seas*. They have all been accomplished through collaboration with the skilled Italian craftsmen of Studio Sem in Pietrasanta in Italy.

"The workshop's nucleus is comprised of three brothers. They can do anything, and a little bit more," describes Sitter. "But they are wary when a new artist appears, and they wonder what kind of person you are. I had to use all sorts of tricks in the beginning to get them to relax, including charm in appropriately small doses. Now they like me and the feeling is mutual. When I come in we shake hands and kiss cheeks. And I buy quite a load of wine before I leave. I always miss Pietrasanta when I am away; coming back is like coming home," sighs Sitter.

"I have many homes, and that is a good thing. I have lived in Belgium, Norway, France, Italy and the U.S. If I had had just one home, I wonder what kind of person I would have been. I've traveled and met new people, been immersed in new environments. All this requires that you keep yourself in good shape – it can be exhausting, but you get back ten times what you put in," she says.

Sitter, who works in several different media, says: "I have a great advantage in my ability to express myself both in painting, graphics and in marbles. It is a gift to be allowed to do this. And the different genres cross-fertilize each other with all their possibilities for variation.

"My relationship with marble, and Carrara and Pietrasanta, began with a competition to decorate the Main Police Station in Oslo. I made a proposal for a work to be made in marble. A colleague said that I should go to Carrara to get a model made. They had the skills and traditions there, and they could deliver first-class results.

"I had a fantastic experience. I saw once again the white marble mountains that I hadn't seen since I was seven years old and sailed in the Mediterranean with my father, who was a coxswain on a Norwegian ship," recalls Sitter.

In Carrara she found a craftsman who made her model in just a couple of days. "I was extremely impressed," recounts Sitter. "They had know-how and technical expertise above and beyond anything I had seen before. I had no idea you could work with marble that way. They put a variety of different stones together – almost a collage – at the same time as they modelled a relief.

> *"Pictorial art deals with the same themes as music: rhythm, energy and movement, a play of forces that can't be described in words."*
> *Inger Sitter*

"When I was 'given' a large wall on the S/S *Norway*, I left immediately for Carrara. I worked there for three months and started to wonder if I should become a resident. That never happened, but I've become more and more infatuated with the 2,000 year old traditional craft that has been maintained since the Roman era."

Sitter also points out that this history was fraught with tragedy. She says that many lives were lost to the extraction of the colossal marble blocks. "They worked in a primitive way up in the mountains,

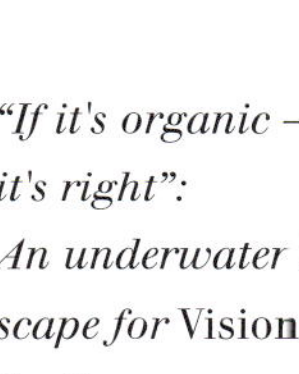

"If it's organic – it's right": An underwater landscape for Vision of the Seas.

and rolled the blocks down towards the coast on huge log beams with the assistance of manpower, oxen, and other animals" she explains. "This in itself is a very dramatic and fascinating history.

"I was so satisfied that I was eager to get more commissions in marble," says Sitter. 'The next one came three years later, for Norwegian Cruise Line's *Seaward.* That same year, I resigned as a professor at the National Art Academy and moved out of Norway. I seriously considered moving to Pietrasanta, but I chose Paris in the end because I could speak French," recalls Sitter.

Like Knut Steen and Helaine Blumenfeld, Sitter works with Studio Sem, which is considered to be the last of the major marble workshops. "Studio Sem was established by the legendary Sem, who was the first one I approached 20 years ago to get an estimate for the art project for the police station. The estimate was unfortunately too high – three times the total budget.

"I didn't know Sem well, but his face was the finest I have seen – except for Giacometti's. And he had a generosity unlike any I had ever experienced. That was probably why he attracted the world's greatest sculptors. He liked women and the first thing he did was to invite me to his home. I was a bit suspicious, but he pulled out a drawer full of small models and he said that these were what Henry Moore had come to him with. 'These small things are the beginnings of the sculptures we have done for Moore,' he said. Then I posed a question: 'Isn't it the same with sculpture as with painting, that is, that the size is given? That you base it on one size when you make a model?' 'No' Sem answered. 'A good sculpture can be made in any size.' That was an amazing piece of information. I had never heard anything like that before.

"I later asked the sculptor Jørgen Hougen Sørensen about this, and he confirmed it. You can follow the model completely accurately. That's what they do at Studio Sem just as it has been done for 2,000 years. And the techniques they use are so advanced that the training is nearly on par with a university level education.

"They'll make a large version of anything. Many years ago, at the Venice Biennial, I saw some lumps of marble that were formed by an artist who had taken clay and squeezed it. This was then translated into marble. Of course it was Sem who had done the job. They can do anything there."

However, Sitter says the artist must follow the entire process closely, even at Studio Sem. "It's not as if you can just deliver a model and come to inspect the final product after four months," she explains. "I would never take a chance like that. There's one thing in particular you have to watch carefully, which is why you have to be at the workshop, and that is the actual material finish. They'd like to polish everything glossy. And that's not always so interesting."

Sitter describes the process of creating one of her marble sculptures: "It starts with me coming to Studio Sem with a model made out of balsa on a 1:10 scale. I make the model myself and paint it in the colors I have conceived. Together with the current head of the workshop, Keara McMartin, I choose the stone. We take our time; she proposes things and I think about it. Eventually, as things develop, my good collaborator Giancarlo joins in with his opinions. This is very important. In my life I have found that this is one of the most interesting and valuable things: a collaborative situation in which

Inger Sitter portrays reefs and large rock formations which meet and struggle for power. She tries to show points of gravity that are displaced and currents that press between the big blocks of rock. In reality, therefore, her art is a symbol for cosmic struggle, and she feels that the human frame becomes a part of this cosmic whole. Inger feels that this description applies to a lot of her art works as she sees it existing as a whole.

you work well together with two or three other professionals. This is in complete contrast to painting, which is a solitary activity," declares Sitter.

"There is a myth that the process of sculpting is extremely long," she continues. "I can debunk this myth: If you work with first-rate craftsmen and know exactly how you want the product to be, you don't have to do things over again and the marble workers don't need so much time. But if the colors and materials do not fit together with the other stones, you can be forced to start over, with a whole new stone. That's expensive. On the other hand, the finished relief is invulnerable and everlasting, assuming nobody attacks it with a hammer. The marble pieces I did for the *S/S Norway* 20 years ago have withstood absolutely everything, while the original oil paintings had to be removed a long time ago because they were so damaged."

For the RCI ships, Sitter also mainly works in marble: reliefs and sculptures. But she has also done some paintings, photos, montages in different materials, and lithographs for the fleet. "I think RCI has put together a good mixture," Sitter points out. "After all, they have to keep their passengers in mind. A cruise ship can't be a floating exhibition space for Scandinavian art. The goal isn't to educate the cruise public to like art."

Sitter says there haven't been many guidelines for her work for RCI. "I've actually only met the architect, Njål Eide, once," she says. "That was in connection with a drawing I made for a Viking ship for the Viking Crown dancing floor on the Splendour of the Seas. They didn't know exactly what they wanted, so I suggested they use the bow of a Viking ship. Njål Eide thought it was a pretty good idea, and that's how it landed in my lap. We got one of Norway's best woodcarvers, employed at the Viking Ship Museum, to do the work," Sitter recalls.

"The road from painting to sculpture isn't as long as you might think," says Sitter. "Many of my paintings are about stone. What impressed me early on, and continues to impress me when I work in marble, is that the process happens by itself, completely effortlessly. It's strange, and I've often wondered how and why it's that way. I think it has something to do with the surroundings I started out with. I use them as inspiration: Norway's slopes of bare rock. I've worked with them intensely for many, many years.

Now they just come out – completely naturally. I know exactly what should go up, and what should be scaled down, what should be red or black. It's just there. This has surprised and delighted me – and it's beautiful. All this adds up to a double pleasure: a continuity that takes place in collaboration. It's completely organic. And if it's organic, then it's right. If it has grown out of something, it also comes alive for the viewer," concludes Sitter. ■

This interview with Inger Sitter took place in her home in Villa Faraldi, Italy.

CV

Inger Sitter, b. 1929, Norwegian.
Lives and works in Norway, USA, France and Italy.
Educated National Academy of Fine Arts, Oslo, Norway 1945. Institut Superieur des Beaux-Arts, Antwerpen, Belgium 1946–50. Studies with André Lothe, Paris 1948.
Inger Sitter is best known as a painter and graphic artist, but has also produced many public installations in marble. Among the most important is the Olympic Hall in Hamar, Norway and several works on board cruise ships.
Inger Sitter has had several solo exhibitions in Norway, Denmark, Sweden, Finland and Italy. She is represented in many private and public collections, such as: The National Gallery, Norway; The National Museum of Contemporary Art; The National Touring Exhibitions; the Norwegian Council for Cultural Affairs; University in Oslo; the Oslo Municipal Art Collections; Bergen Art Museum; Henie Onstad Art Centre; Trondheim Art Museum; Stavanger Art Museum; The National Museum, Stockholm; Arkiv for Dekorativ Konst, Lund; The National Museum of Art, Copenhagen; Peter Styvesant Collection, Amsterdam; Pietrasanta Museum, Italy.

Maura Smolover and Peter Zsiba

"Our goal is to evoke an emotional response in the visitor who will share our experience."

– Maura Smolover and Peter Zsiba

Maura Smolover and Peter Zsiba have made multimedia works of art for several casinos on the Vision class and Voyager class and Radiance class ships. Their most recent commission was for the Casino Royale on the *Adventure of the Seas.*

Their complicated pieces, which combine a variety of elements, are actually stage productions that involve everything except actors. They utilize sound, light, sculpture, metal work, painting and glass-work, all incorporated into computerized sequencing. There are so many disciplines represented in these features; in some cases, there is a different craft or technique for each element.

Smolover and Zsiba describe their work in the *Voyager*'s Casino: "At the aft entrance to the Casino Royale, we created an animated invitation, beckoning passengers to join a celebration of singing and dancing chorus girls. Passengers are invited to stroll in, tapping and humming along as they enter the casino's enchanted world, where good luck and fortune are 'here to stay'. In what might be the production number from a Hollywood musical, two lines of chorus girls flank the passenger, tapping out a thunderous version of 'We're in the Money'.

"An imaginary script tells the story of the debonair and ever-lucky Diamond Jim who has plucked one of the chorus girls from the line and offered the newly bejewelled Diamond Jane a huge gem, celebrating their good fortune. From another song of the period, 'Pennies From Heaven', the companion feature inside the casino celebrates the good things in life: sunshine and rainbows, clouds with silver linings, and giant copper pennies that are offered to us by fairies of good fortune," explains Smolover.

Both Smolover and Zsiba were educated in painting and sculpture during the rebellious 1960's, when the fashionable question was: 'Is painting dead?' In response to this question, they joined the many young easel artists who moved 'off–canvas' and began creating 'visual events' or 'performance pieces' that attempted to involve viewers in what were called 'installations' and 'happenings'. Realizing that these experiences were actually theatrical events, Smolover went on to receive an MFA in production design from Yale, while Zsiba went to New York to design and paint for the Metropolitan Opera. They spent the first fifteen years of their professional careers as production designers for theater, film and opera.

"The commissions to create features for Royal Caribbean's Casinos have taken us back to our roots," Zsiba says. "Creating these theatrical features brings us back to our first love – the theater." But while theatrical productions create an experience for the viewer, the audience remains in a passive role – observers of the actor and scene. Smolover and Zsiba wanted to find a form in which they could create interactive experiences in 'real time', with and for their viewers. "The perfect venue for our theatrical training and interest in experiential design came with the advent of thematic architecture, where patrons become participants in a fantasy environment. RCI has provided a wonderful opportunity to create just such

"Pennies from Heaven" in the Casino Royale, Voyager of the Seas.

entertainment features," says Smolover.

"The process of successful theatrical production design has guided the way we approach the collaborative process of designing site-specific work in two ways. First, we have come to view our clients as authors or composers with whom we have a partnership in realizing their intent and delivering their message. By entering our clients' world as part of a conceptual team, we hope to create a focal point, which will help establish its ambience. Our goal is to evoke an emotional response in the visitor who will share an experience that the owner hopes to create."

Smolover says the stylistic versatility developed while designing operatic and theatrical repertoires has influenced the way the couple approaches the diverse cultures and tastes of their international client base. "Whether commissioned by corporate landmarks such as Rockefeller Center, rich cultural heritages such as the Government of Kuwait, or the flights of fantasy offered by RCI, we hope our designs will most eloquently epitomize their different messages," she says.

As Smolover and Zsiba's installations are not autonomous artworks, but complex multimedia features, the creation process must take many factors into account. The works must comply with the ship's electrical limitations, air ventilation systems and fire codes. Many of the dramatic effects must be miniaturized. Many a great idea has been thrown overboard because it couldn't comply with the ship's stringent codes.

"Sometimes, as the fabrication process evolves, we sort of have to second-guess ourselves," he adds. "The design and the technique must be closely knit. For the design, the ultimate goal is to marry the assemblage with its environment so that it functions with the life of the casino. All of the work is for naught unless it does its job of delighting the passengers. The sound and lights of the casino's interior design and gaming activity are extremely vibrant. The challenge is to create something that allures but does not intrude, that is, something that stands out but does not infringe.

"The evolution of the soundtrack is an interesting case in point. We have found that it adds to the effect of the feature. Because the ships must maximize economy of space, every inch – from the staterooms to the engine room – is utilized. For us, that means that there are no closets or basements in which to house our equipment. So all of the projectors, the relays, the transformers, the dimmers and the audio equipment must be part of the artwork.

"The advantage to this is that the equipment is centralized. The problem is how to ventilate this mass of electricity. Keeping thirty projectors cool means that a lot of air has to be moved. So each piece of equipment is customized with its own fan, which is intended to extend the life of the bulb and surrounding electronic equipment. When you add the other airflow control fans, the feature would hum like an old refrigerator. That is not the impression that we want the viewer to leave with. Thus, the addition of sound has both an aesthetic and technical reason for existence," Smolover explains.

"Casinos are complicated stuff. You cannot compromise too much or make big changes during the installation period. We always try to build in a little extra in case something doesn't work properly. We can scale down if we have to. If everything works perfectly, we have 125 percent. And in a casino, nothing is too much. More is better. If it captivates quickly, if it smiles and if it gives an impression of happiness, then it's good."

There are many challenges that accompany the installation of these artworks onboard the ships, say Smolover and Zsiba. "But most challenges are dwarfed by the wonderful experience of becoming an active inhabitant of a 'global village'," Zsiba remarks. "We were amazed by the number of languages being spoken at the shipyard by craftsmen from all over the world. Faced with an impending deadline, everyone is competing for the yard's resources and attention. Lift time and staging space become precious commodities, as well as the time and attention of related trades. So the challenges are the ones that come with the interfacing of craft and schedules. We are constantly aware that although our work is most important to us, there is a master schedule in which we are only a very small part.

"What continues to astound us is the scale on which all of this happens. Our features for the casino onboard the *Voyager of the Seas* alone had more than eighty crates of artwork, parts and supplies. Each of the features was first fully assembled in our studio in the US with all of the lights and sound working for a dry-run technical rehearsal. They then had to be disassembled, crated, trucked, shipped, trucked again, off-loaded, stored and then hoisted onboard in a precise order, because the ship can only accommodate regulated amounts of supplies stored on the decks for brief periods of time without damage and interfering with other trades. The marvel is that all of this happens with very little damage.

"The lovely thing about commissioned art is that the owner has already decided that there is a purpose for it. He has made a place for it. He might not know what it is, but he knows why he wants it there. You join into a partnership with a client to fulfill the purpose they are looking for. For the casinos, the art has a double purpose.

"We believe that the purpose of the artwork in this particular site is to engage and entertain the passenger; coming from a theatrical background our orientation is to create designs which fulfill for the specific purpose of each site and express the unique character of each client.

"Another blessing of commissioned art is that it gives you an opportunity to perfect your craft. You may find yourself doing things that you never thought about because someone asks you to do it. Commissioned artwork is different from creating fine art, which is a solitary experience with one vision and one creator. With commissioned art, you don't have the pleasure that your decision is entirely yours and you may have to force yourself to find a better way to do it. But that doesn't make it any less exciting.

"We often feel that being commissioned is like being asked to dance. The client becomes a partner in the creative process. Commissions keep an artist connected and responsive to the world around him," states Smolover as Zsiba nods in agreement. ■

This interview with Maura Smolover and Peter Zsiba took place in Turku, Finland, when they installed their Casino Features on Voyager of the Seas.

CV

Maura Smolover, American.
Education: M.F.A. Yale University School of Drama, University Scholarship. M.F.A.: Brandeis University, University Scholarship and Fellowship. B.F.A. Carnegie Melon University, Carnegie Fine Arts Award.
University teaching experiences: Dartmouth College, Oberlin College, University of Wisconsin, University of Maryland.

Peter Zsiba, American.
Education: Art Students League, New York and Italy.
Professional experience: Metropolitan Opera, Scenic Artist. Major Motion Pictures, Scenic Artist, Chargeman.
University teaching experiences: University of Wisconsin.

Selected Corporate Commissions: Abraham and Strauss; American Express; Angels Cummings; Bloomingdales; Chateau Briand; Christian Dior; Clarins; Clinique; Elizabeth Arden; Consulate General of France; Fuji Securities Inc; Guerlain; Hotel de las Artes, Barcelona; Kuwait Mission to the United Nations; Lancome; London Contemporary Art; Ralph Lauren; Rockefeller Center; Royal Caribbean Cruise Line; Trump Plaza; Yves St. Laurent.

Maria Veronica L. Solem

Maria Veronica L. Solem's studio looks out over the Oslo Fjord, with a view of the blue hills and green water. A rowboat is anchored nearby and the seagulls screech overhead. Solem stands in her studio, a former oil warehouse by the small harbor, and puts the final touches on her crated 12-meter paintings that will be picked up in two hours' time to be sent to Kværner Masa-Yards in Turku, Finland.

Solem is feeling happy and relieved but also a little melancholy. This is the end of a long process. "These pictures are my children, you know," says Solem, gazing at the wooden crates. She appears to be wondering what will happen to them in the months that will pass before she sees them again when they are installed on the ship. In three months, they will be on the wall behind the Golf Bar in the Viking Crown onboard the world's largest cruise ship.

Her 'children' are big: one measures 9x3 meters, and the other is 4x4. Plus a half-meter on each side – just to be safe. Solem paints on rolls: a 12x4-meter easel wouldn't fit on the studio wall. She has been painting these pictures, which have a theme of golf, for six months. The next step is to make sure they are hung properly on the ship; only then will they truly be completed.

"It is important for me to finish the paintings on site," says Solem. "Not all artists feel the same way. They complete the work and send it off. But you are never really finished with a painting. You have to decide yourself when it's done. It's an art to know when to stop."

The huge painting rolls are well packed and ready to be picked up. Solem learned the hard way how important the packing is. "For the *Rhapsody of the Seas*, I made some mahogany sculptures with waxed surfaces," recalls Solem, adding: "Wax and water do not mix. The boxes with the sculptures were left on the pier in the rain and the works were badly damaged because the crates were not watertight. Four men laboriously scraped off all the wax and everything had to be treated again."

Three months later: Solem is in action at the shipyard in Turku. She has had to improvise a border behind the paintings because the wall turned out to be larger than planned. "Sometimes you encounter great challenges at the last minute," she says, and recounts another installation. It was on the *Legend of the Seas*, which was the first ship in the *Vision Class*. "It was built in France. I traveled down to participate in the installation, which was to take place on a certain date. But it didn't happen and they finally hoisted the pieces up on deck the night before the ship was to sail. There were more

"It's fine to make small pretty sketches, but when they are going to be 12x4 meters, it's a whole different world."
Maria Veronica L. Solem

than 800 men onboard working to finish the interior furnishings, including the artwork, as the ship sailed across the Atlantic to New York. Thank goodness it was a large picture – six meters – easy to get a grip on. It went well, but I had nightmares about it being hung upside down."

Solem recalls another commission installation, this one on the *Vision of the Seas*: "They had to take down some art because people could cut themselves on it. It was right before the ship was to leave the yard at St. Nazaire. I had finished my job and was in Paris with my five-year-old son. It was Easter vacation, at least until the telephone rang and Gro Nesjar from LCA said: 'Veronica, can you come back?' I told her I had my son with me and she said 'Bring him with you!'

"Then I was given three days to paint something to fit into a hole that was left by one of the works of art that had to be removed. Gro Nesjar was my babysitter. I began on the morning of Thursday and finished the night before Easter. I crawled back into my hotel room and to my son, who was beaming with satisfaction over all the toys he had been given by the nice lady from LCA."

Solem says she is normally "hard-edged and stringent." Indeed, art historian Olga Schmedeling writes: "Solem's universe consists of conflicting hard-edge metallic lines and curves, seemingly deprived of human touch like a Mondrian." But Solem didn't have time to work that way when she was called in at the last minute to fill a hole on the *Vision*. "Afterwards, I saw something," she says. "The blending of something stringent and a kind of wildness represented a step forward. One grows as an artist from these kinds of challenges. That's been one of the most exciting things about working with these ships. The commissions have been light years away from what I would think of as gallery art."

"An Odyssey". Metal and oil on canvas. Centrum. Vision of the Seas.

Solem has a solid background in craftsmanship, having studied at L'Accademia di Belle Arti in Florence. She didn't even apply to any Norwegian art schools, but went straight to Florence, and into a strict regimen: the gates to the academy were shut at 8:15 a.m. and those who didn't attend at least 90 percent of the classes did not get certification. In her four years of study, Solem learned the different techniques from the ground up. In fact, she liked it there so much that she continued to live in Italy for six more years.

"With the Renaissance, art took a huge leap forward," clarifies Solem, "mostly because the princes built churches and palaces. They wanted them to be big and grand, and to have art everywhere. This gave continuity in the form of large commissions to the best artists. Even in ancient Egypt they already had professional artists because their construction activity was so enormous. The end result was very good not because of the money, but because the artists were continually challenged on a large scale. You would never get close to this kind of approach while sitting alone in your little studio, preparing for your next exhibition. You can't even dare to think on such a level if such possibilities didn't exist. And then along comes RCI. They want a lot of art, and in big formats for exciting spaces. And it doesn't dry up. You develop and learn more than you could dream of, both artistically and technically."

However, Solem adds: "On the ships you work with themes, and you have to come up with something concrete to show. It's not like working freely, allowing the picture to develop almost unconsciously. When you have your sketches completely ready after several months of working on them, the rest is craftsmanship."

Solem admits that the Golf Bar on the *Voyager* was a difficult commission. "I started out on the wrong track and made a lot of unsuccessful sketches. I didn't know the first thing about golf. So I went to Marbella in Spain and got up at six o'clock every morning and walked around the golf course with a camera. I was searching for the feeling of what golf is. Then an idea started to develop. I suddenly realized that silence was central. People play golf to calm down. I therefore tried to capture the stillness of it.

"The same thing happened with the South Pacific paintings I did for *Grandeur of the Seas*," says Solem. "Njål Eide sent me out to the Pacific. I hadn't liked the film "South Pacific" very much. The reality is that people actually live in containers. I had to break away from the romantic notion in the theme and design the whole thing as a tribute to the Polynesian people. You go first to the source to find your material, through books and travel – then you translate your impressions into abstract pictures.

"When I was making works for the *Vision*'s Centrum, I had already been through *Grandeur* and *Enchantment*, with themes from South Pacific and Carousel. And then suddenly I was completely free to do what I wanted. I was given the Photo Gallery, the Purser's Desk and the Atrium. I was so accustomed to working according to a theme that I made my own work model and theme. *The Odyssey* became the theme for all my work in the Centrum.

In preparation, I read Homer once again. I took a trip to Ithaca and ambled around in February, taking pictures. This got me going. It was a new and nice way to work."

Solem is not bothered by the characterization of her work as 'hard-edge.' "This implies tight borders and clear images. For me this is a way to make order out of chaos," she says. "Music is the same – organized. A poem can be a way of putting thoughts in order. That's what I try to do. Without being aware of it, I have been working on this project since I was a child and more consciously later on. Life can be chaotic – it needs order. The pictures you make are a reflection of yourself.

"I've tried to make completely wild pictures, but the impulse to make order out of things is so great that the final expression becomes hard-edged anyway. The need for order is probably the worst strait-jacket I have," comments Solem. ■

This interview with Maria Veronica L. Solem started in her studio at Nesodden outside of Oslo on the same day that she sent two large paintings to the Voyager of the Seas, which was under construction in Finland. The interview was continued three months later during the installation of the paintings on the ship.

CV

Maria Veronica L. Solem, b. 1949, Norwegian.

Education: L'Accademia di Belle Arti, Florence, Italy, painting. Diploma 1976.

Solo exhibitions: Italy, Switzerland, Germany, United Kingdom, Norway.

Group Exhibitions: Italy, Norway, United Kingdom, Bulgaria.

Represented in the National Gallery, Oslo; National Museum, Sofia; Graphic Basis, Varna; The Permanent Gallery, Tolbuchin; several cruise ships in the RCI-fleet. Also represented in various public buildings in Norway and the Royal Yacht, *Norge*.

Oil on Canvas. From South Pacific Lounge, Grandeur of the Seas.

Yolanda Sonnabend

Yolanda Sonnabend studied both painting and stage design, and has done the stage designs for more than 60 ballets, operas, theater productions, films and TV shows. Although she paints with abstract elements, her style is clearly influenced by her experience with theater.

In her painting, Sonnabend has for many years rejected the idea of abstract solutions to pictorial problems. Her abstract paintings are more connected to the abstract expressionism of the 1940's and 1950's, personal expressions using color and light.

"Paint and canvas impose certain simplicity," explains Sonnabend, "and ideas from the theater encourage me to focus on the subject, not the image: theater design experiments, manipulations, plays with quotation, reference, style and pastiche. And perhaps I counterbalance this by directness in painting, and a resistance to building up surface textures on the canvas. So there is always a tension between the two activities.

"As a designer, I'm conscious of style and pastiche, and therefore use a rather blatant illusionist image. The influences on my work are disturbingly multiple: Pussin, Courbet, Fayum, Borromini etc., with echoes of the movies."

Sonnabend admits it is obvious that the pictures from Swan Lake that she made for the *Grandeur of the Seas* were done by someone with extensive theatrical experience. "I am unashamedly ready to paint theatrically," she says.

"I did the design for the production of Swan Lake for the Royal Ballet in London's Royal Opera House in 1993. It was a very big operation, and I had lots of ideas that I could not realize for that production. There were people who loved it, and people who hated it. You can't please everybody; if you do, there's something wrong.

"It was an ideal subject, and it was always in my mind to do more of it – and then LCA asked for it! I had done a lot of work on the theme. I knew the ballet well. I knew the characters. On stage you saw it through a broken mirror in a way; one side was gold, the other metal. So I used metal in the paintings for the ship as well. I used a lot of elements from the stage set, including colors. So in a way, I didn't start from scratch. It was very elaborate. Very Fabergé, actually."

Sonnabend says it is challenging to both work for the stage and sustain a growing portfolio as a painter. "Artists should have this freedom to move freely from one form to another if they want to, although it is not easy to do so. There is an element of risk. I don't work exclusively for the Opera. I am very much a painter. But for this commission, the scale and the challenges of the mixed media, I worked with craftsmen in a very good studio. I would go up there and say: 'A little bit more of that, a little bit less there.' They enjoyed it – I know them well, as they are the same people I work with for big stage productions, and they understand my language."

Sonnabend received the *Grandeur of the Seas* commission through her agent, who had been approached by London Contemporary Art.

Yolanda Sonnabend in her London home. (Photo Gemma Levine.)

"I make no distinction. As far as I'm concerned, a stage design is just as much a work of art as a painting or a sculpture."

– Yolanda Sonnabend

"They wanted something theatrical on the themes from the Swan Lake," she recalls, "and I gave them exactly that. The pictures are very related to the set decor I made for the opera production. They were completely modified and abstracted for where they would be placed on the stairways. I did not want it overly detailed, but it also had to be quite rich when you saw it close up. I had nothing to do with the architects. I just got the measurements and brief from LCA who was very helpful in the process.

"It was nice doing the figures. It was of course different, since it was two-dimensional and because you can't see all the paintings at once. But I wanted people to see as much as possible of the one big piece. There was a railing that disturbed me, but people have been saying that my picture absolutely kills the railing. I hope they are right. I was so worried about it. I wanted it to compete successfully with the rich environment. But at the same time, I want a commissioned work to fulfill the necessities. Whereas in my own work I can indulge in all kind of liberties, except for the portraits that I have in the National Portrait Gallery."

For Sonnabend it comes naturally to work in different media. Her father was an anthropologist who settled with his family in Rhodesia after studying among the African Bantu. His Jewish origins prevented him from returning to his native Dresden under the Nazis. As a result of her background, Sonnabend found that her sense of culture was wider and different than those of the art students with whom she studied. She has herself explained that much of her work in painting is an attempt to integrate and bring together the widely dispersed elements of her childhood and youth when Europe was still a remote and exotic place.

"I make no distinction," says Sonnabend. "As far as I'm concerned a stage design is just as much a work of art as a painting or a sculpture. There are no borders." ■

This interview with Yolanda Sonnabend took place in her home in London.

Sonnabend's powerful paintings with scenes from "Swan Lake" dominates the Main Staircase on Grandeur of the Seas.

CV

Yolanda Sonnabend attended Academie des Beaux Arts, Geneva in 1951. Since 1954 she has been a resident of England where she studied painting and stage design at the Slade School of Fine Art 1955-60. She has been a lecturer at this school since 1990 and visiting lecturer at various other Schools of Art.

Sonnabend has had solo exhibitions in Whitechapel Art Gallery, Serpentine Gallery, Fischer Fine Art, Music Theatre Gallery and Long and Ryle, all in London. She has taken part in several important group exhibitions in UK, France, Prague, Cologne, Basel, Milan.

Public collections: Arts Council of Great Britain, British Council, British Theatre Museum, Victoria and Albert Museum, National Portrait Gallery, Science Museum, London, Library of Performing Arts and Lincoln Center, New York.
Yolanda Sonnabend has designed more than 60 ballets, operas, theater productions, films and TV shows, notably for the Royal Ballet, Covent Garden; Saddlers Wells, London; Staatsoper Stuttgart; La Scala, Milan; Staatsoper Ballet, Berlin; Old Vic Theatre, London; Oxford Playhouse; Aldwich Theatre.

Janet Stayton

Janet Stayton's oil paintings make an immediate impression with their size and color. Large spaces are filled with a contrast of light and shadows in her enchanting combination of still life and landscape paintings. With a very sophisticated handling of colors utilizing bold, broken brushstrokes, she captures on canvas the glow of sunshine and the starkness of moonlight.

Stayton, who grew up in Louisiana, now lives in Italy, which she considers her spiritual home. She finds her inspiration in the classical architecture, the natural beauty and the lifestyle of her Mediterranean surroundings.

For several years, Stayton commuted between New York and Italy, but she became weary of the city life and art scene in New York, and moved permanently to the sculpture town of Pietrasanta. She doesn't travel much anymore. She is too busy working.

"I just found New York irrelevant," comments Stayton. "To be a part of the art world game is very demanding. I don't want to go out to openings every night. I'd rather go out and feed the chickens – be more autonomous. You are never your own boss in New York. Someone always has his eye on you."

Yet she is ready to point out that New York, where she has exhibited her work extensively, is a very important place for the development of art. "It is a city generous and hospitable to artists," she states. "Art assumes a social dimension there with the many dinners and parties after openings – artists' studios always full of people – the phone ringing all day long. Expressive freedom manifests itself at a very high level there. The problem is: how can you work with all this going on?"

So Stayton began to escape to Italy for solitude, and for long stretches of time dedicated herself only to painting. "For many years I commuted back and forth between my loft in Soho and my marble barn studio in Pietrasanta," she recalls. "Italy has been my spiritual home; the source of inspiration for my work, as it has been for so many painters through the centuries. America has given me the great gift of a sense of wide-open space, and unlimited expressive possibilities, particular to American painting from the luminists on.

"Here I can do as I please. I am my own boss," says Stayton. However, she admits that doing commissions, such as those for RCI, forces her to be humble: "If you are working for a client, you have to swallow your pride and listen to them when they make comments, and you must do it with great respect. You do it the way you want to, but you must listen," she says.

But Stayton is intrigued by the unique qualities of art onboard ships: "As a site for art it is architecturally and aesthetically unique, especially a cruise ship, which exists for pleasurable activities, for fantasy. Everyone is a king or a queen onboard. You could stretch this idea further and say that the art presented onboard is like an updated Medici collection."

In addition, Stayton feels that artists who do commissioned work for these ships know they have a special forum and are inspired by that. "After all, we have a captive and repetitive audience within the

"The idea of the painting may be revealed not in looking at it, but in walking by it."

Janet Stayton

Janet Stayton finishes her paintings for "Moonlight Bay Lounge" for Rhapsody of the Seas *in her Pietrasanta studio.*

"Ship jobs are elite public work", says Janet Stayton.

time-span of each cruise," she says. "Ashore, viewers visit museum shows usually once, maybe twice. The public spaces on ships in many cases are de-constructed from the architectual norm: sweeping curved walls, gigantic atriums, idiosyncratic spatial relationships, baroque-modernist ceilings and lighting, fanciful carpets designed by the architects themselves. And on and on. All this is great fun, as well as challenging, for the artist."

At first Stayton was a little skeptical to the idea of creating artwork around themes, as RCI often requested. "These themes can seem banal to the artists," she says, "a bit like summer camp." When she was commissioned to do the paintings for a huge lounge-ballroom on the *Vision of the Seas*, which had a South Pacific theme, she recalls her first reaction: "Oh God!" But then she remembered that she had loved the movie when she was a child. "As we were working on the many paintings in my Italian studio one winter day, a package arrived from Oslo," she says. "It was a video cassette of the musical 'South Pacific' with the original cast, Ezio Pinza, etc. We put the music on high volume and we were jumping and dancing around the studio for a few wild moments just loving it! We then returned to our painting with renewed energy."

Now Stayton feels that a theme is not necessarily a constraint. "You can abstract it. It is a point of reference, a mood, even a point of celebration," she says thoughtfully. "The sea and the palm trees were wonderful images to play with. The theme doesn't mean you have to paint two lovers holding hands silhouetted against a blazing sunset – unless you want to, that is."

Stayton says that another interesting aspect to making paintings for ships is that the shapes and sizes are often irregular: "Many times they must be long, thin, and curved; other times concave, sometimes convex. If you have to make a painting one meter by 11 meters, it's a pretty strange dimension, one you would never choose unless someone asked.

"On a ship project, the artist must ask himself: 'How is this painting going to be experienced?' One of the things people do on a ship is wander around. They keep seeing the same things over and over again, and they stroll by the paintings repeatedly. In a museum or a gallery you stand back and look directly at a painting, then you look at other paintings, and then you go away. You have a short experience in a short period of time. On a ship, looking at art is multi-experiential in terms of intervals and duration of time. As people walk by, they may discover something new each time. The artist must foresee this when he creates the paintings. Thus, the idea of the painting may be revealed not in looking at it, but in walking by it."

Stayton calls the ship jobs 'elite public work.' She says there are elements she uses in her personal work that she wouldn't use in this context because it would be too intimate. "I even had to take a second studio for my personal work so that my time wouldn't be shared; the commissions ate all my energy." ■

This interview with Janet Stayton took place in her studio in Pietrasanta, Italy.

CV

Janet Stayton was born in the southern American State of Mississippi. She grew up in Louisiana.

Janet Stayton has had solo exhibitions in several places including Chicago, New York, Washington DC in USA, Hong Kong, Taiwan, Italy, France, Denmark, and Norway. She has participated in a great number of group exhibitions in USA and Europe.

Her works are found in several private and public collections, among them: Chicago Art Institute, Chicago; Ministeres des Affaires Culturelles, France (for French Museums); Brooklyn Museum of Fine Arts, New York; Westmoreland Museum, Maryland; Chase Manhattan Bank, New York; Coca-Cola, Atlanta; J.M. Kaplan Inc. New York; Arthur Young & Company, Chicago.

Knut Steen

"Art is something everyone thinks they know something about and they think they have the intelligence to have an opinion about it. I have taken a lot of flak for my work because it was supposedly avant garde and modern, but that has never been my intention. I have always tried to reach people with what I have done. The objections have gradually died down and the things I have made have steadily become more accepted."

– Knut Steen

"Fire" (Detail). Red Persian travertine relief. Vision of the Seas.

"As a sculptor, it is a great gift to be able to be here in Pietrasanta," says Knut Steen. "One lives and work as a part of an historical tradition. But the best thing is that there are good artisans here. The artisan tradition here has continued unbroken for several thousand years. There is a marble tablet inlaid in the wall of the Bar Michelangelo in the piazza proclaiming that it was on that spot that Michelangelo signed a contract with the Pope for the massive marblework for the Medici Chapel in Florence.

Michelangelo settled down in Pietrasanta. He had lived first in Carrara, where the great marble quarries are, but it turned out that the Medici, who were his patrons, did not control Carrara; the border was near Massa. The Medici Pope commissioned huge works from Michelangelo, but he insisted that the artist get his marble here as he would not buy marble from his enemy. Since that time, Pietrasanta has been known as the town with the very best artisans.

"Here you can always find specialists who began to carve marble with their fathers when they were 12 years old. They also knew how to do mosaic and advanced ironwork, making gates and portals. This town has had experts in nearly every material. But now the trades are dying out. The young do not want to work with such things. We are heading toward the end of a rich tradition. Even in marble-working, there are more and more industrialized methods and the craftsmen who sculpt using the old techniques are dying out," laments Steen.

"It has been wonderful working with the Italians here," says Steen. "When something is difficult they find it fun! If the task is nearly impossible, they get a charge out of it. Once you have them on your side, there is no limit to what they will do. Each new block of marble is equally exciting. You can come upon many strange things in the stone. Often there are veins which can ruin things, but which can also be exploited artistically if one is lucky. It can be a matter of a shadow or a line; sometimes marble with pronounced veins has been used to emphasize a motion. When that happens, it is really interesting.

"There is a certain amount of hope in the attempts to recruit young people to marble working, but this must happen soon, while the elderly are still with us," says Knut Steen. "When they leave us, we will lose their knowledge. But most young people would rather become sculptors themselves than work with a traditional craft." (Photo: Morten Krogvold)

"I made a fountain for the Hotel Sheraton outside of Oslo. It was old Sem who helped me with it. He was a real artist and could see what was inside a block of marble. I was going to carve a head hovering on some kind of wings. I told Sem that I would really like to have some veins which ran around the relief but not in the face. Yes, that should be possible. He showed me a block of stone which looked rough and strange. I had little faith in it, but Sem insisted. 'Okay,' I said. 'But if it turns out there is a vein which ruins the face, I don't want it.' He split the block and it was exactly as he said it would be. It was unbelievable. But he grew up around marble. He had it in his blood."

Steen came to Carrara by chance. His brother, an auditor, was working for a stone company in Larvik, Norway, which was owned by Thor Lundh. "They were traveling down to Pietrasanta and gave me a call," recalls Steen. "I was living in Sandefjord; it must have been 1973. They were on their way to Italy by car. Thor had a beautiful car with a phone, even at that time. He asked me if I'd consider a consulting job. Of course I would!

"The next day, there was a ticket waiting for me at the Oslo airport, and I flew down to Viareggio, where I met up with the guys, along with some Italians working in the stone industry there. I had taken a book by the Norwegian poet Harald Sverdrup with me; I had just illustrated his love poems. They were line drawings – long black lines on white paper. I showed the book to these people. 'But that's marble!' they said. 'You must come down here to work!' That's how it happened. I came here on my fiftieth birthday, found a house and settled in. I launched into my work and I've lived here ever since. And it's gone very well."

Steen is impressed by how much emphasis RCI has put on art for their ships. "It's like a floating gallery with easy access for everybody, not just a chosen few," he says. "More and more the acquisition of serious art has become very exclusive, reserved for a few elite collectors, many of whom buy for the sole purpose of speculation. Even in a museum, one has only limited access, being pushed along so that others can also see, forbidden to touch the art or even get close.

"These vast ships filled with art are actually quite generous projects – especially since everyone tries to make the visual arts so exclusive that one pushes everything away with intellectual snobbery. Much of today's art tries to be elitist and avant garde at all costs, pushing limits so much that I think it has become a form of neurosis. It's almost as if artists are making art for each other," declares Steen.

"But RCI puts their money behind art and believes it means something. The intention is that the art onboard the ships should communicate. It must create a dialog. What's fun about making these things is that there are always new people coming and getting impressions – or maybe not getting them. But there will always be some who are receptive.

"An atmosphere is created wherein the works melt together to create a whole – a whole which

"Aurora". White Carrara marble. Champagne Plaza, Grandeur of the Seas.

Main stair,
Voyager of the Seas.

is the ship; a totality which travels. That is an interesting concept. What is more, they start thinking 'art' right from when they begin planning the ship. That is completely unique. Usually art is something people think about at the end. Here it is a part of things right from the start. And in a way, a ship is a project which is completely defined, a closed world," says Steen.

Like other artists, Steen is aware of the role that commissioned work has played throughout history. "You can just look at what is important in Italy today – the art that was made 500 or 600 years ago," he points out. "That is what is important. It's what they live on and what people come to see. The reason for this is that people with money at that time were determined to make something beautiful. You see beauty everywhere in the old towns. Each house is unique – people have taken aesthetics into consideration. All the elements come together to make a whole, something which is spiritual and beautiful – and which speaks. When houses are built today, they only think about profit. Profit is beauty. Generosity is what is lacking. Everything is done as cheaply as possible and art has become a luxury."

But, as Steen has discovered, this is not the case when one builds a cruise ship. He says it has been 'a blessing' to work on these projects. "It is dangerous to undermine the spiritual," he says. "On land people only talk about keeping the price down. But it is precisely the spiritual which makes humanity interesting, the capacity to transcend mere necessity. It is that surplus which is culture.

"Culture has always been important. Look at what we have built in times past, all the opera houses, theaters and museums. What do these things mean today? Today they mean nothing. And what will remain after us? What has our era to show for itself? Nothing.

Except perhaps the cruise ships." ■

This interview with Knut Steen took place in his studio in Pietrasanta, Italy.

CV

Knut Steen, Norwegian, born 1924 in Oslo. Works and lives in Carrara and Pietrasanta, Italy since 1973.

He was educated at The National Academy of Fine Art in Oslo under Professor Per Palle Storm and Stinius Fredriksen.

Knut Steen has had several solo exhibitions in Norway, England, Italy, Denmark, Spain and Taiwan.

The list of his monumental sculptures and public works is very comprehensive: The Whaler Monument in Sandefjord, Norway (1960); The Daughters of Okeanos, The City Hall of Oslo (1975); Aurora and Sapfo, The Concert Hall of Oslo (1981); Aurora, House of Government, Oslo (1982); Metamorphose, The Norwegian Embassy, Washington DC; and Olav Kyrre, Bergen, Norway (1998).

Knut Steen is represented in several private and public collections in Norway, including The National Gallery, Oslo; The National Touring Exhibitions, Oslo; The Stenersen Collection, Oslo; The City Art of Collection, Bergen; The Gallery of Trøndelag, Trondheim.

Works onboard RCI ships include the Centrum Sculpture for *Grandeur of the Seas* and several important works for *Rhapsody, Vision* and *Voyager of the Seas.*

Gunhild Strømnes

"The images are like pictograms – frozen in time."

– Gunhild Strømnes

Gunhild Strømnes got in touch with RCI via the architect Petter Yran. He had seen a painting incorporating cast polyester she had made in a Norwegian office building. "He wanted to know whether I did full-room installations, and I answered that an entire room is the most exciting thing you can work with if you can get the job," says Strømnes. Yran stopped by her studio and looked at several works. London Contemporary Art entered the picture and it was agreed that she would make an art installation for the Viking Crown on the *Vision of the Seas*.

"These kinds of commissions are challenging; one must proceed according to different needs on various levels," explains Strømnes. In this case her theme was to be the Viking era. The installation forms a large circle, a series of paintings with eggs cast into them on the upper level, while boat forms and many-colored feet 'walk' around the elevators. All the artwork in the Viking Crown is by Gunhild Strømnes, except for the glasswork over the bar: 'Aurora Borealis', a large installation featuring the Northern Lights by British artist Mike Newby.

The overall impression is new and groundbreaking. Polyester is a challenging material that is seldom used by artists; the processes are slow and relatively toxic. But Gunhild Strømnes had already had a good deal of experience in this area prior to the beginning of the project. She was fascinated with the material because, among other things, it is dense, yet gives the impression of transparency. Liquid polyester can be formed and colored, and objects can be cast into it, as though frozen in time.

"My ambition was to give passengers something to wonder about in these surroundings. I hoped that they might experience a kind of poetry emanating from the Viking era," says Strømnes.

Before she started her work for the *Vision of the Seas*, Strømnes had the opportunity to see "her room", the Viking Crown, on the *Vision*'s sister ship, the *Rhapsody of the Seas*, when it was under construction in France. She took a number of photographs there, which turned out to be quite useful. "They gave me a completely different feeling of the room than I would have had merely from drawings," she says. "in general I believe you do better work if you can see the space beforehand. You absorb many details you don't see in a drawing, and you think much more clearly while working.

"There was a steady stream of visitors to the Viking Crown while I was installing the work," she recalls. "Some probably thought the polyester was rather experimental. I would gladly take on more jobs like this. You learn from each commission, not least how the creative process functions. It was good working for RCI. They have respect for art and that is important."

For this installation, Strømnes used wood, metal, paint and various objects cast in polyester. The pieces were inspired by the Viking era both physically and symbolically. The artwork consists of several freestanding sculptures, objects and paintings.

Strømnes has collaborated with many knowledgeable people on the work in the Viking Crown, including the talented carpenter Tor Erling Gransæther, who carved copies of Viking objects. These pieces were then cast into the polyester. "The project actually began as a commission to make some columns for the Viking Crown, but it gradually grew to become quite substantial," says Strømnes. "I came up with ideas and proposals, went to the Historical Museum and the Viking Ship Museum in Oslo, borrowed books from the library and immersed myself thoroughly in the imagery of the Viking era. The Viking era is a very exciting and nearly inexhaustible theme; I could work with it indefinitely.

"I was given great freedom in this commission. After the initial sketches were approved, I received no strong directives, either from the employers or the architects," says Strømnes.

Including the planning, the job took a little over a year. Strømnes also participated in the installation of the work at the shipyard at Saint Nazaire, where she collaborated with Ola Christian Sommerfelt, who was hired specially to work on the project. The mounting couldn't be left to the yard. It had to be done by people skilled in working with polyester, which can be more difficult to handle than glass; one little error could cause instant cracking. It took three weeks just to complete this final part of the job. ■

This interview with Gunhild Strømnes took place in Oslo.

CV

Gunhild Strømnes, born Sarpsborg, Norway.
Education: National College of Fine Arts, Crafts and Design 1982–85. National Academy 1985-90.
Gunhild Strømnes has participated in nine Group Exhibitions since 1985.
Solo Exhibitons since 1990: Wang Art Gallery, Atelier Gourdon, Artist's Association, Norway. Grignan, France.
Commissions: Lorentzen & Stemoco, Royal Caribbean Cruise Lines, Art Link, Radisson Seven Seas Cruises, Creditreform.
Collections: Kosmos, Telenor, Eiedomsspar, Pecunia, Conoco, Thranegruppen.

(Photo: Thanaszewitz)

Index

Names of persons, institutions and ships: (The name Royal Caribbean Cruise Lines and the abbreviation RCI is not included in the index as they occur on most pages).